BROTHERS IN ARMS
Memoirs of Veterans, Victims, Heroes, and
Survivors of World War II, Korea and the Vietnam War

James Downey

Second Edition © 2025 James Downey
©2019 James Downey. All rights reserved. No part of this publication may be reproduced or used in any form or by any means, graphic, electronic or mechanical, including photocopying, recording, taping, or information and retrieval systems without written permission of the publisher.

ISBN Paperback: 978-1-64873-533-2

Published by New Freedom Books
Prescott, Arizona

Original Editor: Harley B. Patrick
Book design: Michael Campbell
Cover design: L. Redding

Imprint Writers Publishing House
Prescott, Arizona

BROTHERS IN ARMS

Memoirs of Veterans, Victims, Heroes, and Survivors of World War II, Korea and the Vietnam War

JAMES DOWNEY

To the men and women whose stories of selfless service and sacrifice unfold in this book, and to those countless thousands of American servicemen and -women, living and dead, to whom we, and much of the rest of the world, owe the freedom we enjoy every day. May we never take for granted or forget the price that you, and your families as well, have paid for the rest of us.

Contents

Introduction . . . . *xi*
Abbreviations and Definitions . . . . *xv*
Preface to Chapters I, II, and III *1*

Chapter I: LT. COL. DAVID HAMILTON 1922– 3
    Off to War *10*
    Pathfinders *12*
    Post-War Flying *28*
    On to Korea *31*

Chapter II: MAJ. GEN. PIERPONT MORGAN HAMILTON 1899–1982 43

Chapter III: MARISE CAMPBELL 1899–1995 55
    Body Count *71*

Chapter IV: REFLECTIONS ON THE VIETNAM WAR 73
Preface to Chapters V and VI *79*

Chapter V: COL. RONALD E. (RON) BYRNE, JR. 1928– . . . 81
    Seven Years as a POW *90*
    The Son Tay Raid *104*
    The Prisoners Revolt *105*
    Another Moving Day *106*
    Freedom *107*
    Back to the World *110*

Chapter VI: 1ST LT. CHARLES EDWIN (CHARLIE) TAYLOR 1942 – **113**
   The Battle of Snoopy's Nose. *117*
   Postmortem to Vietnam *143*
   Post-Traumatic Stress Disorder (PTSD). *148*

Chapter VII: THE ROYAL RABBITS OF KOREA **151**

Chapter VIII: A SNAPSHOT OF THE KOREAN WAR **155**

Chapter IX: LT. COL. ELVIN (AL) BAKER 1932 – **159**
   Preface *159*
   The Howze Board *169*
   Heinz Prechter *177*

Chapter X: RADIOMAN 1st CLASS ALBERT ANTHONY VILLAR 1912-1983 . . . . **179**
   Preface *179*
   The Civilian Conservation Corps (CCC). *180*
   U.S.S. Barnstable *183*
   Kamikazes. *184*
   Life Aboard the U.S.S. Barnstable *187*
   The Surrender of Japan. *190*
   Life in Manila, 1945. . . . . *198*

Chapter XI: WILLEM ("BILL") DE LANNOY, JR. 1932 – . . . **209**
   Preface *209*
   Indonesia *210*
   The DeLannoy Family *212*
   Life in a Japanese POW Camp. *216*
   The Burma Railway *223*
   A New Life in Holland *228*

  Corrie Ten Boom *236*
  Coming to America *237*
  Next Stop, Communist Eastern Europe. *241*
  1985 – Another Giant Step *247*
  South Africa and Apartheid *251*
  East Timor, Indonesia. *257*
  A Trip to Mainland China. *260*
  Taoism *264*
  A Return to South Africa *266*

Chapter XII: BEGINNINGS AND ENDINGS **271**
  V-Mail *273*

Appendix A: Bob Hoover *277*

Appendix B: William Linzee Prescott *281*

Appendix C: David Niven. *283*

Appendix D: Why Do Pilots Wear Silk Scarves? . *285*

Appendix E: the Cold War and Significant
 Incidents – 1950s and 1960s. *287*

Appendix F: the Berlin Wall:
 a Cold War Memoir. *293*

Acknowledgements *303*

Bibliography *305*

About the Author. *307*

x

Introduction

About three years ago, my brother in law Al and I were lamenting the loss of unique war memories with the passing of our veterans. Few World War II survivors remain. The numbers from Korea and Vietnam are likewise dwindling.

Al noted that his father, Albert, was a WWII Navy veteran. He had returned home with an exceptional collection of wartime documents and pictures he had taken. Before his death, Albert confided to Al that some of the pictures portrayed forbidden subjects. In addition, he had spirited back an official telegraph that was supposed to have been destroyed. Al kindly offered to share them with me. I was blown away by what I saw. Albert experienced and documented slices of history that truly needed to be preserved and shared.

While Albert's artifacts did not constitute enough subject matter for a book, it seemed to me that if I combined them with other noteworthy war stories, a book would be feasible. So, I began searching for other material. Two friends shared dramatic wartime, as well as life, experiences. One survived a Japanese prison camp in Indonesia during WWII as a child. A neighbor referred me to a local Korean and Vietnam War veteran, who in turn referred me to others. Each of them had remarkable stories to tell.

Some had participated in historic events. Most provided pictures, news articles, and official documents that brought their adventures to life. Many still bear physical and mental scars. Their valor is attested by Purple Hearts, Silver Stars, and even a Congressional Medal of Honor.

We tend to mischaracterize "war stories" as tales of personal exploits flavored with liberal doses of exaggeration, whose details become grander and more exciting with each telling. Fueled by a few drinks among friends, these tales can blossom into epics. But true war stories aren't just accounts of the glories of battle. They are the stories of the people in those battles—who they are and where they came from. The unembellished true war stories that are rapidly vanishing with the passing of our veterans bear witness to significant chapters from our past. Unless these first-hand accounts are preserved, it is all too easy for their truth to be lost as history is forgotten, or worse, revised and rewritten. These individual tales, woven together, form a tapestry of what really happened.

While other books have been published that recount wartime events and experiences, they tend to narrowly focus on single battles, episodes, or individuals. This book is designed to be quite different. It is a hybrid combination of war memoirs, life stories, and a multi-family photo album, spanning three wars, with history and context stretching back as far as four hundred years.

To help provide a framework for better understanding, several of these stories are interwoven with the larger geopolitical history to which they are attached. Side trips are taken to introduce notable people, including some well-known celebrities, whose lives sometimes intersected with those of the principal subjects. Unusual civilian experiences share the stage with wartime events. Comic episodes punctuate the many absurdities of military life.

It is hoped that the reader will be encouraged to further explore other sources that delve into the wars and events visited in these pages. Their unvarnished history may prove to be quite different than what one has been taught in school, or perhaps reflect things that are never taught at all.

Some of the pictures and documents that appear in this book are of less-than-stellar quality. Older historic images are difficult to reproduce well. Many of the originals are over 70 years old and have deteriorated, or were not pristine to begin with. Please accept them as they are, perhaps assigning "character" to their appearance as we do with other age-worn things that we value enough to save.

The diffuse nature of this book may be a challenge for some. The variance of its subject matter does not lend itself well to the systematic, chronological format of most books. Approaching it as an anthology of short stories with war as a common denominator might place the reader in a better frame of reference. The appendices at the end of the book cover related topics and areas of geopolitical history germane to the stories which, if included in the stories themselves, might tend to distract or diverge from the flow of the narrative.

Wars are painful and lethal episodes in our history, filled with darkness, misery and regret. But the people who rise to the occasion of serving their fellow humans through selfless sacrifice demonstrate a character and resilience that highlights the best qualities of the human spirit. Amidst sorrow, there is laughter. Amidst inhumanity, there is nobility. Amidst despair, there is hope. Through preserving these stories, in all their sadness and humor, I hope to do some bit of justice to the greatness that is in those who have fought, those who have died, and those who — by God's grace — remain. May the stories contained herein serve as a reminder that there is always a light that shines, even in the darkest of times.

Abbreviations and Definitions

Military Ranks
RM: Radioman

Sgt: Sergeant

Lt: Lieutenant

Capt: Captain

Maj: Major

Col: Colonel

Gen: General.

Other
AFB: Air Force Base, used typically for locations within the U.S.

AB: Air Base, used typically for overseas bases

APC: Armored Personnel Carrier; a tread-driven weaponized assault vehicle somewhat similar in appearance to a tank

ATC: Armored Troop Carrier; an armored weaponized Navy boat about 60 feet long used in river warfare in Vietnam

CIA: U.S. Central Intelligence Agency

CCC: Civilian Conservation Corp

CBS: Central Broadcasting System

Hooch: A usually thatched hut; a dwelling (Per *Merriam-Webster Dictionary*, definition 2)

ICBM: Intercontinental Ballistic Missile

NASA: National Aeronautic and Space Administration

NVA: North Vietnamese Army

PBY: An amphibious aircraft widely used by all U.S. service branches in WWII

POW: Prisoner of War

PTSD: Post-Traumatic Stress Disorder

RAF: Royal Air Force (of Great Britain)

ROTC: Reserve Officer Training Corps; high-school and college level programs for military training

RPG: Rocket Propelled Grenade

SRO/RSO: Senior Ranking Officer/Ranking Senior Officer

TDY: Temporary Duty Yonder

TWA: Trans World Airlines; a U.S. commercial passenger airline, no longer in business

UDT : Underwater Demolition Team

UPI: United Press International

UN: United Nations; a coalition of European countries and the U.S. formed after WWII to counter Communist aggression

VC: Viet Cong; a political and military organization primarily located in South Vietnam and Cambodia which shared Communist ideology with, and fought alongside of, North Vietnam against South Vietnam. The VC employed guerrilla warfare and organized peasants to fight in areas it controlled.

WWI: World War I

WWII: World War II

WPA: Works Progress Administration

★

Preface to Chapters I, II, and III

The first time I walked into David Hamilton's home, I was stunned. It was a veritable museum of military memorabilia. Models of the planes he had flown in training and combat abounded. Photographs, news articles, medals, and ribbons reflected years of living history before my eyes. His mother's leather-bound scrapbook depicting her years with the Red Cross in Europe during WWII sat proudly on a credenza. His father's mission into North Africa echoed from a framed 1944 magazine article hung in a hallway, which was lined with even more history in the form of images, documents and mementos of all sorts.

The first three stories in this book comprise a glimpse of the history I saw that day—the amazing saga of an entire family that cast aside the American equivalent of royal family heritage to lay their lives on the line in service to their country in a war that killed three percent of the world's population. Their story depicts a nation wherein everyone, famous and common, rich and poor alike, banded together to defeat a common enemy and preserve the freedom we enjoy today.

2

Chapter I:
LT. COL. DAVID HAMILTON
1922 —

"A national treasure." This is how David Hamilton was introduced to the audience at Embry Riddle Aeronautical University.

The auditorium was buzzing with the energy of older veterans and young students alike, all eager to hear his experiences during the Korean War as a B-26 pilot. The introduction was more than fitting. At 96 years of age, he is the last surviving Pathfinder pilot from WWII, full of energy and a great sense of humor.

It is uncommon to encounter veterans of WWII. We are rapidly losing its few remaining survivors. Even more unlikely is finding one whose father was decorated as a hero in that war, and whose mother also served the war effort in Europe. David Hamilton may be unique in that regard as well as in others. If that were all, his story and his family's would be remarkable. But there is far more to tell. His life journey has intersected with Hollywood celebrities, world-famous pilots, and a general who would one day become our president.

David's family lineage is noteworthy by itself. He was born in 1922 in Wayford, England to Marise and Pierpont Morgan Hamilton. Pierpont was the grandson of bank magnate and financier

J.P. Morgan, and the great-great grandson of one of our founding fathers, Alexander Hamilton.

Pierpont was engaged in London and Paris on behalf of J.P. Morgan & Co. Bank, hence David's British birthplace. In 1928, Pierpont returned to New York where David attended Saint Bernard's day school. A move to California came next, where David attended Santa Barbara Boy's School for Junior High and his freshman year of High School.

Well before David began his military career, he embarked on a life-long side career of running into celebrities. David's parents divorced in 1930, and by 1934, his mother had a house in Oahu, Hawaii. One day, while on Oahu, David was surfing at the beach when he ran into Walt Disney—literally. He accidentally hit the film mogul with his surfboard while walking on the beach. David apologized, and the two began talking. Disney was on a combination vacation and business trip. On the business side, he was there to study the feathered clothing of the old Hawaiian emperors that was on display in the Bishop Museum. Unfortunately, the museum was closed for renovation. This gave David an idea of a clever way to make up for his errant surfboard. He contacted his mother, who was able to get Disney into the museum. On the way back to California by boat, David and his mother ran into Disney again—figuratively this time—and he drew them a sketch of Mickey Mouse on one of the ship's menus.

Another relocation after California took the family to Pennsylvania where David completed High School at Hill School in Pottstown. After graduation, David attended night school at the RCA Institute of Engineering, studying basic electronics and the use of a slide rule. In June of 1941, David began a short stint working at the Canadian Aviation Bureau in New York City. The Bureau closed down following the Japanese attack at Pearl Harbor on December 7, 1941.

David's father Pierpont had trained as a military pilot during the First World War, so the United States' entry into WWII precipitated his recall to military duty. The adventure of flying captivated David, drawing him to enlist in Army flight training. After passing the pilot's exam in 1942, he eagerly headed to Kelly Field in San Antonio, Texas (now Lackland Air Force Base) for three months of ground school. A troop-train ride next carried him to Grider Field in Pine Bluff, Arkansas for primary flight training.

At Grider Field, David discovered that the upper classmen were West Point Military Academy cadets. Having been subjected to hazing (initiation rites) as freshmen at West Point, the upper classmen thought it only fitting that the incoming trainees suffer the same treatment. However, the hazing had a practical aspect. For example, before each meal, the trainees were required to go through the starting procedures for the Fairchild PT-19 trainer airplanes they flew *(Plate DH-1)*, complete with pantomime hand gestures for each step. Meals ended with the same pantomimes for the shut-down procedure.

The PT-19s were a leap forward from the biplanes in which David's father had trained. The biplanes were so forgiving and easy to fly that they almost flew themselves. As WWII approached, the Army concluded that the biplanes created a false sense of accomplishment and the potential for failure as cadets moved up into the newest generation of faster and more powerful planes. The PT-19s were a closer match to the more demanding WWII combat fighters.

Cadet life had its share of military-style drama. David recalls one cadet who had an enlarged ego with an attitude to match. Although the cadet washed out of pilot training by failing his qualification flights, through some bureaucratic mishap he was mistakenly authorized to take a solo flight in a PT-19 . The cadet apparently thought it would be humorous, or maybe payback for being washed out, to taxi his plane through the mud puddles on the field, which he did both on take-off and landing. The base commander, a full colonel, did not find this amusing and was waiting for him when he parked his plane after landing. The colonel ordered the cadet to fetch his toothbrush and drinking glass from his barracks, and scrub down the muddy airplane with his toothbrush. Each time he needed more water, the cadet was ordered back to his barracks to fill the glass. It didn't hold much. He later faced a court-martial for misconduct.

DH-1. Fairchild PT-19A Army flight trainer.
Photo:National Museum of the U.S. Air Force.

Basic flight training, including night flying, formation, and instrument flying followed at Perrin Field in Sherman/Dennison, Texas. Although civilian instructors had previously been the norm, military instructors were now doing the teaching. David's next stop was Blackland Army Flight School in Waco, Texas. The calendar hadn't yet flipped forward to another year. It still read 1942.

Blackland taught advanced twin-engine aircraft flight, using Curtis AT-9 Jeep's (nicknamed "Tadpoles" by the cadets), *(Plate DH-2)*, Beechcraft AT-10s, and Cessna "Bamboo Bombers", so named for the wooden spar that was part of their construction. They were not well-liked by the cadets compared to the other training planes, which may account for their disparaging nickname. David graduated in 1943 as a 2nd lieutenant in the Officer Reserve Corp. Training was close to ending, but there was a bit more to come.

DH-2. Curtis AT-9 "Tadpole" Army flight trainer. Photo: U.S. Air Force.

Texas was beginning to feel like home. Thirty more hours of flight training ensued at Bergstrom Field, in Austin, Texas, with flight time in the Douglas Aircraft DC-3, and the modified military version, the C-47, used by the Army. A trip to Kansas City, Missouri to fly a civilian TWA DC-3 Airliner to its destination provided some real-world experience. This was the first I had ever heard that military pilots trained in WWII by flying civilian airliners full of passengers.

There was no letup. In Alliance, Nebraska, David learned to drop paratroopers while training with soldiers from the 507th Parachute Infantry Regiment. Cargo flights as far away as Chicago, Illinois were also on the menu. But one final training step awaited before heading overseas into the war.

At Laurinburg-Maxton Army Air Base, North Carolina, which is near Fort Bragg and Pope Airfield, David continued training with airborne units on parachute drops, and was instructed in towing and dropping gliders into combat zones with the Waco CG-4A Glider *(Plate DH-4)* behind a C-47. The Wacos, flown by a pilot and co-pilot, could carry 13 troops—or a jeep—or a ¼ Ton Truck—or a 75 mm. howitzer, weighing as much as 7,500 pounds fully loaded. Gliders were made by some unusual companies, such as Gibson Refrigerator.

Laurinburg-Maxton had its own postcards, allowing soldiers to share a sample of their training adventures with family and friends *(Plate DH-3)*.

DH-3. *Postcard from Laurinburg-Maxton Army Air Base showcasing the varities of training done there. Photo: U.S. Army Air Force, courtesy of Wikimedia.*

DH-4. Waco CG-4A Hadrian. Photo: National Museum of the U.S. Air Force.

The Army experimented for a short time with double glider towing, but found that the weight of one extra glider burned up C-47 engines, an expensive lesson. While stationed at Laurinburg, David discovered a way to make some extra money. On a flight to Willow Grove Naval Air Station to pick up gliders to take back to Laurinburg, he noticed that the dimensions of an aircraft carrier deck had been painted on the runway. David got to talking with a Navy fighter pilot who was pretty proud that he could take off from a carrier. David bet the pilot $50.00 (a lot of money in that day) that he could take off a C-47 from the (painted) carrier deck while towing a glider. Of course the fighter jock took the bait. Each of them gave the Base Operations Officer, a Navy lieutenant commander, their $50.00 as the stake holder.

David knew that an empty glider would lift off the ground before his C-47 (which it did). David won the bet, and got $100.00 in the mail later.

Off to War

With his training completed, excited and a bit nervous, David headed to Baer Field in Fort Wayne, Indiana to pick up his C-47 to fly to his overseas base assignment in England. Plate *DH-5* shows a typical C-47 Skytrain. Since in-flight refueling wasn't possible, with a range of 1,600 miles, regular stops were necessary. Winter weather dictated a roundabout Southern route to his ultimate destination, with a stopover in Morocco in North Africa. Getting there wasn't easy.

DH-5. Douglas C-47 Skytrains carrying paratroopers for the invasion of Southern France in Operation Dragoon. Photo: U.S. Air Force.

West Palm Beach, Florida, with an arrival on Christmas day in 1943, was the last American soil David would see for quite a while. From there he hopped across the globe on an odd series of ten refueling stepping-stones: Puerto Rico; British Guiana; Belem, Brazil at the entrance to the Amazon River; Natal, Brazil; Ascension Island west of Africa; Accra, Africa; Freetown, Liberia; and Dakaar, Senegal where the French had a regiment of tough Senegalese soldiers. Upon encountering them, David knew they were nothing to mess with. The last stepping-stone before England was supposed to be Marakesh, Morocco. But sometimes things don't go as planned. David's plane lost an engine on the way to Marakesh, forcing him to divert to Agadir, Morocco—which turned out to be a pretty good place for any airplane to break down.

Agadir was a winter resort for French travelers, with swank hotels and amenities. A U.S. Navy PBY submarine patrol unit was based there. The PBYs were amphibious, equipped to take off and land on either water or land. Although the PBY used the same engine as the C-47, the Army wanted no part of using a Navy spare engine in an Army plane for some reason. The Army insisted on sending a replacement engine from Florida, leaving David with eleven enjoyable days to kill. He quartered in one of the opulent tourist hotels. To pass the time, he went along on a PBY patrol looking for German submarines, which lasted twenty-one boring hours with nothing sighted. Later, he went ibex hunting and dove hunting in some of the many citrus groves nearby. Eventually, his new engine arrived, and it was time to get back to work.

Before heading for Bottisford, England, to catch up with his unit, the 436th Troop Carrier Group, 9th Army Air Force, David was required to stop over in Casablanca, Morocco, to have a maintenance officer approve his engine replacement. The officer who did so was named Bob Hoover. Hoover was also a fighter pilot who would shortly depart to fly combat with the Spitfire-equipped 52nd Fighter Group in Sicily. (The Spitfire was a British airplane). Unbeknownst to David, he had just met a future war hero who was destined to become an aviation legend after the war. (See *Appendix A* for Bob Hoover's amazing story).

After a stop in Marakesh, David arrived in Bottisford, England in the January cold of 1944. He was recommended for a newly-formed volunteer unit known as the Pathfinders, and agreed to join. What had he gotten himself and his C-47 into? Please permit a slight detour for some background.

Pathfinders

As is frequently the case in war, disaster is the mother of innovation. Two badly bungled drops of American paratroopers into combat zones, one in North Africa and one later in Sicily, led to the creation of Pathfinder units. The first U.S. Airborne assault of WWII, by the 509th Parachute Infantry Battalion, dropped into North Africa in November of 1942. Because of bad weather, the drop planes got lost and paratroopers were scattered over Algeria and Morocco. In July of 1943, the second Airborne drop of the war occurred during the invasion of Sicily. With many of the same problems, including high winds and poor navigation, men were scattered as far as 65 miles from their intended drop zones. Misplaced soldiers searched for weeks to locate Allied lines. Higher-ups in the Army seriously considered whether to cease airborne operations altogether. Unless drop accuracy could be improved, this was a real possibility. Although American General James Gavin claims credit for the creation of the Pathfinders, the men of the 509th would strongly disagree. After their disastrous experiences, they feverishly sought ways to improve drop accuracy. The 509th had piecemeal knowledge of successful British Airborne practices, and sought to incorporate them into their own operations. The British parachuted small units into enemy territory drop zones to set up transmitters and other devices that would guide planes full of paratroopers to the drop zones. The drop planes would follow about 15 minutes behind these small units, using the transmitted signals to help insure drop accuracy. The 509th cobbled together men and equipment to form similar advance scout units, which saw mixed success in September of 1943. A jump in Paestum, Italy was on target.

But the jump in the mountainous region of Avellino, Italy did not go so well. The mountains deflected the radar guidance signals, causing pilot disorientation.

In addition to the question of whether to stop airborne operations, the effectiveness and desirability of scout troop drops was hotly debated by the higher-ranking officers involved in Airborne operations at that time. Airborne and Pathfinder troops saw little to no action after that, until preparations began for the massive Allied invasion at Normandy, France on June 6, 1944, known as the D-Day Invasion. Thus, the Pathfinder concept was not brand new when David joined the unit. It was simply polished up and sold as something new to the Army. It was also now an official unit, which came with full funding and equipment support.

David Hamilton is now our last surviving Pathfinder pilot.

In January of 1944, David's Pathfinder unit began the four to five week process of forming up and organizing at Cottismore, England. David remarked that he was glad to know he wouldn't be towing gliders, as it was an assignment he greatly disliked. The British, who had been very successful with their own pathfinders, partnered with the Americans, contributing training and highly sophisticated equipment. C-47 airplanes were fitted out with radar domes underneath. Inside, the planes were equipped with about $500,000.00 worth of equipment, an enormous sum at that time. This equipment included a Rebecca/Eureka radio receiver; an SCR 717; a Shoran "G Box"; a Loran; and a radar altimeter. David quipped that the military put $500,000.00 worth of equipment into a $100,000.00 airplane. The C-47s carried no military insignia or markings of any kind, save for their factory tail numbers.

Pathfinder pilots and airplane crews received special training, including parachuting out of airplanes themselves. Although they would not be parachuting into the drop zones with scout or combat paratroopers, they needed first-hand experience of what it was like to jump out of a perfectly good airplane to help them better perform their drops. David recalls that he wasn't worried about his first parachute jump; he was too nervous to worry about it. The Pathfinders did well on their training jump, suffering only one broken ankle. The British Royal Air Force trained the U.S. navigators on the advanced British navigation equipment installed in the planes. Pilots learned low level night flying and formation flying for dropping paratroopers.

The Pathfinder C-47s carried a crew of five: pilot, co-pilot, navigator, crew chief/engineer, and radio operator. Twenty scout paratroopers flew as passengers to their assigned drop zone, where the scouts would parachute in and set up a transmitter, halophane directional lights, and other devices with which to guide in the C-47s which would later follow, loaded with combat troops, to the drop zone. The scouts had to work precisely and quickly. The first C-47s with combat paratroopers would reach their designated drop zones thirty minutes after the scouts had activated the navigation devices.

The halophane lights could be configured in the shape of an alphabet letter, such as a "T," to designate the code letter for each drop zone. Several of the scout paratroopers would carry firearms to guard the perimeter of the drop zone, protecting the other scout troops who were setting up the guidance devices in case of an enemy attack. One paratrooper would carry the Rebecca/Eureka transmitter strapped to his leg. The transmitter sent distance and directional data to the incoming drop planes. If the paratrooper failed to release the leg strap and drop the padded transmitter onto the ground before he himself hit the ground, the landing would break his leg due to the extra weight. Twenty two Pathfinder crews were trained, but only 20 saw action on D-Day.

David's crew was exceptional. His navigator, and the equipment they had, were so good that they could safely fly only 25 feet above the ground. They were able to detect, and avoid, obstacles such as power lines and barrage balloons. David's navigator, First Lieutenant Carl "Gbox" Jones, would sometimes ask David if he wanted to fly under or over power lines. David wisely and safely chose to fly over them.

As a new and hastily formed unit, one of the benefits the Pathfinder's enjoyed at their home base was the lack of a Table of Organization designating a chain of command. This left the Pathfinders freedom to function simply as fellow soldiers with a common mission. The Royal Air Force (RAF) liaison, squadron leader John Dewar, was possibly the most popular airman in the unit. His family distilled Dewar's Scotch, a well-known brand of whiskey. The colonel in charge was somehow able to regularly free up a plane for John to fly "training flights" to his family distillery in Perth, Scotland where he would pick up cases of Scotch for the troops. The Pathfinders were held in high esteem by the other units they served with.

In preparation for D-Day, a major training exercise took place in England on the Saulsbury Plain, close to Stonehenge. David was assigned as a ground observer to monitor the exercise. He arrived at the staging area in a jeep, which parked about 300 yards from Stonehenge. The unit's designated musician/guitarist, an enlisted man named William Linzee Prescott, (known as "Linzee") was in the back of the jeep singing "Babaloo" as they drove in. Linzee was also the 82nd Division's artist who designed the Pathfinder insignia *(Plate DH-6)* and painted the images adorning the walls of the officer's club at the unit's base in England *(Plate DH-7)*. (Linzee went on after WWII to some notoriety with an intriguing career with military art, including a mural which adorns a wall at the West Point Military Academy. See *Appendix B* for more of his story).

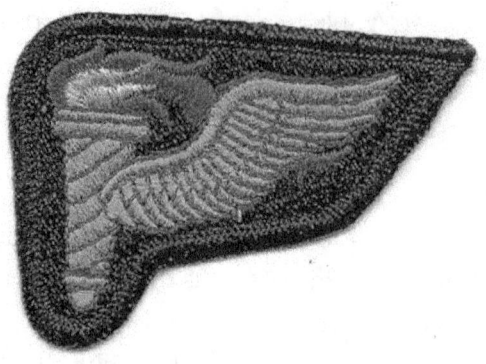

DH-6. *Pathfinder insignia designed by William Linzee Prescott. Unit patch: David Hamilton.*

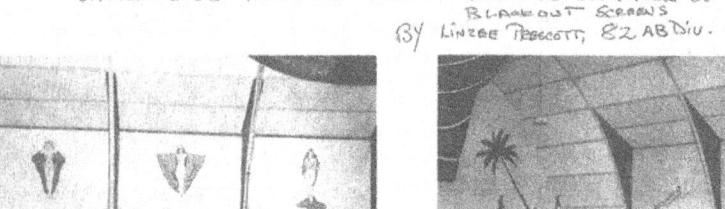

DH-7. *Wall décor, 436th Troop Carrier Group officers' club by "Linzee". Photo: David Hamilton.*

As David and Linzee sat in their jeep on the Saulsbury plain with Stonehenge looming as a backdrop, they watched five hundred C-47s thunder across the skies above the English countryside in the massive pre-D-Day exercise. Between 7,000 and 10,000 paratroopers floated down onto the plain. The planes arrived in waves of three three-plane "V" formations configured thusly:

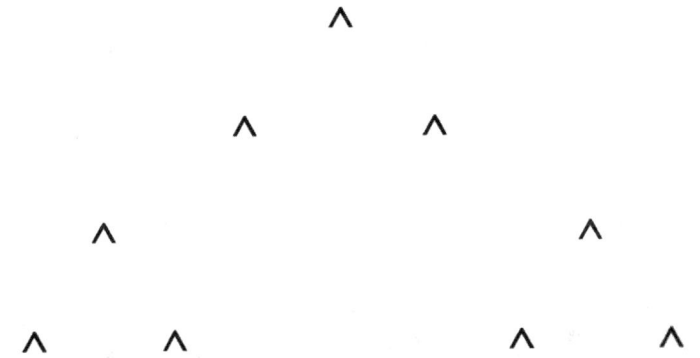

Each wave was separated by only 25 seconds, giving them that small increment of time to drop their troops. Fifty six waves of C-47s flooded over the plains. The sight and sound must have been apocalyptic.

On May 28, 1944, it was obvious that something big was about to happen. The base was sealed.

No mail or phone calls were allowed in or out. No leaves were granted. All soldiers were required to surrender their military ID's, so that nobody could leave the base. Training flights were restricted to take off and land at the same base. Mission briefings were increased. Throughout the time David flew for the Pathfinders, he was required to carry a card *(Plate DH-8)* showing he had clearance to enter the planes carrying the secret equipment. Every day, sand tables, (scale accurate reproductions of terrain and buildings created to present three dimensional pictures of military objectives) which displayed all of the drop zones, were reviewed and studied *(Plate DH-9)*.

DH-8. *David's secret security clearance card. David Hamilton collection.*

DH-9. *WWII sand table usage. Photo:Library of Congress.*

Excitement mixed with fear permeated the base as D-Day drew nearer. David noted that the C-47 pilots shared larger worries than the others. While fighter pilots had only themselves to worry about, the Pathfinder and drop pilots had planes full of troops plus their crew's lives in their hands. On top of that, they flew planes with no guns with which to defend themselves.

Briefings for the invasion began on June 1. The original planned date of June 4th was postponed 24 hours because of bad weather. Early in the afternoon on June 5th, the Pathfinders gathered for their final briefing, *(Plate DH-10)*, after which they were treated to a meal of steak and eggs (with shells), likely hoping it wouldn't be their last. Look closely at the picture to see the varying emotions playing across the pilots' faces.

Around 8:00 pm. the crews gathered around their airplanes for photographs. England is far enough North that it still had summer daylight at that hour of the day. David graciously signed a picture of him and his crew for me *(Plate DH-11)*.

DH-10. Pathfinders gathered for their final briefing before D-Day. DBH (front row, third from left) is David. Photo: David Hamilton.

Twenty Pathfinder C-47s parachuted their scout units into Normandy, marking drop zones for the paratroopers and gliders that would follow. Gliders were the last drops, after the combat troops had been sent in. Gliders typically carried light artillery weapons such as 75mm. howitzers, and support troops such as medics and military police.

DH-11. David Hamilton and crew prior to D-Day departure. David is in the front row, first flier on the right. Photo: David Hamilton.

The first Pathfinders lifted off at 9:30 p.m. on June 5th with only their formation lights illuminated, reaching their drop zones at 1:15 a.m. on June 6th. David's plane departed at 10:30 p.m. Pathfinder scouts from the 82nd and 101st Parachute Infantry Regiments (PIR) were the first American soldiers to set foot in Normandy, charting the course for thousands who would follow onto the six drop zones and two glider landing zones they established. David's plane flew the number two position in a flight of three planes, carrying scout paratroopers from the 507th PIR who had been assigned to the 82nd. An intelligence officer, Captain E.G. McElroy, joined the crew. The Pathfinders flew alone into danger, with no fighter escort.

David's formation forged across England 1,500 feet above the countryside at 155 miles per hour. Reaching the English Channel forty five minutes after takeoff, he dropped his altitude to 50 feet in order to avoid German radar. As he approached the coast of France, he climbed to 900 feet. Two minutes after he hit the coast, he snapped on the red jump light alerting the paratroopers to get ready to jump. Two minutes later, things went sour.

His plane plunged into a dense cloud bank which the weather briefing had failed to detect. Those clouds would hinder all of the other airplanes to follow, but David couldn't warn any other planes because radio silence was required. Then the Germans heard them and started shooting at them with .25 caliber Schmeisser machine pistols and 20mm. Bofors flack guns. The Germans couldn't use their big flak guns, the 88s, because David's plane was too low, but the other weapons were getting the job done. David lost a wing tip. The magnetos in the cockpit were shot out. When he got back to his base, there were over 300 .25 caliber holes in his plane. His air crew chief nicknamed it "The Sieve."

Another two minutes brought them out of the cloud bank into full moonlight, which David says was "bright as hell". Not only could the Germans see them now, but David had to slow down to 110 miles per hour and drop his altitude down to 800 feet. The Germans continued to hose his plane with their Schmeissers. Suddenly, Lt. Jones yelled "Green Light", allowing all of two seconds before the drop zone: (1) for David to hear him say that, and (2) switch on the green jump light, (3) for the jump master to see the light, and (4) send the troops out the door. All the paratroopers made it out the door in 10 seconds, while the Germans continued spraying them and the airplane with gunfire. David later learned that six paratroopers were hit on the way down, and that Stick Commander Ralph McGill broke both ankles when he landed (the groups of paratroopers to be dropped into a landing zone were referred to as "sticks").

Amidst the hail of ground fire, David's crew chief and the intelligence officer frantically hauled in the static lines trailing outside the

C-47 that had been attached to the troops parachutes to pull them open, exposing the plane to 15 more seconds of flying bullets. The crew chief ran forward and yelled "static lines all aboard", which was David's cue to boogie out of there. David hit the throttle and headed for the deck to escape the gunfire. Almost immediately the co-pilot shouted "lift your right wing!" David looked out the right window and blanched at the sight of the steeple of St. Mere Eglise Church fast approaching his right wing. He lifted his wing and nose up a little, averting disaster.

The route home passed over Marcouf Island, which, according to the mission briefing, had heavy German gun emplacements. David thought to himself, "we better haul ass." He climbed to 2,500 feet and increased his speed to 160 miles per hour. When they flew over the island, nobody shot at them.

They later learned that Navy demolition teams had destroyed the German guns.

As they escaped homeward over the English Channel, Lt. Jones invited David back to marvel at the radar view of the channel. What he saw was a portion of the largest naval invasion in history, totaling 6,939 vessels—uncountable dots on the radar screen. David said they looked like measles. The co-pilot was invited back to look as well. David was "filled with pride and excitement" to be part of this historic day. At the same time, he was "overwhelmed" by the enormity of the invasion.

David's plane became separated from the other two in his formation when he flew into some cloud banks. His plane returned home alone; his other two planes arrived just before he did. Since his magnetos had been shot out, he couldn't shut down his engines in the normal fashion. He had to starve them of fuel by shutting off their fuel supply until they died. David later learned that all three of his formation planes had dropped their paratroopers on their drop zones with 100% accuracy within 45 seconds of each other.

Unfortunately, the cloud banks disoriented later drops, particularly the combat soldiers, scattering them away from their drop zones. Some analysts later concluded that there may have been a good side to this. The paratrooper force appeared to the Germans as far larger than it really was, causing the Germans to incorrectly position some of their own forces.

Only one Pathfinder plane was lost in the invasion. With one of its engines shot out, it was forced to ditch in the channel. Its crew and Pathfinder unit were picked up by a British Corvette, to be sent ashore in a landing craft with the infantry soldiers. No doubt they had to endure some good natured harassment for having their bacon saved by the Navy, and wading ashore with the ground pounders.

David and his crew finished their debriefing and were having drinks in the officers' club at their base in North Witham, England by the time *That's All Brother*[1] took off for its mission.

After D-Day, the intensity of David's flights moderated, but only for a short time. Missions included supply runs, paratroop drops, and some "shuttle runs" to the French coast. The Allies constructed a steel planking runway above the D-Day landing site, Omaha Beach, on the French coastline. Pilots rotated duty for the daily round trips mandated by General Eisenhower from England to that landing point, carrying liaison officers back and forth, and bringing high ranking German prisoners back to England. On a few runs, David delivered gasoline to U.S. General George Patton's unit. The long English summer daylight enabled his unit to fly two missions per day when required.

David's penchant for celebrity encounters was never thwarted by such mundane things as major world wars. A British Intelligence

---

1 That's All Brother is the name of the lead C-47 that carried combat paratroopers into Normandy on D-Day, guided by the drop zone beacons emplaced by the Pathfinders. Four hundred C-47s would follow behind in triple V-wave formations separated by 1,000 feet, the same formations the Pathfinders flew. The drop planes flooded 13,000 soldiers onto the fields of Normandy from 700 feet above the ground. That's All Brother is still flown and maintained by the Commemorative Air Force (CAF) Central Texas Wing in San Marcos, Texas.

captain named David Niven was scheduled to head from Normandy to England aboard an LST, one of the boats with drop-down ramps that were used to transport and disgorge loads of combat troops and equipment onto the beach. It promised to be a wet, long and miserable trip. Niven spotted David near his C-47 and approached him to ask if he could fly back to England with him. David recognized Niven, a famous English film star, and told him to go over to the sergeant with the machine gun who was guarding his plane and tell him that David had authorized him to board the plane. Niven was grateful, and promised David he would repay him one day with the best steak dinner he ever had.[2] (A brief summary of Niven's D-Day related mission and career is included at Appendix C.)

David "flew into" another celebrity encounter in Italy in July of 1944. Actress and opera singer Lily Pons and her orchestra-conductor husband Andre Kostelanetz, who were on tour entertaining the troops with their traveling entourage, needed air transport from Naples to Caserta to Rome, and then back to Naples. Their talent level was such that they were able to perform using local musicians on the spot, including soldiers. The entourage was small, maybe 7 to 10 of their regulars, David recalls, including makeup artists and a violinist. David knew that before the war, his father, Pierpont, who was by then a full colonel in the Plans and Operations Division in the Pentagon, had gotten Lilly Pons her first movie role with RKO Pictures. Pierpont had served as JP Morgan's representative to RKO Pictures, for whose pension JP Morgan acted as the trustee. This regular contact with RKO had given Pierpont the influence with which to help Ms. Pons land the role. David therefore suspected that this assignment to transport Pons, along with her husband and

---

2 In 1973, David took his daughter to the well-known New York restaurant 21 for her 18th birthday. As they walked in, they spotted Niven sitting at a table towards the back. After all those years, David and Niven recognized each other and exchanged warm pleasantries in an unexpected reunion. That evening, Niven bought David (and his daughter) the steak dinner he had promised almost 30 years prior.

entourage, had his father's fingerprints all over it, but his father later disavowed any knowledge.

In August of 1944, David flew into the South of France as part of the "Champagne Campaign," participating in the last nighttime drop of paratroopers in the European Theatre. The tide of the war was turning in favor of the Allies and they met little air resistance.

Wartime flying, though, presents more dangers than enemy fire. Bad weather and poor weather forecasting can be just as deadly. On August 18, 1944, David dropped a stick of British Pathfinders into Southern France. On August 22, coming back to North Witham from Gibraltar, David was exhausted, having flown all night. He stopped for fuel, breakfast, and a badly needed break at an RAF base in Newquay, Cornwall, England. Before taking off, his crew received a horribly inaccurate weather briefing from the RAF indicating safe flying conditions back to their home base.

Once airborne, David was still exhausted, so he tried to catch some sleep by turning the airplane over to his co-pilot. The weather briefing had lulled them into false security. Shortly after takeoff, without warning, they plunged into a pilot's worst nightmare. An unexpected driving rain storm rendered visibility near zero. Before the co-pilot could react, the plane crashed into a mountain top near Cornwall. David later remarked that the crash "ruined his nap."

As the plane skidded towards a 200-foot-high cliff, the radar dome on the bottom of the plane dug into the ground, arresting the craft's skid, and saving them from plunging over the cliff. Although David and his crew survived, there were casualties: three cases of Italian wine, which David allowed was not particularly good wine anyway, were lost. David made his way to a farm house where he telephoned the nearest RAF Base in Barnstable to send ground transport for him and his crew, and air police to guard the airplane. The airplane later had its wings removed and its fuselage loaded onto a flatbed truck. The pieces were hauled to a base where the plane was repaired and reassembled. It flew again — but not with David as its pilot. One has to wonder if the pilots of those planes were ever told about such things before they were assigned to fly them.

DH-12. Allied paratroop drop into Holland, September, 1944. Photo: National Archives.

In September of 1944, missions were flown into Holland over a five-day period. Four of those were regular paratroop drops of 82nd **PIR** troops. One was for medical evacuation. Antiaircraft fire was a constant danger. Although Allied fighters had some success in destroying German gun batteries, the Germans developed a new tactic unique to Holland. They installed flak guns on innocent-looking civilian boats they had commandeered, intermingling their flak boats with the many other civilian boats traveling Holland's plentiful canals, covering the guns to conceal them. There was no way for Allied planes to detect the guns until they were uncovered and began firing.

British paratroopers under the command of British General Montgomery participated in the first run into Holland. Montgomery had, and still has, his share of detractors. David refers to Montgomery's tactical deployment of his paratroopers as "Monty's Mistake," which was a lot worse than it sounds.

Under his direction, his troops were dropped in Arnem about eight miles from German heavy gun emplacements. The Germans encircled the helpless foot soldiers and simply trained their artillery into the circle, killing thousands of British troops.

During the October-November time period, David flew 1st Army Commanding General Courtney Hodges to a classified location in order to meet with Army Group Commander Omar Bradley, 3rd Army Commanding General George Patton, and General Dwight Eisenhower, commander of SHAPE (Supreme Headquarters, Allied Powers in Europe) *(Plate DH-13)*. The generals seem to be in good spirits, perhaps optimistic about the outcome of the war. David wasn't close enough to hear what prompted Patton's upraised arm.

David's last combat mission was on December 23, 1944, delivering desperately needed food, medical supplies and ammunition to American troops in Bastogne, Belgium, during the largest land battle of WWII, The Battle of the Bulge. Bastogne was located in the boggy, hilly Ardennes region of East Belgium, Northeastern France and Luxembourg. German troops had surrounded the American forces holding Bastogne, a key strategic road chokepoint. The Americans were so short of ammunition that it was being rationed. David's supply mission was critical to the Allied victory in that battle.

The winter of 1944 was one of the coldest on record, but David observed that many of our troops at Bastogne did not even have winter uniforms. Between December 22nd and December 27th, four airborne supply drops flew into Bastogne. The bitter cold winter produced "ice fogs" in England, which left the runways dangerously coated with ice. In order to melt the ice, burning embers and cinders from the coal stoves used to heat the buildings were shoveled onto the runways. On December 23rd, David led a formation of twenty-seven planes whose route took them along a road in Belgium. Flying at 1,500 feet, the formation encountered a Panzer formation about a mile long, which began to rain gunfire on the airplanes. Breaking radio silence, David moved his airplanes a couple of miles to the right of the road and out of the Panzer's firing range. The Panzers kept firing anyway. This mission was dangerous and costly. Only nine planes, including David's, made it back to their home field in England. Damage was heavy.

Sixteen planes were badly damaged and forced to land at other fields in France and Belgium, or at other fields in England. Two planes were shot down but managed to land. Their crews blew up the planes to prevent the Germans from recovering the advanced electronic and navigation equipment within. The crews were recovered safely, though. One of David's crew members who was hit with shrapnel received a Purple Heart for the mission.

On December 26th, 1944, General George Patton's 3rd Army relieved the troops who had fought so bravely to hold Bastogne.

February of 1945 brought a welcome change. David headed back to the U.S., having survived the war in which so many others gave their lives to defeat a murderous dictator and his regime, and to restore freedom to Europe.

Post-War Flying

After the war, David's piloting skills found a home with Trans Air, a non-scheduled carrier that flew a passenger route from Newark, New Jersey, stopping over in Miami, Florida, and terminating in Havana, Cuba. A new opportunity later arose with American Overseas Airlines (previously known as American Export Airlines), a scheduled carrier. David flew the elegant three-tailed Lockheed

Constellation from LaGuardia Airport in New York to Frankfurt, Germany, carrying diplomats, military personnel and their dependents, military mail, and high priority freight.

DH-13. *Foreground, left to right: American Generals Eisenhower, Patton, Bradley, Hodges. Background, left to right: David's co-pilot Vanwyck, pilot David Hamilton, navigator Geebox Jones. Photo: U.S. Government, David Hamilton collection.*

For five years, David flew as co-pilot to Captain Charles F. Blair, Jr., another wartime pilot who would achieve a measure of fame. Blair set three flying records, including piloting the first jet fighter (an F-100, profiled later in this book) to fly nonstop over the North Pole, from England to Alaska. Blair retired as a Brigadier General. He would marry fiery Irish movie actress Maureen O'Hara in 1968. They enjoyed a close marriage until his death in an airplane crash some years later. David enjoyed socializing with Charles and Maureen in those years, yet another celebrity involved in David's life.

During the time David flew the Constellations, the planes began experiencing engine fires caused by carburetor problems, grounding the entire fleet. Howard Hughes, who was then the majority stockholder of both TWA and Lockheed, met in an airplane hangar with some engineers who were examining dismantled carburetors from failed engines. Hughes was one of those bigger-than-life figures that America produces — wealthy beyond measure, Hollywood producer, founder of Hughes Aircraft Company, holder of world flight records, Las Vegas developer, and in his final years, an eccentric recluse.

Hughes, who had significant knowledge of aircraft, decreed that, rather than trying to remediate the carburetors, they should simply throw them away and install fuel injection. They did so. The fleet was up and running again in a couple of months with fuel-injected engines which the pilots loved. In 1950, American Overseas Airlines was sold to Pan American Airways. This was a non-event for David, as he had been called back into the military for the Korean War.

In 1947, the Army Air Corps had matured sufficiently to become a separate branch of the U.S. Military. When the Korean War started, the newly-created U.S. Air Force, rather than the Army, welcomed the pilots who were recalled to duty. David's father, who had remained in the military after WWII, knew a general named Lawrence Kuter. They had lunch one day and concluded that David would be well suited for the honor of being the personal pilot for General Dwight Eisenhower (known as "Ike"), who was being recalled from Columbia University to join the war effort as the commander of NATO. Eisenhower's command plane was one with which David was quite familiar, a Lockheed Constellation.

After receiving that assignment, David flew the plane, but never with Ike in it. He flew it from Washington National Airport to what is now JKF airport in New York to be outfitted for Ike. David realized that this assignment would keep him away from his wife for extended periods and therefore decided it wasn't for him. He was able to find another qualified pilot to take his place, a single man named Charles Draper who jumped at the chance to fly Ike around. Though both David and Charles were happy with the situation, General Kuter, who felt he had landed David a prime assignment, was a little put out.

David moved into a desk job, not the best assignment for a pilot who wanted to be in the air. He immersed himself in the development of the air evacuation unit of the MATS (Military Air Transport Service) which brought back wounded soldiers from Korea. David describes his service caring for the wounded veterans as a "very rewarding" experience. From time to time, he was able to log some hours in a MATS DC-6, flying military personnel between stateside bases. Torn between wanting to fly more and not wanting the prolonged separations from his wife that overseas duty entailed, David discussed two options with her: an assignment in France, where she could join him after a year's wait, or a seven-month "over and back" tour in Korea without her. The second option seemed preferable to her, so Korea it was.

On to Korea

David trained for two and one-half months in the Douglas A-26/B-26 *(Plate DH-14)*, the only American bomber to fly in three wars: WWII, Korea, and Vietnam. He learned to level bomb, dive bomb, and strafe with machine guns. He loved it, taking to it, he said, "like a duck to water." Now qualified as a B-26 pilot, David joined a flight of nine B-26s to head into the Korean War. Their flight to Korea was led by a B-29 and its navigator. Departing from Hamilton Air Force Base in San Francisco, California, they flew first to Hawaii, then to Wake Island, and then to Japan where David was assigned a new plane fully armed with ammunition in its guns. The reality that an enemy with jet fighters and antiaircraft guns would soon be shooting at him hit home.

DH-14. Douglas B-26C Invader. Photo: National Museum of the U.S. Air Force.

The B-29 abandoned David's flight group in Japan, leaving them on their own to find Korea.

They arrived safely at K-9 Airfield in Pusan, a coastal city in Korea where Allied ships unloaded ammunition and other military supplies. By the time of his arrival, David had logged over 4,000 hours of flight time, more than his squadron commander had.

David was attached to the 17th Bomb Wing, 37th Squadron, commanded by Lt. Col. Rhodes Elam. (The 17th had produced all of the volunteers for Jimmy Dolittle's famous raid on Tokyo in April of 1942). His new duty assignment, "B" Flight Leader and Operations Assistant, awaited him after he completed three "Dollar Flights." These are flights with an instructor pilot: first, to familiarize new pilots and crews with mountains, fields and other local navigation aids; second, to achieve a broader familiarization with other airfields by flying hops in and out of them; and third, an actual combat mission. For David, the latter was a night reconnaissance flight to look for enemy truck convoys. They didn't find any. David thinks "Dollar Flights" were a military custom. The pilot being trained gave his instructor pilot a dollar after each training flight.

David later conducted dollar flights himself as an instructor pilot for trainees. He commented that he "didn't like not having control in combat."

The "mascot" of the 37th Bomb Squadron was movie star Marilyn Monroe, who graced the first cover of *Playboy* magazine in December of 1953. The squadron pilots' flying scarves had Marilyn's picture embossed on them. *Plate DH-15* shows David in uniform wearing his squadron's silk flying scarf. The men in his squadron were ordered to not wear those scarves with dress uniforms or on other official uniform occasions for obvious reasons. Why do pilots wear silk scarves? It's not just to look jaunty and cool, although they do. See *Appendix D* for the interesting answers provided by David.

DH-15. David adorned with his squadron's Marilyn Monroe flying scarf. Photo: David Hamilton.

Two versions of the B-26 saw action in Korea. David primarily flew the glass-nosed version, naming his plane *Sweet Miss Lillian* after his wife. The bombardier sat in the nose, using the Norden bomb sight (later replaced with a better British low-level bomb sight). The other version, sometimes flown by David, had a solid nose containing eight guns which could be fired by the pilot. The bombardier sat next to the pilot in the solid-nose versions.

All the B-26s had three fifty-caliber machine guns in each wing, which were fired by the pilot.

Rotating gun turrets were located in the back of the aircraft, facing backwards. Each gun was loaded with 800 rounds. Every fifth round was a tracer to allow the gun operator to see where his rounds were heading.

David bore-sighted his wing guns at different distances to match the varying trajectories the bullets followed during a four to five-second strafing run. Each pilot bore-sighted the guns in his own plane to match his own individual strafing attack pattern, which varied from pilot to pilot. The ordinance crews that cleaned and maintained David's guns were so good at their jobs that he never experienced a gun jam in all of his missions. *Sweet Miss Lillian* is now on display at the Air Museum at March Field in Riverside, California.

B-26s were sometimes accompanied by fighter planes flying cover overhead. A worn-out South Korean F-51 that could barely keep up with the B-26s came along on an early mission. Things improved when jets were assigned to cover later missions, flying weaving patterns above the 26s. In all the missions David flew, he never took fire from an enemy fighter. Ground fire was another matter. David took ground fire on every mission, a constant deadly threat.

Some missions fell into categories. "Tadpole Missions" tended to be somewhat boring. (David called them "Mickey Mouse Missions." It wasn't clear to the pilots where the official name Tadpole came from). When the weather was socked in, medium altitude missions, typically at 16,000 feet, were dispatched to bomb a predetermined location. The crews never knew what they were bombing, only the types of bombs that made up their payload. Planes were directed to their targets verbally by radio, told when to drop their bombs, and then sent home. They didn't know the results until after they returned. The planes were directed by "Shirley," who was not a cute little curly-haired girl, *ala* child movie actress Shirley Temple who was popular at the time. Shirley was the code name for Combat Command in Seoul, Korea, though she changed her name from time to time. In order to avoid hitting American ground troops, a "bomb line," which changed daily, was established about 200-500 yards north of the troops front lines. Bombs were dropped at a prescribed distance north of the bomb line. The directions to target and then back to base were controlled by radar trucks on the ground. One of David's Tadpole missions was flown in thick cloud cover and weather from take-off to landing, totally on instruments, an incredibly nerve-wracking flight.

Night reconnaissance ("recce") missions were a little hairier. Crews flew in the dark looking for trucks, tanks, convoys or boats. The planes were not equipped with infrared target detectors, so they had to rely on reflections or anything else that disclosed targets. Enemy vehicles traveled over mountainous roads, keeping their lights off to avoid detection. But some road sections were so dangerous that lights were needed. When the lights came on, the vehicles or convoys became targets. When targets were spotted, parachute flares were dropped to illuminate them. David then decided whether to only bomb, or to bomb and strafe as well. Strafing was prohibited until bomb loads were gone. Otherwise, the wings would be overstressed. Attacks continued as long as they were getting results. Sometimes the planes took enemy fire from a convoy or nearby ridges.

At the end of one recce mission, David's navigator spotted an enemy harbor patrol boat in Wanson Harbor. The wing guns were set up to fire on the boat. The B-26 began its strafing run, blowing a hole in the boat at the water line. The gunner watched the boat go down. The gunner wanted to paint a boat on *Sweet Miss Lillian* to notch the kill, but David declined.

Train killing missions formed part of the squadron's routine. Trains moved enemy troops and supplies through the North Korean countryside. Stopping those trains was an important strategic objective. David flew three of these missions. The first was a single plane mission in partnership with an offshore Navy destroyer along the Northeast coast from Wonson to a point about fifty miles south of

Vladivostok in Russia. A Navy underwater demolition team (UDT) [the forerunners of today's Navy Seals] based on the destroyer infiltrated the surf line close to the railroad tracks using an inflatable rubber boat. The team belly-crawled across the ground up to the tracks and attached clips to the rails to detect an oncoming train. The UDT monitored the clips from their boat, signaling David's plane when a train was detected. The UDT team then fired star shells — pyrotechnic munitions used for illumination — to light the tracks and the tunnel into which the train was heading. David's plane then went in ahead of the train and bombed the tunnel to close it off, trapping the train. He then came around and bombed the trapped train, finishing up with a strafing run. Another B-26 came in after David, finishing the destruction of the train.

The second and third missions were similar but in different locations. In one, the train was trapped inside a tunnel so it couldn't be attacked. In the third, another plane had trapped a train outside of a tunnel, allowing David and his crew to finish it off.

The trains were not sitting ducks. After suffering a series of losses, the North Koreans began mounting anti-aircraft guns on their trains, making the train runs dangerous and deadly.

A hydro-electric plant on the Yalu River kept the lights burning in North Korea. David and his crew were handed the opportunity to turn out the lights. Three B-26s from his squadron were selected to drop phosphorous bombs on the plant. Phosphorous munitions create fires that can't be put out. David's B-26s lit up the target for a strike group of multiple B-29s which finished off the plant with explosive bombs. As an in-your-face touch, the phosphorous bombs were colored red, white and blue. David flew the lead plane in a trail formation (one plane behind another). Hastily dropping their flares, the planes were gone by the time the B-29s arrived. As his plane headed south, David's gunner reported large fires and explosions.

All the lights were out in North Korea for a couple of weeks, as well as the trolley cars and mining operations.

The most dangerous mission David recalls was a night mission to destroy search lights on the South bank of the Yalu River, a location far from his home base. In addition to the threat of being shot down, trying to nurse a damaged plane home over a long distance added another fear. B-29s were dispatched on bombing runs along an arc where the Chinese and North Koreans had set up POW (Prisoner of War) camps. Those planes couldn't conduct higher-altitude bomb runs along that route for fear of hitting their own troops, who were imprisoned in the camps. They were therefore forced into lower altitude runs in order to insure greater accuracy. Search lights were set up in an area somewhat away from those camps that lit up the B-29s like daylight, making them easier targets for anti-aircraft fire. The search lights made the B-26s easy targets as well.

David's flight was assigned a fifteen square mile area to look for search lights. They found some, and began taking fire. There was a huge concentration of anti-aircraft batteries around the searchlights. The North Koreans really didn't want them put out.

A twin-engine night fighter that was flying cover for the B-26s piloted by a Marine colonel was shot down. The butterflies churning up David's stomach wondered if they were next. They were flying very low, between 1,000 and 1,500 feet. David's flight managed to put out some of the searchlights with bombs and machine guns. His heart was pounding, but they got the hell out of there alive. Taking ground fire was a part of every mission, but this was the closest he and his crew came to being shot down.

Some missions fell outside of any categories. David's navigator got him lost on his 9th mission, after which the navigator was replaced. On occasion, B-26s were sent out on "hunter-killer" missions to take out radar or search light sites. On these missions, the lead plane would act as a decoy to prompt the enemy into activating the radar or search lights. The second plane would then try to pin down the location of the radar or lights and proceed to destroy the site with bombs or guns. (These missions were the forerunners of the "Wild Weasel" jet fighter squadrons in Vietnam that would do the same thing. The U.S. lacked electronic systems capable of detecting and marking such sites for targeting in the Vietnam War, thus some very brave pilots acted as bait to force the enemy to reveal its positions. To complicate those missions, the enemy would move its sites around so they never remained in the same positions very long).

Only nine of David's missions were daytime flights. The rest were more difficult and dangerous night flights. B-26 and B-29 pilots flew 50 missions on their rotations in Korea. Fighter pilots flew 100. David flew his fifty missions from May through October of 1952. He remarked that each one carried the threat and fear of being shot down.

The pain of seeing friends killed in action was always present. A pilot named Pete had missed combat flying in WWII. He thought he had been cheated out of seeing action. After civilian flying as an airline pilot after that war, he was back in Korea flying B-26s. Disregarding David's warnings, Pete set out on a night mission with a full moon, which was the equivalent of a full-time spotlight on his plane. Pete was killed on that mission.

Although flying was in his blood, David was relieved to finish out his tour in Korea without becoming a casualty. He returned to the U.S. for further pilot training, this time in jets. Starting with the T-33 trainer, he progressed through the F-80 and F-84 to the most advanced U.S. jet fighter of that time, the F-86 Sabre Jet. As his time in active duty came to an end, David transitioned to the Reserves, as a reserve officer attached to the 329th Fighter Squadron of the Air Defense Command at Stewart Air Force Base in Newburgh, New York. In 1961, then a lieutenant colonel, he was assigned to the DIA (Defense Intelligence Agency) in Dover, Deleware.

Like others in this book, David was involved in the Cuban Missile Crisis in 1962 (detailed in later stories). He was employed in the civilian work force at the time. Much to his employer's consternation, he was recalled to active duty and sent to Miami, Florida for thirty days to analyze spy photographs of missile bases under construction in Cuba, which had been taken by the high-altitude U-2 spy plane. The U.S. was preparing for the possibility of a full-scale war in which the missile bases would be prime targets. Fortunately, that war never came, but the U.S. did suffer the loss of a U-2 which was shot down over Cuba.

DH-16. David Hamilton's service medals. Author's photo.

David's military career ended in 1963. The medals he was awarded include the Distinguished Flying Cross for his missions in Korea plus nine air medals; the Korean Service Medal with three battle stars; the European Service Medal with nine battle stars; the Order of William, awarded by Holland; the New York State Gallantry Cross; and the French Legion of Honor, which was presented by the French Consul in Phoenix, Arizona, in 2015. David's medals are proudly displayed in a shadow box in his home *(Plate DH-16)*. Yes, his name is on his nametag in both English and Arabic, reflecting the North Africa component of WWII. The French Legion of Merit is at bottom center.

David's first civilian endeavor was in sales management for G.F. Heublein Company, headquartered in Hartford, Conneticut. Heublein was a major player in the food and beverage industry, producing or distributing products including A-1 Steak Sauce, a wide variety of pre-mixed cocktails, Smirnoff Vodka, and at one time products for KFC (Kentucky Fried Chicken). David's sales management work took him to Portland, Oregon where he managed several states, and worked with the Governor of Oregon on the Wine Advisory Board to develop Oregon's wine industry. He retired in 1973 when Heublein merged with another company.

In 1976, David moved to San Francisco, California to care for his mother whose health was declining. While there, he spent some time as a winery consultant. In 1981, he returned to the work force as a sales manager for the Orvis Company, a Vermont retailer of hunting and outdoor goods and clothing. Orvis was opening their first retail outlet outside of Vermont in California. David remained with Orvis until 1994, when he really and truly retired, moving to Prescott, Arizona. But not really. Since then, he has enjoyed a safari in Africa, worked for ten years with the Yavapai County Sheriff Search and Rescue Team, given frequent lectures at Embry Riddle Aeronautical University, and has been active in veteran organizations.

Not all of David's encounters with famous people are sweet refrains. In 2000, the Pathfinders were holding a reunion in New Orleans, Louisiana. A newly-constructed WWII museum was about to open. One of its sponsors and founders was a famous author named Stephen Ambrose. Ambrose was a university professor who wrote many notable books including *Nothing Like it in the World*, recapturing the building of the transcontinental railroad, and *Band of*

Brothers, a collection of the stories of WWII veterans that was made into a PBS TV series. The museum was scheduled to open in about a week. A group of eight or nine Pathfinders got permission to tour the museum before its official opening. David was quite upset to see that there was nothing about the Pathfinders in the museum's D-Day displays.

After the tour, David and a navigator named Leonard Luck ran into Ambrose on the sidewalk outside of the museum. They recognized him from a picture they had seen. Leonard asked Ambrose, "do you know who the Pathfinders were?", to which Ambrose replied, "No." Wrong answer. David and Leonard went back inside with Ambrose and gave him a very frank education about the Pathfinders.

How could Ambrose not have known of their key importance to the success of D-Day? To this day, David does not know if Ambrose ever included any information about the Pathfinders in the museum.

In 2019, at age 96, David traveled to France for the 75th anniversary of D-Day celebration and reunion. Later that same year, Embry Riddle Aeronautical University in Prescott, Arizona, organized an air show at the local airport in his honor. David is truly a national treasure. His parents are equally remarkable; their stories follow.

Chapter II:
MAJ. GEN. PIERPONT MORGAN HAMILTON 1899–1982

War heroes come from all walks of life. WWII united our rich, our poor, and those in between, from our cities, our small towns, and our vast countryside. All fought and died together, side by side, for a common cause. Although his lineage could be considered aristocratic, Pierpont Hamilton undertook one of the most dangerous missions of that war in order to save thousands of lives. His military service, however, began well before that.

Born in 1899 in Tuxedo Park, New York, Pierpont was the grandson of financier and banking magnate J.P. Morgan, and the great-great grandson of one of our nation's founding fathers, Alexander Hamilton. Graduating from Harvard in 1917, Pierpont pursued his dream of flying by joining the Aviation Unit of the U.S. Army Signal Corp. He trained at Ellington Field, Texas in a DeHaviland DH-4 *(Plate PH-1)*, but the war ended as he completed his flight training. Pierpont attained the rank of captain by the time he completed his three-year enlistment term. Like his yet-to-be-born son David, he had a penchant for intersecting with yet-to-become-famous people. He made the acquaintance of Colonel Carl "Tooey" Spaatz who would later hold significant command positions in WWII, and ultimately become the Chief of Staff for the newly-created U.S. Air Force in 1947.

PH-1. DeHaviland DH-4 Army trainer. Photo: National Museum of the U.S. Air Force.

Some 24 years later, Brigadier General Spaatz would pin the Congressional Medal of Honor onto Pierpont's uniform. The traditional awarding of that medal calls for it to be hung around the recipient's neck on a blue cordon. However, General Spaatz was about 5'5" tall, while Pierpont stood about 6'4" tall. The General was unable to reach high enough to hang the cordon over Pierpont's head, so it was pinned on.

After WWI, Pierpont joined the JP Morgan banking firm. In 1920, he married Marise Blair. They headed to Europe in 1922 to manage JP Morgan's affairs in London and Paris. Their son David was born in Watford, England in 1922. Pierpont returned to New York in 1928. He and Marise were divorced in 1930. In 1931 Pierpont married Becky Stickney from Arlington, Massachusetts, a fashion editor of the trendy magazine *Harpers Bazaar.*

During the 1930s, JP Morgan served as the trustee for the pension fund of RKO Pictures, one of the largest studio film producers in Hollywood. In 1935, Pierpont and Becky moved to Los Angeles, California, where Pierpont acted as the Bank's representative to RKO until 1938, when Pierpont managed the sale of RKO Pictures to Howard Hughes. (See Hughes bio-sketch in David Hamilton's story.) During his time in Los Angeles, Pierpont socialized with some of Hollywood's many luminaries, even facilitating famous actress Lilly Pons' first role in an RKO film. After RKO's sale, Pierpont returned to New York, remaining with JP Morgan until WWII broke out.

Pierpont was recalled to military duty in the Army Air Corp right after the Pearl Harbor attack on December 7, 1941, commissioned as a major. He was assigned by Major General Hap Arnold, Chief of the Army Air Force, as liaison to British Lord Louis Mountbatten's Royal Commandos (similar to our U.S. Navy Seals). Gen. Arnold was an aviation pioneer in his own right, having been one of the first fliers trained by the Wright Brothers.

On August 19, 1942, Pierpont was stationed on a British destroyer off the French coast as an American observer, posted next to the radio room to monitor the effectiveness of the tactics used on the raid in Dieppe, France that day. Pierpont would report his observations back to Hap Arnold's staff in the Pentagon. He was likely shocked and dismayed by what he witnessed. The Dieppe raid was a disaster.

4,963 Canadian troops, 1,075 British troops, and 237 ships amassed for an assault against heavily-entrenched German forces. Within nine hours, 907 Canadian troops were killed, 2,460 were wounded, and 1,946 captured. The costly lessons learned showed that overwhelming force would be required for a sea invasion of France—exactly the tactic employed on D-Day some two years later.

On the Sunday morning of November 8, 1942, Pierpont embarked on the mission that would earn him the Congressional

Medal of Honor, and an article in the February, 1944 issue of *Esquire* magazine, complete with a full-page hand-drawn color illustration of his mission.

The Allied invasion of North Africa was in full swing, landing troops ashore at Port Lyautey, French Morocco. The invasion was being opposed by Vichy French forces.

Pierpont was dispatched into North Africa, together with two other soldiers, to attempt to broker a cease fire. The message, to be delivered to French Maj. Gen. Maurice Mathenet, who commanded the region, was this: The Allies had no quarrel with the French troops or France itself. In fact the Allies had great affection for France and wanted only to see it liberated from Germany's grasp. Nor did the Allies have any intent of conquering and acquiring the French colonies or protectorates in North Africa. The Allies had hopes of a friendly reception. The invasion was aimed solely at the German forces. By agreeing to a cease fire, it was likely that thousands of deaths among Allied and Vichy forces could be averted.

Accompanying Pierpont were Col. Demas T. (Nick) Crew, who was in command of the air units which needed control and use of the local airport, and Private Orris Corey. Pierpont was chosen for the mission given his command of the French language and knowledge of the country from his prior residence in Europe when he worked with JP Morgan.

The two officers wore their full service uniforms rather than battle dress. In the midst of the fighting, the trio boated ashore in a landing craft carrying a jeep. The landing craft would attempt to make its way up a river some five miles to Port Lyautey. When the landing craft could go no further in water, it would drop its ramp and dispatch the jeep to make its way to the French headquarters.

As the landing craft approached the mouth of the river, all hopes of a friendly reception were shattered. Cannon and machine gun fire began to rain upon the landing craft. The ships off shore began to answer with their own fire. The very thing the trio was trying to prevent was occurring; French and American soldiers were dying. Pierpont knew that it was urgent to get their message through.

The mouth of the river was impassible, forcing them to make their landing further down the beach and work their way inland. They landed in the surf. As the battle raged around them, their jeep bogged down. Three fighter planes approached them at twenty five feet, strafing the beach. They dived under the jeep as it was hit by fire. Fortunately the planes went away. They managed to get the jeep unstuck and onto a road running parallel to the beach. Private Corey Drove. Col. Craw sat in the front passenger seat. Two flags were mounted in a flag-holder bracket on eight-foot poles towards the front of the jeep: an American flag and a French flag. Pierpont sat in the back on boxes occupying the back seat, with his feet dangling outside the jeep, holding a white flag (the international symbol for surrender or truce) in his hands on a similar pole. As they drove around the fort that was firing on the invading forces, they ran into a startled company of French infantry, who stood slack-jawed, too startled to fire on them. Pierpont greeted them, shouting "Bon Jour" ("good day" or "hello" in French) as they drove calmly on. Further down the road they plunged headlong into a French field artillery battery. Before the troops manning the battery could react, Pierpont jumped out of the jeep and approached the officer in charge.

Pierpont must have been an imposing figure, as he stood 6'4" tall, quite tall for that era. Pierpont asked the dumbfounded young officer for directions to headquarters to deliver a message. Follow the road, you can't miss it, was the answer.

As the sounds of the battle fell behind them, for a short time they felt more confident in their chances for success. But as they crested a ridge, they ran point blank into a machine gun nest. The gunner opened fire, tearing Col. Craw to shreds. His body fell over onto Private Corey. Miraculously, neither Pierpont nor Corey was hit.

Hamilton leaped from the jeep, raging in barroom French at the young French officer who appeared. "What in #@$! do you mean killing my Colonel? Has the honor of the French Army sunk so low under German influence that you even fire on the flag of truce? Get me your captain!" The captain appeared, punch-drunk from battle and waving a pistol. He was accompanied by a jittery, trigger-happy bunch of soldiers. The captain shouted something like, "Forget about questioning parliamentary procedure; you are my prisoners!"

Pierpont and Corey were stripped of their sidearms and taken at gunpoint in a car to Port Lyautey. Not knowing what to expect or how long they would be held there, Pierpont ruminated over the fact that he had plotted the location of Port Lyautey on a map in the event the Allies needed to bomb or shell the French headquarters. But fortunately, French Col. Charles Petit, who had a clearer head than the excitable French captain, arrived, and the message was transmitted to Gen. Mathenet, who in turn transmitted it to the Chief-in-Charge of Vichy France, Marshall Petain. It took until Tuesday to get results. Meanwhile, Pierpont and Corey spent their time as prisoner-guests wondering if they would end up being bombed or shelled by the Allies. On the evening of the third day, Gen. Mathenet telephoned to advise Pierpont that his mission had been a success. The French would cease resisting the Allied invasion. An immediate meeting with U.S. General Truscott, who commanded the task force under General Patton, would occur.

After his experience with the French troops ignoring the white flag and the excitable French captain who seemed equally ignorant of protocol, Pierpont demanded that a French officer accompany him to locate an American unit where he could radio Gen. Truscott, in the event they encountered French forces ignorant of the cease fire. He was assigned such an officer, as well as a bugler who had been imbibing too much wine, to trumpet a mangled version of the French call of cease fire as they made their way through the

French forces. Some hours later they found an American unit and made the radio call.

That part of the war was over, except for making a dignified disposition of the body of Col. Craw. Thousands of French and American troops' lives were saved, which would have been lost had the battle raged on to its conclusion.

Pierpont wrote to his wife that he couldn't fathom how he and his driver were not cut down as Colonel Craw had been. Perhaps, he mused, St. Christopher had persuaded the Lord that he wasn't worth taking. But he did conclude that from then on, he was living on borrowed time.

The drawing of Pierpont's mission that appeared in the February, 1944 issue of *Esquire* magazine hangs framed in his son David's home.

After his overseas tour ended, Pierpont rotated to the Pentagon in Washington, D.C. in the Plans and Operations section. He authored both the Act of Military Surrender for Germany *(Plate PH-2)* and the Instrument of Surrender for Japan *(Plate AV-8;* see Albert Anthony Villar chapter which follows later). He was awarded the Legion of Merit medal for each surrender document he authored. His son David noted that the surrender articles for Japan had only one word changed from Pierpont's original draft.

The strain of military service on a marriage is extreme, particularly in wartimes. Pierpont and Becky were divorced in 1946. In 1946 or '47, Pierpont was given charge of the purchase by the U.S. of airports in Morocco and Spain for use as military bases.

When the Korean war erupted in 1950, General Dwight D. Eisenhower (known popularly as "Ike") was named as chief of the NATO forces. Ike had previously met Pierpont when the two of them served in the North Africa campaign. Ike chose Pierpont, then a major general, as his Chief of Intelligence. Pierpont's son David had the honor of flying his father from Washington, D.C. to Westover Air

Force Base in Massachusetts for his flight to Paris, where NATO headquarters was located at the time. In 1952, a heart problem while on active duty brought about Pierpont's retirement from active duty.

> Only this text in English is authoritative
>
> ACT OF MILITARY SURRENDER
>
> 1. We the undersigned, acting by authority of the German High Command, hereby surrender unconditionally to the Supreme Commander, Allied Expeditionary Force and simultaneously to the Soviet High Command all forces on land, sea, and in the air who are at this date under German control.
>
> 2. The German High Command will at once issue orders to all German military, naval and air authorities and to all forces under German control to cease active operations at 2301 hours Central European time on 8 May and to remain in the positions occupied at that time. No ship, vessel, or aircraft is to be scuttled, or any damage done to their hull, machinery or equipment.
>
> 3. The German High Command will at once issue to the appropriate commanders, and ensure the carrying out of any further orders issued by the Supreme Commander, Allied Expeditionary Force and by the Soviet High Command.
>
> 4. This act of military surrender is without prejudice to, and will be superseded by any general instrument of surrender imposed by, or on behalf of the United Nations and applicable to GERMANY and the German armed forces as a whole.

5. In the event of the German High Command or any of the forces under their control failing to act in accordance with this Act of Surrender, the Supreme Commander, Allied Expeditionary Force and the Soviet High Command will take such punitive or other action as they deem appropriate.

Signed at Rheims at 0241 on the 7th day of May, 1945.
France

On behalf of the German High Command.

[signature]

IN THE PRESENCE OF

On behalf of the Supreme Commander, Allied Expeditionary Force.   On behalf of the Soviet High Command.

[signature: W. B. Smith]   *[signature: Souslaparov]*

[signature]
Major General, French Army
(illegible)

PH-2. Act of Military Surrender drafted by Pierpont Hamilton officially declaring Germany's surrender in WWII. U.S. government document.

In addition to the Congressional Medal of Honor he was awarded for the mission to quell the Vichy French resistance in North Africa, and the two Legion of Merits he was awarded for drafting the

German and Japanese surrender instruments, Pierpont received the French Legion of Honor for his North Africa service, and the Order of the British Empire for his service with Lord Mountbatten's staff and in North Africa.

Meanwhile, Eisenhower had entered the political arena as a Republican candidate for the U.S. Presidency. Pierpont, who had moved to Santa Barbara, California, became Eisenhower's California Campaign Finance Director. When Eisenhower accepted the party's nomination in Chicago, Pierpont was one of a small group of people standing together with him.

Drawing of Pierpont Hamilton's mission in Port Lyautey originally printed in the February, 1944 issue of Esquire magazine. Reprint permission requested without response.

During the ensuing years, Pierpont founded the Santa Barbara Bank & Trust, Lear-Sigler, (which operated a radio station), and Channel Industries, which owned the land on which Lear's transmitter and tower were located. The latter two companies have since merged into Alta Properties. Pierpont was also President of the

Valley Club in Montecito, California. Pierpont passed away in 1982 in Santa Barbara.

Although his family was considerably well off, all three of his sons proudly and gladly served in the military in WWII. Pierpont's portrait is displayed in the Pentagon in Washington, D.C. and in the Air Force Academy (AFA) museum in Colorado Springs, Colorado (the AFA portrait is shown at the start of this article).

Chapter III:
MARISE CAMPBELL 1899–1995

America's success in WWII was a group effort, a collaboration between civilians and our military. Each played a vital role in winning the war. Among civilian agencies, the Red Cross stood out in its support of our troops at home and abroad. Of the many dedicated women of the Red Cross who served our troops overseas, some shined exceptionally bright. Marise Campbell was one of them. Born Marise Blair in Peapack, New Jersey in 1899, the youngest of four girls, she was crowned the New York State Amateur Figure Skating Champion in her teens. Her love of the Red Cross started at an early age. In 1918, she starred in a benefit performance for the organization at Madison Square Garden in New York City, towards the end of the First World War. In 1920, she became Marise Hamilton, marrying Pierpont Hamilton. They would have three sons together.

Marise and Pierpont parted ways in 1930 by way of a divorce. She moved to Reno, Nevada, where she struck up an acquaintance with another recently-divorced lady named Claire Booth Luce. Marise shared her son and ex-husband's penchant for intersecting their lives with people who would one day become famous. Luce became the editor of two trendy magazines, *Vogue* and *Vanity Fair*, between 1930 and 1934. She also became a successful playwright, served in the U.S. House of Representatives, and was the first woman appointed to a major ambassadorship (Italy) in 1953. She was an influential figure in politics for many years after that.

During her time in Reno, Marise's godfather passed away, leaving her an inheritance of $10,000.00, an enormous sum in those days. Marise embarked on a journey around the world, spending six months in Peking (now known as Beijing), China and an extended time in India as a guest at the estate of the Maharaja of Jaipur. A letter of introduction from an influential friend in the U.S. paved the way for that visit. She also spent time in New Zeland, where she wrote several magazine articles to supplement her inheritance and cover travel expenses.

After Marise married a neurosurgeon, Doctor James B. Campbell, WWII would pull both of them overseas. Before America entered the war, Marise, her mother, and all of her sisters, were engaged in activities with the Red Cross, as well as with the Friends of France, an organization started by her aunt (her son David's great aunt), Ann Morgan. Friends of France had chapters across the U.S. Its members knitted socks and scarves to send to the people of war-torn France. When the U.S. entered the war, it was a natural next step for Marise to join the Red Cross full time. In addition to her pre-war involvement with the civilian organization, her three sons were all serving in the military. In 1942 she headed to Washington, D.C.

Meanwhile, Dr. Campbell was dispatched to the Pacific war theatre. In 1942 he was sent to Australia as an Army Captain and head of the first Harvard University medical unit sent overseas to operate on war casualties. He was later transferred to the battlefields of New Guinea, and then to the Philippines, performing surgery in the midst of battle. One of his operating tents was next to an actively-firing 155 mm. cannon emplacement. Dr. Campbell was told each time the gun battery was ready to fire a round, so he could stop cutting with his scalpel. The concussion of the gun firing was so great that the ground shook. His delicate surgeries would have gone disastrously wrong had he been making an incision when the cannon fired.

After the war, Dr. Campbell's experience with badly injured soldiers led him to undertake research at Massachusetts General Hospital in order to explore methods of repairing the spine and neck injuries that left soldiers as quadriplegics. One of the research labs studied the nervous systems of cats, which have some similarities to those of humans. David Hamilton wryly referred to it as the "cat house." In later years when David was employed by the Heublein company in Oregon, David met a veteran by the last name of Green whose life Dr. Campbell had saved during WWII by implanting a metal plate in his head.

MC-1. Princes Garden Officers' Club, London, England. Photo: Marise Campbell.

Marise served with the Red Cross in Washington, D.C. from 1942 into 1943. Later in 1943 she headed to England by ship to manage and operate a rest and recuperation camp for the 8th Air Force in London. Once again, her path intersected with a future celebrity. One of her fellow passengers and bridge partners aboard ship was a young 26-year-old UPI reporter named Walter Cronkite who was on the way to Europe to report on the war. Young Walter would join CBS (Central Broadcasting System) News in 1950, rising to anchor its evening news television broadcast from 1962 to 1981, appearing on millions of television screens across America. He became one of the most recognized and respected broadcast journalists in the country. His demeanor, sonorous voice, and fatherly/grandfatherly appearance earned him the moniker "the most trusted man in America".

The 8th Air Force Camp assignment set the stage for Marise to become the manager of the Prince's Gardens Club in London from 1943 to 1944. Located in a stately English building *(Plate MC-1)*, the club was a haven for war-weary officers who temporarily escaped the war there. Marise formed an incredible bond with the officers and engendered such loyalty and affection among her co-workers and the troops who came through there that, on her 44th birthday, she was presented with a leather-bound 54-page scrapbook with her name embossed in gold on the cover, full of photos, letters, newspaper articles, and other memorabilia. Some of the newspaper articles reported the deaths of pilots who had spent time at the club before returning to combat flight. The number of pilots whose pictures and newspaper clippings appear in the book is striking, a testament to the closeness of the ties they forged with Marise in a short period of time. The scrapbook is a treasure trove of war history, a miniature museum in itself. It was difficult to select a small representative sample of its contents that would not overwhelm this book. Here are but a few of the treasures it contains:

Plate MC-2: snack bar of Prince's Gardens Club. Note the black shades over the windows. London was regularly bombed at night by German planes. The city was subjected to night-time blackouts, requiring windows to be covered and outside lights turned off to avoid presenting a visible target to the German bombers.

MC-2. Snack bar, Princes Gardens Officers Club, London. Photo: Marise Campbell.

MC-3. Top: *officers sunbathing, courtyard, Princes Gardens Club, Summer, 1943.* Bottom: *officers relaxing inside Club, 1943. Photos: Marise Campbell.*

Plate MC-4: Marise with club mascot "Inky". The idea of "therapy dogs" is nothing new, just the term.

MC-4. Marise Campbell with club mascot "Inky."
Photo: Marise Campbell collection.

Plate MC-5: a caricature of U.S. wartime President Franklin Roosevelt and British Prime Minister Winston Churchill.

MC-5. Caricature of British Prime Minister Winston Churchill and U.S. President Franklin D. Roosevelt, respective wartime leaders. Marise Campbell collection.

Plate MC-6: the front of a propaganda leaflet dropped in large quantities over Germany by the British Royal Air Force. The back side showed photos of some of the submarines being sunk. The German people were deceived by their press as to how the war was going. This flier announces that 30 German submarines were sunk in May of 1943, not exactly a picture of German victory. Many similar leaflets were printed and dropped during the war.

LUFTPOST *Extrablatt*

Grösste U-Bootoffensive zusammengebrochen

Über 30 U-Boote im Mai versenkt

Im Mai 1943 hat die deutsche U-Bootflotte ihre grösste Offensive gegen die alliierte Schiffahrt auf dem Atlantischen Ozean unternommen. Diese Offensive ist mit furchtbaren Verlusten zusammengebrochen.

Während die Schiffsverluste der Engländer und Amerikaner seit Mitte Mai auf ein Minimum zurückgegangen sind, sind U-Boote in grösserer Zahl vernichtet worden als je vorher in diesem Kriege.

Im Mai sind über 30 U-Boote vernichtet worden. Auch im Juni sind die U-Bootverluste schwer gewesen. Dagegen ist zwischen Mitte Mai und Ende Juni im ganzen Nordatlantik kaum ein einziges Handelsschiff mehr versenkt worden.

Getreu den Ankündigungen Hitlers und Goebbels' haben tatsächlich im Mai 1943 U-Boote in grösserer Zahl und stärkerer Konzentration als je zuvor im Atlantischen Ozean britische und amerikanische Geleitzüge angegriffen. Diese „Rudel" sind von britischen und amerikanischen Patrouillenflugzeugen aufgespürt, durch Bomben- und Torpedoflugzeuge, Zerstörer, Korvetten, Kanonenboote und Fregatten von den Geleitzügen weggetrieben, in tagelanger Verfolgung über Hunderte von Seemeilen gejagt und vollkommen aufgerieben worden. Viele U-Boote sind mit Mann und Maus untergegangen.

An einem einzigen Tage — dem 7. Mai 1943 — wurden im Atlantik 6 U-Boote versenkt und 4 beschädigt. Dabei kam eine neue Geheimwaffe erfolgreich zur Anwendung.

In einer anderen, fünftägigen Geleitzugsschlacht wurden 2 U-Boote mit Sicherheit, 3 weitere wahrscheinlich versenkt und mehrere andere so schwer beschädigt, dass sie ihre Ausgangshäfen nicht mehr erreicht haben dürften. Die Gesamtverluste der U-Boote im Mai 1943 waren mehr als doppelt so hoch wie im Mai 1918 — dem „schwarzen Mai" des vorigen Krieges.

Im Mai übertrafen die Schiffsneubauten in England und Amerika die Schiffsverluste um mehr als eine Million Tonnen. Im Juni ist der Zuwachs an Handelsschiffstonnage noch grösser, und zwar sind nicht nur die Versenkungen erneut zurückgegangen, sondern die Kurve der Schiffneubauten ist auch weiter emporgeschnellt.

In Amerika liefen an einem Tage, dem 26. Juni 1943, Schiffe mit einer grösseren Gesamttonnage vom Stapel, als die Deutschen behaupten, im ganzen Monat Juni versenkt zu haben.

Diese schwere Niederlage der U-Boote im Atlantik folgt auf die Schlappe, die die U-Boote bereits vorher im Mittelmeer erlitten hatten. In der Zeit vom 8. November bis 3. Dezember 1942 waren an der Küste von Französisch-Nordafrika 30 deutsche und italienische U-Boote versenkt worden; seither sind die deutschen U-Boote im Mittelmeer untätig geblieben. Dafür hat Hitler mehr U-Boote als je im Atlantik eingesetzt. Hitler hoffte, durch eine nie zuvor erreichte Konzentration von U-Booten der englisch-amerikanischen Schiffahrt einen Vernichtungsschlag zu versetzen.

Das Ergebnis war, dass diese U-Boote in Massen in ein Abwehrnetz hineinfuhren und in nie dagewesenem Ausmass vernichtet wurden. Deutschland hat einen der entscheidenden Feldzüge dieses Krieges verloren.

Diese Niederlage wird sich bald an allen anderen Fronten fühlbar machen. Denn die U-Bootoffensive hätte die Vorbereitungen für den Sturm auf die „Festung Europa" lähmen sollen. Ihr Scheitern hat gewaltige englisch-amerikanische Schiffsraum- und Materialreserven freigesetzt. In kurzer Zeit werden die deutschen Soldaten und Rüstungsarbeiter wissen, was das für sie bedeutet.

Die Hitlersche Strategie des Kolossaleffekts hat zur See dieselben katastrophalen Folgen gezeitigt wie zu Lande. Die Niederlage der deutschen U-Boote im Frühsommer 1943 ist das Stalingrad des Atlantik.

G 42

MC-6. British propaganda leaflet dropped into Germany, front page. Marise Campbell collection.

MC-7. *Officers on leave in Egypt. Seated left to right on camels: Lt. Col. Shelton; Dick Wright; Lt. Col. Ellis. Marise Campbell collection.*

Plate MC-8: a British political cartoon. Their dry sense of humor helped them cope with the German bombings of London. The German rockets were called "buzz bombs" because of the buzzing sound they made when flying towards their targets.

MC-8. *British political cartoon, an example of their dry sense of humor and fortitude during the German rocket bombardments of London. Marise Campbell collection.*

Plate MC-9: P-51 Pilot J.J. Jack. Marise referred to him as one of her Three Musketeers.

MC-9. P-51 pilot J.J. Jack in the cockpit of his plane. Marise Campbell collection.

MC-10. B-17 Bombers en route to their new field. Photo: U.S. Army Air Force.

MC-11. Pilots Don Gentile and Johnny Godfrey in front of Don's P-51 Mustang Fighter. Both were former RAF pilots in the Eagle Squadron. Marise Campbell collection.

MC-12. *Major General Henry J.F. Miller busted to Colonel and sent home for blurting out sensitive information. Marise Campbell collection.*

Plate MC-12: Even Generals get in trouble when they blurt out classified information.

Plate MC-13: An article outlining raids in Germany and France. *Upper left:* ace pilot Claude Weaver featured in the article is later reported missing in action.

Plate MC-14: Tin foil dropped by German planes to confuse British radar, found in the club garden in March, 1944. The Germans thought they could bring about Great Britain's surrender by sustained bombing, and later V-1 and V-2 rocket attacks on London. The Germans severely underestimated British resolve.

Claude Weaver, reported missing over France, Feb. 1944.

GREATEST U.S. DAY RAID ON GERMANY

FIGHTERS' DEEPEST PENETRATION

The greatest daylight raid of the war on Germany took place yesterday, when American Flying Fortresses and Liberators, presumably utilising the newly announced device for bombing through clouds, attacked important targets in South-West Germany.

United States Army H.Q. announced last night that the largest number of fighters ever despatched by the American Army Eighth Air Force escorted the record force of United States heavy bombers. The operation was the deepest penetration into enemy territory yet attempted by the fighters.

Spitfires and other Allied fighters also took turns in escorting the American force.

Some 23 bombers and 12 fighters are missing, while 23 enemy fighters were destroyed, 11 by the bombers and 12 by the fighters.

The American armada must have comprised more than 1,300 planes, the number which attacked the Pas de Calais area on Christmas Eve—up to that time the greatest American force despatched on a single mission. The bombers yesterday numbered well over 600.

Of five enemy aircraft destroyed by R.A.F. fighters, two F.W.190s and two Me.109s fell to members of Royal Canadian Spitfire squadrons.

One of the successful Canadians was Flt.-Lt. George ("Screwball") Beurling, D.S.O., D.F.C., D.F.M. and Bar. He chased his victim for 20 miles and shot him down to the north-east of Paris.

"The F.W. blew up as I hit it," said Beurling. "I saw the pilot bale out and passed him in the air about 100 yards away."

Another of the Canadian squadron's victories went to Pilot Off. C. Weaver, a 21-year-old American pilot serving in the R.C.A.F. He destroyed one of the Me.109s.

Weaver escaped from an Italian prison camp after being shot down in North Africa, and he and Beurling between them have now destroyed 45 enemy aircraft. Beurling's score is now 31 and Weaver's 14.

PAS DE CALAIS ATTACKS

Military objectives in coastal areas of Northern France were heavily attacked throughout yesterday by strong forces of Allied aircraft.

The attacks, which began in the morning and were continued at intervals, involved sorties by nearly 500 medium and fighter-bombers escorted by a strong fighter formation.

The heaviest attack of the day was launched by Marauder medium bombers upon targets in the Pas de Calais. Returning crews reported good bombing.

The Marauders' raid followed closely on an earlier attack on similar targets by a strong force of Mitchell and Boston bombers, escorted by fighter squadrons. Good bombing despite cloud was reported by the Boston formations, which included a Fighting French squadron. No enemy aircraft were seen and the flak was light. Bombers and fighters returned without loss.

GOOD BOMBING RESULTS

Later in the day the assault was taken up by squadrons of Hurricanes and Typhoons. Again good results were seen. No enemy aircraft appeared to challenge the bombers' escort of Typhoon fighters.

No medium or fighter bomber was lost throughout the day's intensive operations, but two American fighters and one R.A.F. fighter are missing.

The total number of planes employed in the air offensive yesterday must have exceeded the Christmas Eve daylight figure of more than 2,000.

NIGHT BLOW

Targets in Northern France were probably attacked again last night. After nightfall R.A.F. bombers were heard going out over a South-East Coast district for half an hour. They were flying towards the French coast west of Boulogne.

Within two hours aircraft were returning from the other side of the Channel.

MC-13. Article outlining raids in Germany and France. Upper left: ace pilot Claude Weaver featured in the article is later reported missing in action. Marise Campbell collection.

MC-14. Marise's scrapbook contained a piece of the tinfoil chaff dropped by German planes on London to confuse British radar. The only thing we can glean from the photocopy is its shape and size. Original size is 6" x 3 ½" x ¾" wide.

MC-15. Black and white copy of color pastel drawing of Marise done by a French girl when Marise worked at Versailles. Marise Campbell collection.

Within a month after the D-Day Invasion, Marise went ashore in Normandy to bring coffee and donuts to the front line troops, such was her devotion to our soldiers. Shortly after that, she was transferred to Gen. Eisenhower's headquarters in Versailles, France, where she took charge of the food preparation and service. Marise continued to earn the respect and admiration of those around her. One of the French girls who worked with her at Versailles painted a pastel profile of Marise as a gift to her *(Plate MC-15)*.

The use of the Versailles Palace for Eisenhower's headquarters probably did not sit well with some of the French. Versailles is one of those timeless historic and architectural treasures that defies description, with artifacts such as the gilded furniture of kings and queens dating back to the 1700s. While on leave from the Army in 1971 I took some pictures at Versailles. Unfortunately only two could be found *(Plates MC-16, 17)*. David Hamilton mused that, "Ike probably moved in before [French General] DeGaulle could gripe about him moving in there."

MC-16. Versailles Palace near Paris France, 1971. Author's photo.

After the war, Marise returned to New York. Dr. Campbell had not yet returned. Marise was told that his ship would make landfall in San Francisco, so she headed there. When she arrived there, she was told that, no, the ship wouldn't be arriving in San Francisco, but rather New York. So, back to New York she went.

Marise and Dr. Campbell eventually moved back to Tuxedo, New York, where Dr. Campbell passed away prematurely in the early 1970s. After that, Marise moved back to England for about five years. She had friends there, and told David that she was tired of listening to the "body count" all the time in the television news of the Vietnam War. Her own wartime experiences gave her a particular compassion for the soldiers who were dying in that conflict.

MC-17. *Versailles Palace, 1971. Author's photo.*

Body Count

The news reporting of the Vietnam War forty-plus years ago included a daily mantra that went something like this: "American troops engaged in a firefight yesterday in [pick a name] province. [Big number] of Viet Cong were killed. [Little number] of American troops were killed." This went on for so long that one marveled that there were any Viet Cong left to eliminate. Marise was not the only one disturbed by this.

Lt. Col. James D. Johnson, a retired Army Chaplain who served in Vietnam, in his book entitled *Combat Trauma—A Personal Look at Long Term Consequences* details the still-persistent effects of PTSD (Post-Traumatic Stress Disorder) on veterans of that war. He confirms, and laments, that body count was a misguided official measuring stick for success in that war.

On page 50, he writes: "....combat veterans were abandoned [by the government] in several ways. First, we were abandoned on the battlefield. Our national leaders decided to fight this war by 'out-body counting' the enemy. We became expendable! Individual life was seen as having no value. We were only a number."

After living in England, Marise moved to San Francisco, where she passed away in 1995, a heartfelt influence on her family and the many soldiers whose lives she touched with care and compassion.

Chapter IV:
REFLECTIONS ON THE VIETNAM WAR

Two of the following stories plunge deeply into the uncomfortable reality of the Vietnam War. They include graphic battle and POW camp descriptions which may be difficult for some to read. But reading is one thing. Let's consider, and appreciate, how much more difficult those years were for the soldiers who endured them, for the sake of freedom for others.

Not since our Civil War has the U.S. been so divided and torn apart by a war as it was by the war in Vietnam. Its effects on our country and on the veterans who fought in it linger to this day. In addition, the political overlays from the way it was managed by our government make it nigh on impossible to produce a commentary that will find universal agreement. My own perspectives as an observer of the entire war saga (and as a 1970 Army draftee—who did not see combat) will occasionally bleed over into the narrative. There are ample published materials, as well as other perspectives, on the war for those who want to dig deeper.

Before WWII Vietnam was a French colony known as French Indochina. The Japanese invaded and occupied Vietnam during that war. After the war, Japan's occupation forces were ousted, sparking a communist-led rebellion against French rule. By 1950, opposing sides were cast that would remain antagonists until the end of the Vietnam War.

Communist China and the Soviet Union chose to recognize a Hanoi-based Northern faction as the legitimate government of the country. The U.S. and Great Britain chose to recognize the French-backed South faction based in Saigon as the legitimate government. In the early 1950s, the U.S. began trickling in money, military advisors and trainers to aid the South. Like a giant quicksand patch, the conflict would slowly suck the U.S. in deeper and deeper.

In 1954, the French surrendered, leaving a power vacuum. Hostilities between North and South Vietnam pressed on. U.S. involvement continued at a lower level until about 1962. After the failed Bay of Pigs invasion of Cuba in 1961 and the Cuban Missile Crisis in 1962, (see Appendix E), some historians suggest that U.S. President John F. Kennedy felt pressure to take a more active position in order to counter communist military aggression. U.S. aid was ramped up. Following President Kennedy's assassination in 1963, Vice-President Lyndon Johnson, who had an even more aggressive position on Vietnam, became President and greatly escalated U.S. involvement.

On August 2, 1964, three North Vietnamese torpedo boats attacked the *U.S.S. Maddox*, a destroyer on routine reconnaissance in the Gulf of Tonkin. Report of a similar skirmish a few days later came in, although its accuracy was debated. On August 10th a joint declaration of both houses of Congress known as the Gulf of Tonkin Resolution was passed, giving President Johnson unilateral power to launch any military actions he deemed necessary in order to aid members of the Southeast Asia Defense Treaty, without a declaration of war. U.S. involvement in terms of money, military equipment, and troops quickly escalated. An initial influx of 13,500 U.S. troops in 1965 quickly grew to 200,000 by that year's end.

In 1968, President Richard Nixon was elected to inherit the war. The U.S. began a program of gradual withdrawal of its forces, with a face-saving strategy called "Vietnamization," claiming that the forces of the South would ultimately be able to take over all of the fighting and succeed in winning. In 1975, under yet another president, Jimmy Carter, the U.S. pulled its last troops and government officials out of South Vietnam, whereupon the communist forces from the North overran and conquered the South. As of this writing, Vietnam remains a Communist-run country. Over 58,000 American soldiers died in that war.

The Vietnam War left wounds on America that have never healed. Although more than forty years have passed since it ended, far too many veterans who fought there continue to struggle with permanent psychological damage as well as physical injuries. Significant numbers of veterans who fought there (as well as in other wars) won't talk about it. Not to friends, not to family, not to anyone. There is a very good reason for that.

The Vietnam War had everything going against it. The general sense of patriotism which created a common base of support among most Americans during the Korean War in the 1950s had eroded away. America had become prosperous, comfortable, and perhaps complacent. Beginning in the 1960s, America embarked down the road of divisive groupthink. What social cohesiveness existed began to unravel. The first groups to draw lines were generational: an older generation (my parents' generation) vs. teens and 20-somethings (my generation, the Baby Boomers).

Womens' Liberation pitted women against men. Racial divisiveness rose to a new level. Suddenly we were a country at war with itself. Legitimate grievances were manipulated and hijacked for political purposes, polarizing the country. Creating "victim" groups rather than discussing and solving problems was the goal of those who wanted a divided country.

Generational warfare is nothing new, but this time the break was dramatic. Leftist ideology became trendy. The fact that it was abhorred by my parents' generation made it even more attractive. Favorite slogans of the time included "Question Authority," and

"Make Love, Not War." In keeping with the siren song of the left, civil disobedience and protests worked their way in. By the late 1960s and early to mid-1970s, mob behavior wasn't all that unusual any more. The riots at the 1968 Democrat National Convention in Chicago (over the Vietnam War) were bell cows for the flourishing protest movement.

Within this social upheaval, the Vietnam War took center stage as the best candidate to divide the country; and it did. Countering Communist aggression and fighting for democracy were no longer unifying concepts. In fairness, there have always been those with anti-war sentiment in the U.S., as well as leftist elements, but not to this degree. The unpopularity of the war was exacerbated by the way it was fought. In the public's eyes, there was no apparent strategy or plan for victory. It simply dragged on, with our forces hamstrung by mystifying rules of engagement—limitations on our soldiers imposed by our own government.

Our Vietnam Veterans were treated horribly, by the population at large and by the government they had thought was behind them. The media fanned the flames of discontent continually, echoing the anti-war themes. Many question the accuracy of much of its reporting, as well as blaming it for exacerbating, if not creating, a bitterly divided country.

The war dragged on for years. Those who devised our tactics had the abysmally-misguided idea that the war could be won by "out body counting" the enemy. (Refer back to Lt. Col. James Johnson's remarks in Marise Campbell's story for a first-hand officer's reaction to that tactic). Victory was made impossible by the misguided tactics, strategies, and political decisions that were being made. As the war dragged on into the 1970s with no clear strategy for victory, morale among the troops plunged to the bottom. Death rates were so high that units rarely had their full contingents of soldiers they needed in order to function. Junior officers without combat experience were continually rotated in to replace those killed in battle or who survived to return home. From time to time, enlisted troops reportedly killed unskilled junior officers who insisted on suicidal missions or were so green and inept that they would likely get them killed.

In January of 1973 the Paris Peace Accords were signed ending U.S. involvement in the war. Our POWs began to be released in February. By August, 95% of U.S. troops had been withdrawn. The Accord process committed further U.S. support for the South if the North renewed hostilities. The South would supposedly become independent. But, the North reneged on the treaty, in 1975 mounting an offensive that conquered the South. The U.S. Congress refused to honor the commitment to supply U.S. equipment and arms to counter the renewed offensive, ensuring the fall of the South. The last U.S. personnel were evacuated from Saigon in April of 1975, shortly before the final offensive by the North.

When our soldiers returned home during the war years, many were spat upon and castigated by the very citizens for whose interests they had thought they were fighting. These soldiers had serious medical problems from exposure to the chemical defoliant used to kill jungle vegetation, Agent Orange, which the government failed to quickly and properly recognize and treat. Psychological trauma from battle stress (Post-Traumatic Stress Disorder—PTSD) was rampant, and lingers yet today 40 years later. Anti-war protests and riots plagued college campuses, frequently targeting ROTC programs and students. More than forty years after the last shots were fired, we have yet to fully recover.

As you read on, be mindful that many of those around you—friends, family, co-workers, or strangers you encounter—may be veterans who continue to struggle with the effects of war, although they will never tell you so. Be tolerant of them and thankful for them.

Preface to Chapters V and VI

Ron Byrne and Charlie Taylor represent another face of war, a war that split our country apart rather than uniting it. Their sacrifices are stark reminders that America pays a terrible price to defend the cause of freedom for others as well as for ourselves. While the Vietnam War divided the country, Ron and Charlie's stories demonstrate a tragic unity shared by those who fought in the conflict. Both men returned home from Vietnam afflicted with Post-Traumatic Stress Disorder. Ron suffered seven years of torture as a prisoner of war, while Charlie endured the carnage of savage combat and death on an almost daily basis. But both bear the deep psychological scars that only our veterans can truly understand. It is hoped that the stories of these two men, for whom the words duty, honor and country are more than clichés, will provide some insight into the suffering they endured, both in combat and upon returning home, as well as how the combination of inept, misguided political leadership and media bias can turn a country against its soldiers who fight and die for freedom's sake. Their stories invite us to cultivate a new measure of understanding, respect, and compassion for the Vietnam veterans among us, and demonstrate how faith in God can sustain a soldier through unimaginable horror.

Chapter V:
COL. RONALD E. (RON) BYRNE, JR. 1928—

Greater courage is required from soldiers than from civilians. Most of us will never face death on a daily basis. For those soldiers who are tortured as prisoners of war, one more threshold is crossed. Perhaps the highest level is reached by those who are willing to share those experiences years later. Ron Byrne is one of those rare individuals.

The Great Depression hit the United States when Ron was just a year old. Born in Brooklyn, New York, and raised on Long Island, he dreamed of becoming a pilot through his earlier school years. During our hard economic times in the younger days of aviation, pilots were our adventurers. As they continually strove for new records and frontiers, stories of their ever-expanding exploits hit the newspapers and radio broadcasts, fascinating and thrilling the country.

An early childhood eye injury seemed to put an end to Ron's dreams of flying. As he neared the end of high school, family economics cast doubt on a college education as well. Seeking to continue his education, Ron enrolled in the U.S. Merchant Marine Academy in 1946.

The larger Byrne family had produced a number of lawyers. Following that tradition, he left the Academy after three years, and successfully passed the New York state exam for law school with the intent of pursuing a legal education. But the outbreak of the Korean War derailed those plans for Ron and thousands of others who were destined to be swept up by their draft boards to fight in Korea. Facing the inevitable, in 1951 Ron wisely enlisted in the Air Force Aviation Cadet Program, rekindling his childhood dreams of flying. He also knew that being up in the air over Korea looking down would be far better than being on the ground looking up, wishing he was soaring in that F-86 overhead. Despite his eye injury in his earlier years, Ron qualified medically to fly.

Trading the suburban landscape of Long Island for the dusty Texas plains, he headed to Lackland Air Force Base in San Antonio, Texas, for Basic Training. Basic flight training for six months followed at Bartow Air Base in Florida, where he soloed in the T-6 Trainer *(Plate RB-1)*. Advanced Training at Williams AFB in Arizona propelled Ron into the world of jets — T-33s and F-80s. There, he proudly received his wings and commission as second lieutenant and pilot. The last stop in the U.S. was gunnery training at Nellis Air Force Base in Nevada flying the F-86 Sabre Jet, the plane he would fly in combat *(Plate RB-2)*.

RB-1. AT-6 trainer. Photo courtesy of Pixbay.

Ron headed to Japan for further deployment. Pilots arrived there from the U.S. at different times, and were assigned to units in Korea on an as-needed basis. They had no advance warning of where they would be sent. Ron deployed to combat duty with the 39th Fighter Interceptor Squadron in Suwon, South Korea. His 75 combat missions there had a critical purpose: to maintain U.S. air superiority over the North Korean Mig 15s flown by North Korean, as well as Russian, pilots. (Although Russia continually denied its pilots were flying in combat, claiming they were merely "training" the North Korean pilots, the U.S. was well aware of their dirty secret.)

RB-2. *North American RF-86F Sabre Jet. Photo: National Museum of the U.S. Air Force, courtesy of Wikimedia Commons.*

Ron's missions took to the air actively seeking Mig 15s to engage in combat. But apparently most of the Migs had been scared out of the sky by the American pilots. During his 75 combat missions, he fired at the enemy several times without success, and evaded enemy fire on another occasion. His flight unit's only combat victory was claimed by a Canadian flight commander, who shot down a Mig while flying lead with Ron flying his wing. However, Ron's Squadron boasted a number of Ace pilots (five or more kills). Lieutenant Colonel George Ruddell, the Squadron Commander, downed eight Migs. Captain Hal Fisher shot down ten, before being shot down himself and taken to a POW camp in Manchuria. The leading Ace, not only of the Korean War, but of the entire jet age, Captain Joe McConnell, was credited with downing sixteen Migs.

The 1953 Armistice ended the Korean War. Before Ron returned home to U.S. soil, he enjoyed a bit more flight time over Korea in the enemy-free skies, which he described as a "fun fair." After his return to the States, he served as a flight test maintenance officer at Laredo AFB Texas, moving on from there to maintenance officer school. While posted at Bunker Hill AFB in Indiana (later renamed Grissom AFB after astronaut Gus Grissom), he met a lovely lady named Joanne Kilcline, who became his wife.

Joanne's brother was a Navy fighter pilot who later was promoted to vice-admiral.

Reassignment to England AFB in Alexandria, Louisiana came packaged with a significant promotion to a new plane, the F-100 "Hun," a major upgrade from the F-86 *(Plate RB-3)*. The Hun was the first Air Force plane capable of level supersonic flight, in addition to its nuclear payload capability.

RB-3. F-100D "Hun" supersonic fighter/bomber.
Photo: National Museum of the U.S. Air Force.

The Hun evolved through four versions: A, C, D, (all single seat) and F (2 tandem seats). The F version was later equipped with electronic counter-measures designed to seek out and destroy enemy surface-to-air missile sites with its own Shrike missiles.

Ron continued with flight testing and maintenance duties. A tactical duty rotation to Aviano, Italy with an F-100 squadron provided new scenery for about seven months. Further education ensued under the auspices of the Air Force Institute of Technology, resulting in a Mechanical Engineering degree from Oklahoma State University in 1959.

RB-4. Titan II nuclear ICBM missile, top view, looking down into silo. Photo: U.S. Government.

Moving from aircraft to missiles, Ron was assigned to the Ballistic Missile Division in Los Angeles, California in 1960 as Program Director for the Titan I Missile Launch System, and Program Director for the Titan II silo door system. The Titans were stored in underground silos over 140 feet deep. Titan Is were raised to the surface for launch. Titan IIs could fire from their silos. *Plate RB-4*, Titan II ICBM looking down into its silo.

The Titans were not without problems. From time to time over the years, explosions (non-nuclear) would occur in a silo. Prior to Ron's assignment as Director, a Titan I silo had blown up at Vandenberg AFB in California. While being raised into firing position during a system test, a fully-fueled Titan crashed to the bottom of its silo when the hydraulic system used to raise it to the surface failed. The impact of the fall ignited all of the combustible material on board in an event known as a deflagration, in which fuel burns with intense heat, with the resulting expanding gases bursting the vessel containing the fuel — somewhat akin to napalm. The damage was greater than an explosion that would have created shrapnel, expanding beyond the safety perimeter limits established around the silo. Ron was handed that problem, along with implementing the Titan II silo door system when Titan IIs began to replace the Titan Is. He engaged a research firm to trouble-shoot the failed hydraulic system. They discovered a cracked valve which had leaked hydraulic fluid, causing a loss of pressure in the system.

After a few years of that type of duty, Ron was eager to return to flying. In 1963, he was back at Nellis AFB learning to fly the F-105 *(Plate RB-5)*. On November 22, 1963, the day U.S. President John F. Kennedy was assassinated in Dallas, Texas, Ron and other airmen were in the middle of survival school. More specifically, they were engaged in prisoner of war training. The POW phase was abruptly stopped as the Kennedy assassination was announced. Ron and his fellow trainees at first didn't believe the announcement. They thought it was a psychological gimmick worked into the training. It was hard to believe that such a thing could happen…..until they were taken to see the news on television for themselves.

By 1964, Ron had been promoted to major and assigned to the 67th Tactical Fighter Squadron (TFS) on Okinawa, nicknamed the

"Fighting Cocks." Their F-105s were the most advanced and fastest jet fighters in the Air Force, capable of carrying two nuclear weapons. High-speed-low-altitude missions were their specialty. In November, Ron was rotated into Vietnam. Early missions were flown into Laos. The war was in its infancy at that time, but American involvement would soon explode. 1965 saw an initial insertion of 13,500 troops swell to some 200,000 by year's end. The 67th Tactical Fighter Squadron (TFS), Ron's squadron, under the command of Lt. Col. Robinson ("Robie") Risner, rotated on Temporary Duty to Korat AB in Thailand in March of 1965. They flew a number of successful missions in North Vietnam, including one for which Col. Risner was twice rewarded: with the Air Force Cross medal, and with his picture on the cover of *Time* magazine, wearing his flight helmet with his unit clearly visible on the front. A flight of F-105s, including Ron, was dispatched to destroy a specific bridge as first priority, with two other bridges designated as second and third priorities. In mid-flight, the formation was redirected to one of the lower priority bridges, and then on to the two other bridges. All three bridges were destroyed. Other missions, however, highlighted the cost of the war. On April 4, the Squadron lost its first pilot, who spent almost eight years as a prisoner of war. Ron would later meet up with him when he was shot down and became a POW himself. Following the Korat rotation, the Squadron returned to Kadena AB in Okinawa, Japan, where they resumed training and nuclear alert.

Not all the dangers faced by pilots come from air combat. Fellow airmen who are bad drivers can appear out of nowhere. A number of Airmen, including Ron, owned and used motor scooters to travel over the great expanses of the air base. As Ron was heading across the base taxiway atop his scooter on his way to the operations center, the sun was at his back, creating a blind spot on his windshield by forming a glare in the center from top to bottom. The blind spot didn't obscure any aircraft that posed a hazard; they were big enough to spot. However, the blind spot perfectly concealed another scooter, which flew out of the sun (an old air combat tactic) and crashed into Ron's scooter. The collision broke Ron's collar bone, delaying his rotation back to Korat.

RB-5. Republic F-105 Thunderchief over Southeast Asia. Photo: U.S. Air Force.

On his return to Korat, Ron scheduled all of the pilots for their missions. The arrival of an "expert" led to Ron being shot down, followed by seven years in captivity as a POW. When an "expert" shows up to assess and improve performance in private industry, eyes often roll and puzzlement abounds as to how someone so incompetent can wear that label. However, in the private sector, planes don't get shot down because of an expert's foul ups.

An officer from the Wing Standardization Board arrived on the scene from Kadena Air Base.

Board pilots were supposed to be experienced pilots charged with quality control and procedure standardization among squadrons in order to facilitate movement of pilots between squadrons. Whatever his expertise may have been, he was woefully unsuited to be flying on combat missions with experienced combat pilots.

The first indication of this was revealed in a dangerous way. Ron was flying in formation with an official Air Force photographer in an F-105-F, a two-seater with tandem seats (rather than the single-seat version typically flown in combat). The F-model is heavier and therefore slower than the other F-105 models, in addition to some aerodynamic differences which also reduce its speed. The "expert" was flying lead in a combat formation in a faster F-105. On the way back from the mission, the "expert" left Ron's plane in the dust in a combat zone. Breaking up the formation in that manner left Ron's plane more vulnerable to enemy fire. The "expert" hadn't a clue as to the differing flight capabilities of the planes in his formation, nor, even worse, that he had left one of his planes behind. Ron did not say anything when they got back, but he did not want the "expert" flying with them. Ron delayed his report on the "expert", wanting to be sure. The next day showed how right Ron was. The "expert's" malfeasance got Ron shot down.

Four-plane "fingertip" mission formations flew configured like this:

$$-1$$

$$-2 \qquad\qquad -3$$

$$-4$$

Positions -2 and -4 were Wing Men. A pilot's first fifty missions were flown as a Wing Man. Position -1 was Flight Leader; position -3 was Element Leader. A pilot's final twenty-five missions were supposed to be flown in position -1 or -3.

On August 29, 1965, a four-plane formation set out on a bombing run utilizing computers designed to operate a low altitude bombing system, flying only 100 feet above the ground at 550 knots. The "toss bomb" system directed a plane towards its target at low altitude, providing an electronic signal for the plane to suddenly pull up into a steep climb and release its bomb while climbing, "tossing" the bomb towards its target. The system was designed for the deployment of a nuclear bomb, to allow the pilot to escape from the massive nuclear blast before it detonated. Ron's formation was testing the system's effectiveness with conventional bombs.

The "expert" flew position -3. Despite his misgivings, Ron scheduled himself to fly the "expert's" wing as position -4, where he could further observe the experts "skills." The "expert" failed to maintain the speed required for the formation, lagging his plane and therefore Ron's behind the formation.

Suddenly, the formation flew into anti-aircraft fire. Ron's plane was hit in the nose by a phosphorous round from ground fire, which was probably aimed at the "expert's" plane but hit Ron instead. Despite being hit, Ron flew on to the target, unloaded his bombs, and reported the results back to his formation. But after Ron had climbed to 15,000 feet for the return to base, his cockpit erupted in bright fire from the round that had hit him. The brightness of the flame told him that parts of his plane which were made of highly flammable light-weight magnesium were on fire. Once ignited, magnesium burns extremely hot and the fire can't be extinguished. To add to the crisis, his ammunition began to explode. At 15,000 feet, Ron popped his canopy and triggered his ejection seat to launch himself upward and away from the dying plane. His parachute unfurled, drifting him into the bowels of enemy territory.

Seven Years as a POW

He landed in a bamboo forest atop a hill. A village sat at the foot of the hill. The tall bamboo caught his chute in midair which provided a soft landing as his feet gently touched the ground. Ron detached himself from his parachute harness and looked around. He heard many voices. The hill was surrounded by people. Ron noted that he had no more chance than a sugar cube on top of an ant hill. The first person he encountered was a civilian. Ron simply said "Hi" to him. The civilian wanted no part of this. He turned and walked away. Thirty seconds later, Ron was surrounded by guns.

RB-6. POWs can be seen looking out through barred windows at the Hanoi Hilton. Photo: U.S. Government via AIR FORCE Magazine, February, 1998.

His hands were tied by his thumbs behind his back, bound together with twine. Immobilizing his thumbs was a very effective way to prevent him from using his fingers and thumbs to get out of his restraints. His captors paraded him through the village to show off their prowess, but none of the villagers struck him or did anything to him. This was not always the case. Captured Americans were often assaulted by villagers when marched through local populations. In another stroke of good fortune, they left his boots on. Being forced to walk without them would have torn up his feet badly.

Ron was taken by truck to a camp near the Red River, and from there he endured a five to six hour ride by truck to the main POW camp in Hanoi, officially named Hoa Lo, but christened as the "Hanoi Hilton" by our captured troops. Ron was the 24th American taken captive in North Vietnam. *Plate RB-6:* Prison building, Hanoi Hilton.

He was imprisoned in room 24 before being moved to a cell block with eight cells that the airmen named "Heartbreak Hotel." Early in his capture, he looked out the door of Room 24 at a set of steps leading down to a small enclosed open area about six steps below him, from which he could have jumped.

RB-7. The Hanoi Hilton. Photo: U.S. Air Force, courtesy of Wikimedia Commons.

A concrete trough with a sharp-edged side jutting upwards sat below him. When asked what his lowest point in captivity was, Ron recalled this moment, telling a group of junior ROTC cadets that he thought at that point, "I could end this all" by jumping headfirst onto the concrete abutment. But he dismissed the thought, and never considered that again. Ron's optimism has been a steadying force throughout his life.

Ron was kept in solitary confinement and tortured for thirty consecutive days. The cells had foot stocks where prisoners were shackled during torture. The North Vietnamese favored two forms of torture. "The rope trick," so named by the prisoners, involved pulling the prisoners' arms behind their backs and tightly tying a rope above the elbows, pulling the arms together and nearly pulling the arms out of their attachment to the shoulders. One torturer stood on Ron's elbows while tying the ropes together. The prisoners were left tied like this for hours, the pain becoming progressively more excruciating.

In the other method, ratcheting handcuffs were clamped around the prisoners' forearms half-way up from the wrists towards the elbows, as the prisoner's arms were held behind their back. The ratchets were then tightened further and further until the bones in the forearms were drawn together. Again, the pain was unbearable. To this day Ron feels pain in his right arm from that. Ron's torture took him to the point of death.

Ron notes in a biography published by POW Network (pownetwork.org), that at one point in his captivity, "The North Vietnamese doctor told me I was close to death. A doctor said he would give me nothing to help unless I gave them the information they wanted. I went back to my room and they continued the torture."

Ron confirmed to me that any and all information pulled out of prisoners resulted from sustained torture. When his squadron commander was shot down and joined Ron as a prisoner, the pilots were told to resist as far as humanly possible to the point where severe permanent physical and psychological harm would result.

In the POW Network biography, Ron related that when he was near death he was given intravenous feedings, vitamins, and medications necessary to keep him just barely alive—for propaganda purposes. His survival training and military discipline, as well as his and many others' faith in God, enabled him and the other POWs to survive their torture and deprivation.

One piece of information the captors wanted to extract from Ron, the identity of his unit, fell into their hands from another source. When his squadron commander, Col. Risner, was captured 18 days after Ron, the North Vietnamese had a copy of the *Time* magazine featuring him on the cover. The magazine article disclosed his unit. All they had to do was compare Ron's helmet to get a match. (Ron learned from one of the prisoners who returned to Hanoi in the 1990s that Ron's flight helmet was on display in a war museum in Hanoi.)

Eventually three other pilots from Ron's squadron joined him as prisoners. In addition to Robie Risner, Ray Merritt, "Smitty" Harris and Wes Schierman were captured, all eventually imprisoned in the same building. Harris and Schierman were already there when Ron was moved to confinement with them. Risner and Merrit joined them shortly thereafter.

Around November 17th of the year he was captured, and after about three months of solitary confinement, Ron was moved to another prison on the outskirts of Hanoi referred to as "The Zoo." It was christened as such by the first American taken captive in North Vietnam, Navy Lt. J.G. (Junior Grade) Everett Alvarez who quipped, "this must be the zoo where the animals come to see the people." The North Vietnamese Army (NVA) that held the prisoners moved them around from time to time to prevent any organized resistance or escape groups from forming. Unfortunately, the cycle of torture started all over again. The prisoners at The Zoo who had been there hadn't yet been put through the torture cycle.

Ron was caught up with them. He was confined together with Larry Guarino, a captured pilot from the 44th Squadron, also from Okinawa. He and Larry would live together for the next 44 months.

Larry had flown combat in WWII in North Africa, Sicily, Italy, and ironically in Vietnam as WWII was closing down in Europe.

Larry was a fairly "volatile" Italian from Newark, New Jersey whose temperament would often get him in trouble with the NVA. Larry also had the unfortunate compulsion to constantly talk about gourmet Italian food in great detail while he and Ron were starving. After his release, Larry wrote a book entitled *A POW's Story: 2801 Days in Hanoi* (see Bibliography) in which he credits Ron for saving his life during captivity.

The POWs employed a code tapping system to communicate with each other that was learned by Smitty Harris in survival school. The code matrix was a simple progression of 25 letters, with the letter "K" omitted. "C" was substituted wherever a "K" would be used.

	1	2	3	4	5
1	A	B	C	D	E
2	F	G	H	I	J
3	L	M	N	O	P
4	Q	R	S	T	U
5	V	W	X	Y	Z

The first tap designated the line, the second the column. Thus the letter "B" would be tap—pause—tap tap. At night, the POWs would frequently tap "GN", "GBU"—good night, God bless you—to keep up morale. A loud "bang" signaled the approach of a guard and communication ceased.

At one point, Ron was moved into a cell previously occupied by Robie Risner with walls about 10″ thick. The prisoner in the next cell began tapping at the same spot on the wall. Ron located the spot and discovered that Risner had somehow managed to drill a small hole through the wall, which was concealed by a plug. Ron was able to communicate through the hole with his next door neighbor, a Navy man named "Windy" Rivers. Ron passed cigarettes through the hole to Windy, since Ron never smoked the few cigarettes they were rationed, which he said were really lousy.

In addition to torture, the NVA kept up a steady stream of petty harassment. POWs were required to bow down to the NVA whenever they appeared. The NVA would bounce in and out of the prisoners' rooms every few minutes, forcing them to bow each time. Food was left to sit outside of the prisoners' rooms to get cold and covered with ants before being brought in to the prisoners. The NVA withheld basic hygiene items like toilet paper, soap, toothpaste and clothing.

The prisoners' rooms were infested with ants by the thousands, as well as scorpions and rats.

Mosquitoes were everywhere. Mosquito nets were provided, which gave some protection.

Christmas time in 1965 provided a brief respite. For a short time, better food was provided, and some prisoners were allowed to see a Catholic priest on Christmas Day. The irony of atheist Communists who tortured the POWs recognizing Christmas and involving a priest was not lost on the prisoners. Of course, propaganda photographers were on hand to document how well the NVA were treating their prisoners. Reviewing Larry's memories of captivity when he and Ron were confined together, it shines through that their faith and prayer were sustaining forces for both of them throughout their ordeal. *Plate RB-8*, Christmas Services, 1965.

Although the NVA were interested in strategic information, the torture was primarily designed to get the prisoners to say whatever the NVA wanted them to say. One of the favorites was the lie that they were being treated well, despite constant torture and starvation. In December of 1965, Ron was dragged to an "interview" without any advance warning. The "interviewers" were three Americans who were outright Communists or Communist sympathizers: Herbert Aptheker, the leading U.S. Communist; Professor Staughton Lynd from Yale University; and Tom Hayden, founder of the U.S. anti-war group Students for a Democratic Society (SDS) and, in Ron's words, a "total prick." Professor Lynd seemed embarrassed by Hayden's despicable behavior. The trio of course tried to get Ron to denounce the war and say wonderful things about his NVA captors. Hayden was by far the worst. Ron described him to his cell-mate Larry as hating everything America stands for; one of the most rotten people running loose in the country. Ron was on edge throughout the interview that his failure to say what the NVA wanted would result in further torture after the interview. The "interviewers" failed miserably. After Ron's interview, the NVA began torturing prisoners in advance of future "interviews" to force the prisoners to give the answers the NVA wanted. "Interviews" continued throughout Ron's entire time in captivity.

RB-8. 1965 Christmas services. L to R: Ron Byrne, Jr., Arthur Cormier, Larry Guarino, Father Ho Than Bien. Vietnamese propaganda photo.

Ron described three different stages of his confinement which produced differing treatment for the prisoners. The first stage ran from the time of his capture until the Hanoi March in July of 1966.

The second ran from July of 1966 to the death of Ho Chi Minh, the leader of Communist North Vietnam, on September 2, 1969. The last stage ran from then until the release of all American POWs in February and March of 1973.

On June 29, 1966, U.S. planes bombed oil storage facilities outside of Hanoi, causing severe damage and many casualties. Ron heard and saw the explosions and flashes from the bombing. These were the first sounds of war he had heard since being imprisoned. The North Vietnamese government labeled it "illegal bombing" and decided it needed to stage a propaganda event in response, which became known as the Hanoi March.

On July 6, the POWs were awakened early. The NVA guards were agitated. Something was up. Fifty-two American POWs, including Ron, were assembled, not knowing what for. Their prison pajamas which had no markings on them had been taken from them that morning, then returned that afternoon with non-consecutive numbers stenciled on them. Some of the numbers ran into the high 300s. Ron and Larry's sandals, which were normally very loose, were tied to their feet by the NVA guards with lengths of gauze, for unknown reasons. Ron relates that it was a bizarre feeling to have the guards doing that.

The prisoners were blindfolded and trucked into Hanoi to Hang Day Stadium. After the blindfolds were removed, the prisoners were handcuffed together in pairs, side by side, and lined up to march. Ron and Larry were handcuffed together. They knew then why their sandals had been tied to their feet.

The two-by-two column was marched down the main street of Hanoi for about 1 ½ miles. Each handcuffed pair of POWs had an NVA guard on either side with bayonets attached to their rifles, ostensibly guarding the prisoners but in reality keeping the crowds back. They were unsuccessful in that. Ron and Larry saw thousands of citizens lining the streets in deathly silence as they approached.

Ron heard a single loud shout, at which point the crowd, on cue, erupted in an angry wave of yelling, cursing the POWs as they marched along the street. The event was obviously orchestrated. The crowds were agitated by soldiers with bull horns. Interrogators were interspersed with the NVA guards. One of the NVA soldiers accidentally jabbed an interrogator in the hind end with his bayonet in the midst of the jostling, a rare moment to enjoy.

Two flat-bed trucks were positioned near the start of the march, full of international journalists eager to take still photos and movies of the circus. Some wandered in and out of the throng of prisoners snapping pictures of the staged event. The inflated numbers on the pajamas suggested dishonestly that the NVA had captured far more prisoners than it actually had. Official sources claimed the actual number at that time was less than 100.

As the march returned to the stadium, the crowds morphed into a violent mob which some described as a riot, beginning to beat at the POWs, some with rocks and stones. Ron was struck by a woman wielding a shoe. Bottles were thrown. The safety of the POWs and the NVA's ability to control the crowd deteriorated. The NVA guards were genuinely frightened. As they got close to the stadium, Ron watched an angry woman who couldn't get close enough to the POWs to strike at them reach down and pick up her small child, whom she threw at them. The flatbeds with the photographers had been located where they couldn't see the mob violence erupt. The POWs reached the safety of Hang Day Stadium, from whence they were returned to their camps. There, they were handcuffed to trees until they were taken back to their cells. While the prisoners were handcuffed to the trees, NVA guards would randomly walk by and punch them or kick them in the groin. Some suffered torture that night. Most POWs were not tortured before the march, although some had been subjected to it.

The event backfired to a large extent, drawing widespread condemnation across the globe, and showcasing the mistreatment of POWs. Ron noted that a senior U.S. officer had been asked by the NVA after the march what he thought. The officer thought it had been barbaric. The NVA let slip that it hadn't been their idea, but rather the Communist government's, perhaps showing that the Army hadn't thought it was a good idea. That government had been threatening to pursue war crime trials against the prisoners before the march, but backed off after the condemnation.

The Bibliography at the end of this book lists some sources for information on the Hanoi March.

At least one YouTube video of the march exists, in which Ron can be seen.

The wholesale torture of POWs continued, not to extract information, but to produce lies. The first lie the NVA wanted from Ron was a written statement that he "appreciated the humane treatment" of his captors. On the night of July 8, just after the march, Ron and Larry were tortured with the rope trick all night to get them to write this lie. They heard the screams of other POWs who were being tortured. At one point, while Robie Risner was being tortured, he tried to identify who was screaming…..and realized it was himself.

Larry was the Senior Ranking Officer (SRO) in the Zoo at that time. An older POW, "Pop" Kearns, who had flown in WWII, had been tortured into writing a confession. Pop approached Larry, wanting to turn himself in for treason. Pop was devastated by what he had been forced to do. Larry refused, spending about two hours talking Pop down.

They were soon transferred to another camp about 50 miles from Hanoi known as the "Briar Patch," where they were tortured again, this time with the ratcheting handcuffs. At this point in his story I had to ask Ron the question I wanted to ask from the outset: "How did you endure for so long?" Ron simply said, "there was no choice but to endure." Ron did note during a presentation to students at Yavapai College that at one point, he and Larry were discouraged to the point where they hoped that the U.S. would come in and wipe out North Vietnam with nuclear weapons and end the misery.

The cell walls at the Briar Patch were made of rough stone to discourage prisoners from tapping on them to communicate. The POWs did it anyway. There was no electricity, no lights. The food got worse. The addition of a generator allowed the NVA to introduce the "Bitch Box," a loudspeaker that blared propaganda. Prisoners were sometimes amused at the lame attempts to convince them of exaggerations such as the lie that thousands of U.S. aircraft were being destroyed in battle. But, during their captivity, the POWs also received news of the anti-war protests in the U.S., which had a demoralizing effect.

In late January of 1967, Ron and Larry were transferred back to the Zoo, still receiving torture almost daily. Eventually he and Larry were put in a remote cell to prevent communications with other POWs. The NVA were obviously aware of the strength the Americans drew from each other. Torture continued. Ron spent five months in leg irons. Larry spent eight months.

During the dark times, Ron and Larry developed a routine to fight off despair. They would list everything good they could think of that they had going for them, like the fact that Americans didn't like long wars. They fortunately didn't realize at that point that they had almost seven more years to go.

One day, as Larry was running in place in their cell for exercise, the NVA guards appeared and accused him of trying to communicate with other prisoners by code. For punishment, he was locked into leg irons and had his hands handcuffed behind his back for ten days. He was supposed to be released for eating and bathroom breaks but never was. Ron had to help him sit on the chamber pot they used to relieve themselves, and to feed him with a spoon. After five days of this, Larry was unable to eat and was in excruciating pain. Through the prisoner grapevine, a prisoner in an adjoining cell was able to slip a metal pin into Ron's food bowl. Ron learned how to unlock Larry's cuffs, and then taught Larry to do it himself so that he could periodically get relief from them. Larry learned to unlock and re-lock them quickly and endured his last five days of punishment without being caught.

Cuban officers were among the torturers. The NVA and Cubans used strips cut from tires that looked like automobile fan belts to beat the prisoners. A Navy pilot, Earl Cobiel, was beaten so severely that he went into a catatonic state. The Cuban who was torturing him thought he was faking it and beat him severely on his face, without getting a reaction. Ron noted that nobody could possibly fake not being fazed by that kind of beating. Cobeil eventually died from his beatings.

The Cubans were given access to about twenty American officers. It was thought that the Cubans were there to experiment on the Americans in order to learn how much physical torture it took to break a prisoner.

The Cubans and NVA guards and torturers were nicknamed. Two of the Cubans were "Fidel" (who was unbelievably sadistic) and "Pancho." Fidel had possibly been trained in prison control psychology somewhere in Russia or Europe. The NVA guards were nicknamed largely based on things they resembled: "Bug," "Rabbit," "Duck," "Dum Dum," "Fish," and "The Flea."

Inexplicably, after being isolated from other prisoners, Ron and Larry were transferred to a large cell block with ten cells known as the Pool Hall that housed multiple prisoners. Ron called it "communication central" because line-of-sight communication was possible to most other buildings housing prisoners in the Zoo. The prisoners were able to take advantage of this arrangement by communicating through a form of sign language.

Roommates can only be best friends for so long during the best of times before they start irritating each other. As the years passed, Ron and Larry had their moments. They began to criticize and grouse at each other, one day ending up in a wrestling match when tempers got out of hand. Once they got that out of their systems, they became friends again.

Torture slacked off somewhat, until two POWs escaped from another camp nearby. They were only free for 12 to18 hours before recapture. One of them was killed by the severe torture that followed his recapture.

After the two prisoners escaped, the torture started again, first at that camp and then moving on to Ron's. This time, it was to learn how prisoners communicated with each other. The rattling of keys on a large metal key ring signaled the approach of the NVA to remove a prisoner from his cell to be tortured. To this day, "rattling keys are still a problem" for Ron. Then one day, abruptly, the torture stopped.

Something had happened.

On September 2, 1969, the leader of North Vietnam, Ho Chi Minh, died. He was a rabid, brutal Communist who had been groomed in the Soviet Union early on from 1923 to 1925. His successors did not seem as enamored with torture as he had been.

Ron was moved to a room with three strangers who were captured more than eighteen months after he was. From them, he gained information about what was happening outside the camp. He tried to share his meager food ration with one of the prisoners he felt needed it more, but the rest of the prisoners convinced Ron that he actually looked a lot worse. Ron was down to somewhere between 90 and 100 pounds at that point. His weight was up to 125 pounds when he was released.

For a short time, things got a little better. The prisoners were given packages sent from home, the first ever to be handed out. Some contained playing cards, which the men enjoyed (for a short time; they were later taken away). Some of the prisoners began exercising, doing push-ups and walking (in circles in their small cells). During Christmas, a few men were given Bibles, and POW Quincy Collins formed a choir, which performed over the Bitch Box in the camp.

The Son Tay Raid

In November of 1970 things got ugly again, after the simultaneously successful and failed Son Tay raid. U.S. intelligence received reports showing that about 500 American POWs were being badly abused in a POW camp at Son Tay. Months of planning led to a rescue raid by special forces in November of 1970 involving 29 aircraft. The raid was successful in that some 200 NVA guards were killed and the only American casualty was a broken ankle. Sadly, it was unsuccessful in that all of the Americans had been moved elsewhere in July. There were no POWs in Son Tay. Although the raid had failed, word of it somehow got back to the prisoners. Ron noted that it "energized" the prisoners to know that someone out there cared enough to try to rescue POWs from their years of captivity.

For some reason, on December 26, 1970, the Zoo erupted in turmoil. Prisoners were strip searched, their cells ransacked, and most of what they had gotten in their packages from home was taken away, including their playing cards. They were blindfolded and moved into large rooms in the Hanoi Hilton. The rooms quickly began to fill up. Within three days there were 39 men in Ron's room. The POWs later learned that the Son Tay raid had prompted the move.

After the long periods of prisoner separation, the unexpected reunion lifted the men's spirits. Some shared narrations of their favorite movies. Others attempted to teach their comrades about subjects they knew. One held a class in self-hypnosis. Room-to-room chess games were organized, using the tap system to communicate moves. Consider the ingenuity required to do this.

The Prisoners Revolt

Although the NVA rules prohibited anyone from lecturing, Church services were organized.

When the NVA stopped Robie Risner from preaching in Room 7, and removed all of the senior officers from the room, the roots of a revolt were formed. The prisoners began singing the National Anthem, which flustered the NVA, who didn't know how to respond.

In Room 6 where Ron was located, the SRO attempted to lead the service. The NVA came in and removed the SRO, but the men had previously decided to simply rotate in the next-ranking SRO to continue leading the service as each successive SRO was removed by the NVA. The men began to recite the Lord's Prayer in unison as the removals continued. Their frustration level began to boil over, and the prayer recital turned to screaming as the room lurched out of control. One POW was literally red with rage. After a few removals, Ron became the SRO.

The NVA began to react, in a dangerous fashion. Guards who were literally kids, appeared at the windows with rifles and pointed them into the room at the prisoners. Ron did not trust the judgment of the NVA kids, not knowing what might prompt them to start shooting. It could end up a blood bath if they did. He had to stop the pandemonium before that happened, and brought the POWs activity to a close. But the prisoners were not ready to give up their quest to express their grievances. They just needed a new plan.

A couple of days later, the prisoners began a plan that worked, dubbed the "Stare Program." Individual prisoners would pick out an NVA guard when out in the prison yard and stare at them for prolonged periods without taking their eyes off them. This proved to be quite unnerving to the guards, and ultimately was successful. Ron, acting as SRO at the time, was granted an audience with the Camp Commander to air the prisoners' grievances.

Another Moving Day

In May of 1972, Ron, along with about 240 others, were moved to "The Dogpatch," located forty miles from the China border. They were treated to a 36-hour non-stop truck ride there, blindfolded and handcuffed. Upon arrival, they were placed in cells with thick, rough concrete walls with narrow slits for windows. There were no individual beds. Each cell had one long row of planks laid end to end along the wall for all the prisoners to sleep on, head-to-head or head-to-toe. The planks were uneven heights at their ends, making sleep uncomfortable and difficult.

The buildings were intentionally laid out in a random pattern to make communication between them difficult. Drain holes were located at the floor level at the ends of two buildings that happened to be adjacent, which allowed the prisoners to signal in tap code by passing a stick through one building's drain hole into the neighboring building. One has to marvel at the ingenuity of our POWs.

Dogpatch was dark, both literally and figuratively. The cell buildings had no electricity. On one occasion, prisoners were herded into an auditorium where they were forced to watch generator-powered propaganda films. They ignored the films and instead used the occasion to communicate with each other. Their spirits refused to be conquered.

October of 1972 ushered in another morale booster. The POWs were reshuffled into different cell blocks, based on their order of capture. They knew there had to be a reason for this, but after their move, through November and December, they heard no news.

Unbeknownst to them, the various politicians embroiled in the war were engaged in the Paris Peace Talks attempting to bring an end to the war. Those talks had stalled. In response, U.S. President Richard Nixon had resumed the bombing of North Vietnam with B-52 Bombers, coming as close as 2,000 yards from the Hanoi Hilton. The B-52s brought Vietnam back to the table.

Freedom

Late at night on January 28, 1973, the Dogpatch POWs heard a sizable number of transport trucks driving into the camp. Their hopes lifted, knowing something was up. On January 29, they were loaded into those trucks for a return trip to the Hilton. Upon arrival, they were grouped together, free to gather in the courtyard. Senior officers were no longer separated from the others. Men reunited with familiar faces, and met the unknown faces of the comrades whom they had known only by tap communication for so long. Did they dare hope the end of their captivity was at hand?

Thanks to their new-found freedom to communicate, they formed the 4th Allied POW Wing (counting forward from WWI, WWII and Korea as Wings 1, 2, and 3), consisting of seven Squadrons. The Wing has its own Unit Patch *(Plate RB-9)*.

On February 4, 1973, the POWs were called into the courtyard by the NVA. They formed up by squadrons, anxious and expectant, to hear the incredible news: the Paris Peace Accords releasing them to freedom. The men remained somber. Robie Risner, then the SRO, called them to attention and dismissed them to their rooms, squadron by squadron. Once back in their rooms, they let loose and celebrated.

They had endured and survived a nightmare beyond anything most of us can imagine.

RB-9. *4th Allied POW Wing Unit Herald, created by the Air Force office of Heraldry in 1973. Its colors are those of the U.S. and Vietnam. The chained eagle symbolizes the captured fighting men. Source (with gratitude for their sacrifice): nampows. org— Three's In ***—the Vietnam POW Home Page.*

In one of those inexplicable moments of war, the Vietnamese allowed the POWs themselves to determine their order of release. Ron felt that they didn't want any problems with the process. The first prisoners to be released were the sick and injured. After that, release groups were scheduled in the order in which they were shot down. As I was meeting with Ron for this book on February 12, 2019, he observed that it was the 46th anniversary of his release. His was the first group to be released after the sick and injured, based on their earliest date of capture.

After years of living in rags and deprivation of basic hygiene items, the POWs were given new clothes to wear and bags for toiletries and (nonexistent) personal effects. *Plate RB-10:* POWs brought by bus to Gia Lam Airfield for the return trip to the U.S.

RB-10. Prisoners awaiting return to the U.S. after delivery by bus to Gia Lam Airfield outside of Hanoi. They maintained their dignity by forming up in military fashion as true soldiers. Photo: U.S. Government via AIR FORCE Magazine, February 1998.

The POWs were not the only ones to find release from captivity. Dog lovers, the rumors are unfortunately true. The Vietnamese used dogs for food. One of the returning POWs managed to sneak out with a small dog that had run out of the camp kitchen. He brought the dog home with him on the plane stashed in his toiletry bag.

Sadly, some of the POWs had cooperated with the NVA propaganda efforts during captivity to escape torture and maltreatment. The NVA sneaked a couple of them out on the first airplane that was supposed to carry home the longest-held POWs. Adding to this insult, those identified as collaborators did not face court martial. Ron felt that the higher-ups likely didn't want the bad publicity at such a sensitive time.

One of the collaborators did suffer consequences of a different sort. When he ran for public office in California, Ron and some other POWs took out a full-page newspaper ad revealing his collaboration with the NVA. The collaborator lost the election, and then brought suit against Ron and the others. He lost that as well.

Back to the World

Vietnam was so surreal that the soldiers who served there coined the phrase "back to the world" to describe getting out of there to go anywhere else. Returning to "the world" required four flight stopovers before Ron's final destination. The first was Clark AFB in the Philippines. 14 POWs flew there with Ron. A total of 566 returned home during the 1973 release. Medical care was provided for the POWs at the base hospital. The hospital cafeteria had an awesome array of food. Although the medical staff wanted the POWs to observe a bland diet, they were "having none of that." Steak was one of Ron's first targets.

The next stop was Hickam Naval Air Station in Honolulu, Hawaii. Custom called for the senior officer deplaning on a returning POW flight to act as the spokesman to those greeting the flight.

Although Ron was the senior officer on his flight, the honor was passed on to a Naval officer—the second-ranking officer on the flight—because the flight was landing at a Naval station.

From Honolulu, the POWs flew to Travis AFB in California. As the senior officer on that flight, Ron gave an eloquent statement to those greeting the flight which he well remembers to this day: "We are grateful to the American people who reached out over time and space, took us by the hand, and brought us home. For this we are eternally grateful."

A stopover at Scott AFB in Illinois followed. Ron did not deplane there, and did not act as spokesman to the greeting contingent. As flights passed across the U.S., the POWs were distributed into smaller planes to continue to their destinations. Ron's final stop was Wright-Patterson AFB in Dayton, Ohio, where he was greeted by his wife, his mother, and four grown sons to whom he had been reading bedtime stories the last time he saw them. He underwent a short hospitalization in order to recover from his mistreatment as a POW. The POWs also received field and intelligence debriefings to report their experiences. Ron's arrival at Wright-Patterson was captured by a government photographer *(Plate RB-11)*.

Ron is aware of the treatment our returning Vietnam Veterans received. He commented that returning with fellow POWs had a good side, coming home with comrades who understood each other's pain, and receiving a positive welcome. Sadly, the 17 to 21-year-old young men who fought in South Vietnam were simply turned loose in U.S. airports to make their own way home, where many were jeered at and spat upon. They had been required to wear their uniforms while traveling.

RB-11. *Ron's arrival at Wright-Patterson, being greeted by General Robbins. Photo: The Daily Courier, a newspaper published in Prescott, AZ, July 27, 2015. Original photo from research.archives.gov.*

After returning home, Ron remained on active duty, attending the Air War College at Maxwell AFB in Alabama. Following that, he was appointed Program Manager for the Joint Tactical Information Systems, and then as Director of Advanced Plans with Air Force Systems Command at Hanscom AFB, Massachusetts, where he served until his retirement in 1977.

Ron was awarded two Purple Hearts, three Silver Stars, and the POW Medal. In addition to the 75 missions he flew in Korea, he flew 27 in Vietnam before his capture. Ron remarked that he was proud to have completed his 100 required missions as a fighter pilot, even though it took him two wars to do it.

Adjusting to life in the U.S. after the years in captivity produced some challenges. Ron was dismayed to witness the declining morals and loose behavior prevalent in the country. Walking among crowds and people who were moving about took some adjustment, coming from an environment where he needed to be well focused on every movement around him. But there were certainly pleasant changes.

Mini-skirts were something new. Cars were a lot better looking. Especially Porsches. A Porsche might have been in Ron's immediate future, were it not for their inability to carry him, his wife and their children as passengers all at once.

Although most would consider Ron a hero, he humbly regards what he endured as a matter of duty and service to his country. He remains hopeful that knowing what our POWs endured in Vietnam will pivot public opinion in a positive way towards our veterans from that war. Despite his experiences, he considers himself blessed in many ways.

Ron has not slowed his pace. As of this writing, he remains actively involved in the local Military Pilot's group and various college classes. His lifelong optimism remains a steadying force in his life. We truly owe a debt of gratitude to Ron and all the other POWs who sacrificed so much for the cause of freedom.

Chapter VI:
1ST LT. CHARLES EDWIN (CHARLIE) TAYLOR 1942 —

I first met Charlie about three years ago. He is soft-spoken and strong of faith, a gentleman in all respects. I was honored when he agreed to participate in this book, because I knew his memories of Vietnam were painful and would not be easy to share. In fact, I learned that some of his post-war struggles were described in a book written  in 2010 by his combat Chaplain, Lt. Col. James D. Johnson (Ret.), detailing the effects of Post-Traumatic Stress Disorder (PTSD) in sixteen Vietnam veterans, including Charlie (see Bibliography). Before we talked, Charlie gave me a copy of the book. I tried to read it in one sitting but couldn't. The pain poured out on those pages was too much. The Vietnam War remains a gash in our collective side that refuses to heal.

Flagstaff, Arizona, sits high in the mountains, above seven thousand feet. It is home to Northern Arizona University; the Lowell Observatory built in 1894, where the planet Pluto was discovered; and magnificent alpine scenery. Charlie Taylor was born there in 1942. He loved the outdoors and the crisp, cool mountain air.

In his younger years he thought being a game warden would be the perfect job. College took him in a different direction. In

1964, he graduated from Arizona State University with a Psychology degree. By the time he was 24, he was married, working for a loan company, and facing the specter of being sent into the Vietnam War. Local Draft Boards were scooping up large numbers of young men between the ages of 18 and 26 to be sent off to fight in far-away jungles.

Charlie asked his draft board where he stood in line. He learned that he was the number one candidate to be drafted the following month. Being proactive and wanting to serve as an officer, he started making the rounds of the local recruiting offices to see what was available. Unfortunately, many other young men across the country had the same plan. The Navy, Air Force and Marines had an oversupply of officer candidates. But the Army was happy to welcome Charlie. He enlisted in 1966 to train as an infantry officer. In that year, popular sentiment against the Vietnam War had not yet reached the fever pitch it would soon attain. Charlie was supportive of the war effort and was willing to join the fighting.

In 1967, he plunged into a nightmare that blindsided a generation of young soldiers. Please note: the following story contains graphic descriptions of combat injuries.

What are the worst challenges most of us face when we go to work? Terrible commutes, traffic jams, co-workers or bosses who are jerks, worrying about keeping our jobs, poor pay....the list can go on and on. What was the job of an infantry soldier in the Vietnam War like?

He was thousands of miles from his home, his friends, his family, his wife or girlfriend. He was not in an air conditioned office or building. He was in a jungle infested with oppressive heat, humidity, insects, snakes, and other unfriendly inhabitants. Regularly, he got up in the morning and headed into that jungle. He might be on a patrol boat cruising down a river, or on foot walking through the jungle. He knew one thing: every time he went into that jungle, someone would try to kill him. They might shoot at him with a rifle or machine gun, a rocket propelled grenade, a mortar, or something else. The enemy would hide in the jungle and ambush him and his fellow soldiers. He wouldn't know where or when the shooting would start. When it started, some of his friends and companions would be killed or wounded. He would watch them get their arms and legs blown off, see their bodies shredded by gunfire and shrapnel, and hear their cries as they were wounded and killed. Every time he went into the jungle he would wonder when his turn would come. If he survived the day, he would have to get up another day soon and do it all over again. Every time he returned from a patrol, some of the men he started out with wouldn't come back. He would typically be in Vietnam for a year. If he survived, he would feel guilt that his friends who died didn't make it, yet he did. Charlie points out that Vietnam was different from WWII in one critical aspect: an infantry soldier in WWII typically faced 40 days per year of combat. The rest of his days were spent marching, deploying, and holding territory. In Vietnam, the infantry soldier faced an average of 240 days per year of combat, 4 to 5 days each week. Doesn't this make our gripes about our jobs seem petty?

Let's explore Charlie's story as it is woven into this picture.

Second Lt. Charlie arrived in Vietnam by airplane in June of 1967 after completing advanced infantry training and officer candidate school. He was enthusiastic and optimistic, confident in the excellent training he had received to serve as an infantry officer in Vietnam. Assigned as a platoon leader in C Company, 5th Battalion, 60th Mechanized Infantry Regiment, Charlie was eager for his first firefight. When the shooting started, he moved to the front of the formation and began unloading on the enemy.

After that fight was over, the Company Commander took him aside and provided some on-the-job pointers. Charlie was reminded that his job as an officer was to lead his men. The job of the enlisted ranks of soldiers was to do the shooting. He was to direct his men, to radio reports to the Company Commander, and call in and direct artillery fire and air strikes. The Commander had needed reports and updates from Charlie during the firefight, but Charlie was busy shooting away.

Charlie soon learned that our soldiers were primarily "bait" to draw enemy fire. They were sent out on patrols to do just that. Once enemy troops were encountered, artillery and air strikes were called in to eliminate the enemy troops, together with the fire from the patrols. The goal, sadly, was not to take and hold territory but to kill more soldiers than we lost. Body count was all that mattered; individual soldiers didn't.

On September 12th, 1967, Charlie earned his first Bronze Star medal for heroism. (The recommendation had been for a Silver Star, but by the time the paperwork got through the red tape in May of 1968, some of the witnesses had been killed in action, and it was so late in being processed, that a Bronze Star was awarded instead). One of the platoons in Bravo Company was pinned down by enemy fire. Casualties were high. (A Platoon at full strength is 40 soldiers. Because Charlie's Regiment was mechanized, he had some additional troops such as mechanics in his Company. However, units were never at full strength—ever—because of the constant casualties they suffered in battle).

Charlie's entire Platoon that day consisted of sixteen soldiers. He had them split into three equally sized teams, positioned in a triangular deployment. Charlie and five other soldiers were in the lead at the forward point of the triangle. Two five-man teams were positioned behind them. As he moved forward to assist the Platoon that was pinned down, Charlie thought he had sixteen men to count on. But they had hit the ground in the firefight and moved forward at a crawl. His two teams in the rear never followed him forward.

Charlie and his five men managed to organize and evacuate the wounded from the Platoon that was pinned down, moving in and out through heavy enemy fire. He hadn't known that ten of his men had stayed behind. They later claimed they hadn't seen him move forward.

There was no respite after this battle. Three days later, Charlie and his men, along with Chaplain Johnson (then a captain) would head into one of the seven major battles of the Vietnam War, which would leave indelible memories and scars that linger yet today.

The Battle of Snoopy's Nose

A major battle of the Vietnam war was fought at one of the hairpin turns on the Rach Bai Rai River—a turn whose shape evokes the familiar snout of Snoopy, canine star of the *Peanuts* comic strips, cartoons and films. As such, the battle became colloquially known as "The Battle of Snoopy's Nose."

The description of that battle which follows is a composite of Charlie's recollections and Chaplain Johnson's personal notes on the battle. The largest part of the river battle story features Chaplain Johnson. His detailed and comprehensive notes, reflecting his movement about the battle scene, provide a compelling picture of what took place. I am grateful to Chaplain Johnson, first of all for his service to our country, but also for his permission to use excerpts and accounts from his notes.

At 2:00 a.m. on September 15th, 1967, members of Lt. Charlie Taylor's unit, C Company, 5th Battalion, 60th Mechanized Infantry Regiment, were already awake and active, preparing for an operation that would take them by boat down the Rach Bai Rai River to a landing point known as White Beach 2, where they would engage a large concentration of VC forces. Pre-battle stress affected everyone differently. Charlie had gotten physically ill the previous night, "puking his guts out." This was his unfortunate prelude to all of the missions he went on, born of a fear of the unknown. During the battles there was little fear. Knowing what was happening plus the huge amounts of adrenaline made the difference. One of the sergeants who was about to head out was also nervous, but he responded differently. He tended to doze off when he got on the boats. The diesel vibrations and fumes drifted him into sleep. In darkness, at 4:00 a.m., a single-file convoy of nine Armored Troop Carriers (ATCs) spaced fifty feet apart set out down the river, moving slowly at eight miles per hour towards their objective. The ATC is a specially-designed Navy boat 60 feet long, with armor plating on the sides. The convoy was headed by two mine sweeper boats to guard against mines in the river. The boats and their machine guns were manned by Navy crewmen known affectionately as "River Rats." *Plate CT-1* shows an ATC traversing a Mekong River tributary similar in shape to Snoopy's Nose.

The trip was uneventful until shortly before 7:30 a.m., when a few rounds of enemy small-arms fire began hitting the water near the convoy. At first, Charlie wasn't too concerned, thinking it was just random sniper fire. I had to let that sink in. If I was driving down the road, and a few rounds of small arms fire began hitting the road around me, would I just shrug it off? Would any of us? "Just another day at work. No big deal, only some snipers trying to kill me".

At 7:30 a.m. U.S. artillery batteries were scheduled to lay down fire for five minutes to soften up White Beach 2. At 7:30 a.m. things turned ugly. The river was only 30 yards wide, making the convoy an easy point-blank target. Two RPGs (Rocket Propelled Grenades) exploded against one of the mine sweepers. AK-47 fire began raining down on the convoy from the river banks, mixed with more RPG fire. The convoy had just entered a killing zone about .8 miles long. The enemy had somehow known they were coming, and had constructed bunkers along the river banks about five yards from the water's edge to fire on the convoy. (Later reconnaissance would discover 250 bunkers. Consider the number of enemy troops and the horrendous amount of fire brought to bear on the convoy from that many emplacements.)

CT-1. Mekong River tributary with bends shaped similar to Snoopy's Nose. An ATC is shown at center left. Photo: National Archives

The convoy blasted back with M-16 rifles, M-79 grenade launchers, mortars, and other weapons. When the River Rats manning the .50 caliber boat-mounted machine guns were wounded, Army troops took over firing. The shooting was overwhelming and non-stop. Two U.S. M-60 machine gun barrels melted down from sustained fire. On one boat, M-79 gunners went through three cases of ammunition in twenty minutes. Chaplain Johnson observed that the AK-47 fire that hit the boats was "basically harmless" because of the boats' armor. Again I had to marvel at the combat mind-set that can dismiss certain enemy fire as nothing to worry about. Similarly at ease, Charlie would pop up to take pictures during the firefight, despite Chaplain Johnson telling him to get down and quit doing that. (Rather than keeping a written journal, Charlie chose to keep a photo journal of his experiences).

Damage and casualties were significant. Fighting back against the VC was difficult because they were so close, and positioned so far below the boat decks that the boat-mounted machine guns couldn't be depressed that low.

As the fighting wore on, the enemy rounds began taking a devastating toll. One after another, boats were disabled by RPG fire. *Plate CT-2.* One boat had its steering mechanism knocked away. The pilot managed to beach it and repair the mechanism. It then returned to the fight.

CT-2. ATCs under fire during the Battle of Snoopy's Nose. Photo: Charlie Taylor — taken while bullets were flying.

Casualties mounted at an alarming rate. Boat formations scattered in disarray. More severely damaged boats had to withdraw from the convoy or call for help with their wounded. Chaplain Johnson boarded one to provide medical aid. The first soldier he reached was bleeding but talking on the radio. He would make it. The coxswain was next. He was lying very still. The medic found no pulse, so they moved on to another. A soldier was lying partially under the 81 mm. mortar. Chaplain Johnson was sickened by the sight of his brains spilling out of the left side of his head, his legs kicking spasmodically. There was no other response. It was then that Chaplain Johnson had one of those disjointed thoughts that materialize in traumatic combat. Even though the soldier was clearly dead, Chaplain Johnson was afraid to move him for fear that his brains would fall completely out. Another soldier was lying in a pool of blood. The lower part of his left leg and foot were gone.

Jumping over to another boat to help, Chaplain Johnson bandaged a soldier who had a hole in his chest big enough to put a fist into. He marveled at how dark it is inside the human chest. Miraculously, that soldier survived. Chaos reigned on the boat as soldiers scrambled to balance helping the wounded with fighting the enemy.

Both mine sweepers were disabled by the heavy enemy fire. Standing protocol required that a convoy withdraw if it could not be led by minesweepers. The withdrawal order was given around 8:00 a.m., thirty minutes after the fight began. Gradually the ATCs retreated back in the direction of their starting point, about 500 yards beyond where the ambush began, to regroup and evacuate casualties. The Aid ATC was heavy and fitted with a helicopter landing pad *(Plate CT-3)*.

Neither Charlie nor Chaplain Johnson were happy with the decision to pull back. Although casualties were severe, they both thought that they should press on to White Beach 2 and not lose the ground they had gained. But the most anger at the withdrawal came from the one boat that had reached White Beach 2. They had to return back through the entire length of the killing zone, rather than going ashore where they might have had a better chance of fighting back. The retreat cost them one more fatality and four more wounded from a rocket strike on their .50 caliber machine gun.

CT-3. Huey helicopter evacuating wounded from Snoopy's Nose battle. Photo: Charlie Taylor.

Most of the boats beached and dropped their ramps on land when they reached a safe zone. Soldiers were sent ashore to set up a defensive perimeter to repel an enemy attack. Chaplain Johnson assisted with evacuating the wounded. He was soaked with perspiration and the blood of all those he had cared for medically. He carried litter after litter of wounded men to the evacuation helicopters. Some asked for prayers. A few became hysterical with the shock of their wounds and the din of continuing gunfire, explosions from the artillery, and aircraft strikes continuing to attack the enemy positions.

Chaplain Johnson talked to them as best he could through the roar of incoming artillery explosions, radio chatter and other voices, to calm them down. He told them generally about their wounds, but not in great detail. Around them, two of the boats were on fire. Men worked to extinguish the fires.

The medical evacuation helicopters were easy targets for sniper fire. So were the men carrying the wounded to them. One chopper could only carry three wounded on stretchers, plus three who could walk. After 45 minutes, 27 soldiers were taken out by helicopters, with no damage from snipers. Scores were wounded in the fighting. Those who were not evacuated were patched up and deemed ready to fight on.

The officers in command made the decision to run the gauntlet again. Replacement troops and three new boats were brought in to substitute for the most severely wounded and the three most severely damaged boats. Ammunition was resupplied and redistributed. Chaplain Johnson and some of the others who survived the first incursion didn't think the enemy fire would be as bad the second time in. They thought the artillery fire and helicopter gunships had substantially reduced the enemy threat. They were very wrong.

As the boats pulled up their heavy metal ramps to depart, someone noticed the body of a VC soldier underneath the spot where one of the ramps had dropped onto the beach. He had apparently been hiding there as a spotter or observer, and was now very squashed and dead.

Around 10:00 a.m. the convoy formed up and moved out again, assuming the enemy had been softened up. Despite the artillery and bombing runs by F-4 Phantom jets, as soon as the convoy entered the killing zone, enemy fire exploded into it as viciously as the first ambush. Boats were immediately hit and began taking casualties. The lead mine sweeper took two rocket hits. The second one took seven direct hits, but only three soldiers were wounded.

For the second incursion, our troops had supporting firepower. In addition to the F-4s and artillery, helicopter gunships sprayed the areas where the enemy was thought to be hiding with heavy machine gun fire. But that changed nothing. Just as the first time through, the boats quickly took multiple casualties. About two minutes in, a boat ahead of Chaplain Johnson burst into a bizarre movement pattern. Its radio operator could only keep shouting, "we've been hit, we've been hit!" Smoke and fire poured from the boat. Sailors were screaming at the boat pilot to slow down so another boat could pull close enough to help. The medical aid boat with Chaplain Johnson aboard pulled alongside. The boat on fire rammed into it and bounced off, as if the ramming was intentional. Two navy crewmen were finally able to board the damaged boat. They found five of the six sailors aboard too badly wounded to function. The sixth, who had no experience driving the boat, was in full panic meltdown trying to drive it. He was mentally incapacitated with such fear that he couldn't distinguish between his fellow soldiers and the enemy. The fighting was too intense for the aid boat to call in helicopters to evacuate the wounded. All Chaplain Johnson and the others on the aid boat could do was pray for the wounded…and for themselves.

A panicked call came in from another boat that had taken a devastating hit. As the aid boat pulled alongside, Chaplain Johnson leaped from the guard rail of the aid boat onto the stricken boat before the two crafts were close enough to allow him to do so safely. In his rush to help the wounded, he risked falling between the two boats and getting drowned or chopped up by propellers.

A rocket had penetrated the armor of the stricken boat and exploded inside and under the canvas canopy. Piles of wounded men lay all over the deck. Out of twenty-five platoon members aboard, only two had no injuries. Two were clearly dead. Some were calm, others panicked. In the midst of continuing explosions and raining gunfire, Chaplain Johnson assured the wounded that help was on the way. Some of the casualties were temporarily deafened by the explosion. All were asking for water. Chaplain Johnson knew that most of them would be in surgery soon and should not have water. It hurt him deeply to have to withhold it. He thought to himself, "how do you tell a man with his guts literally hanging out that he can't have water."

No horror movie could match the blood and carnage of the scene. The doctor and two other medics jumped onto the stricken boat to help. Looking around, they realized that some of the worst casualties wouldn't make it. Chaplain Johnson spotted another soldier with parts of his brain hanging out of a large hole by his ear. He would survive but only in a vegetative state for the rest of his life. Another was more psychically wounded than physically. He sat amidst the carnage in shock, staring blankly ahead, seeing nothing. Yet another sat in a pool of blood, his own and others, singing hymns in a low voice. As if to underscore his feelings for the war, one of the wounded seemed compelled to relieve his bowels into an empty C Ration box, adding to the already putrid stench.

As the convoy approached White Beach 2, the firing died down. The boats plowed into the river banks and dropped their ramps. Those infantry troops who were able to function scrambled ashore to establish a defensive perimeter so that helicopters could come in to evacuate the wounded. The entire platoon aboard the boat Chaplain Johnson had boarded to help was wiped out. So were several others.

It took about forty-five minutes to evacuate all of the casualties. Chaplain Johnson continued circulating among the wounded, giving them information and encouragement which seemed to calm them. Some he prayed with, some he simply held hands with. Some asked that their next of kin be notified. After the wounded were evacuated, Chaplain Johnson was finally able to drink some water himself, physically and mentally exhausted. It was about 4:00 p.m.

By that time, three companies had deployed 200 yards inland beyond the river bank. Intense fighting continued. So did artillery fire, some of which was landing uncomfortably close to the boats. Hot metal shrapnel occasionally pinged distinctively against the boats, driving Chaplain Johnson to wisely seek cover under the helicopter landing deck.

Charlie's platoon had moved through thick jungle to a more open area. The underbrush was so dense, and the concealed enemy soldiers so plentiful, that it took three hours to go 150 yards. A shallow ditch provided some cover from VC fire as Charlie led his men through the tangled maze *(Plate CT-4)*. The ever-present deadly snakes were put out of mind in favor of avoiding the more deadly enemy fire. Soldiers particularly dreaded the highly venomous Many-Banded Krait, nicknamed the "Two-Step Snake," whose bite was so lethal that, according to local lore, you could only take two more steps after being bitten before dying.

CT-4. Charlie's platoon maneuvering through the jungle after landing at White Beach 2. Photo: Charlie Taylor.

Upon reaching open ground, Charlie's Platoon was spotted by the VC. They were quickly pinned down by enemy fire, unable to move. A VC machine gun was so close it splattered him and one of his squad leaders with mud. Charlie bravely called in artillery fire to land within twenty-five yards of his position onto the VC who threatened to overrun and eliminate him and his men, saving his platoon. Still, there were minor casualties to Charlie's platoon from the artillery, but they survived.

As the afternoon wore on, a sergeant emerged from the brush carrying another wounded sergeant back to the aid boat. Chaplain Johnson went out to help him. A medic examined the wounded soldier and pronounced him dead. He had been alive when his fellow sergeant had picked him up to carry him back for help. The sergeant who had carried him in broke down, yelling at his dead comrade, "How could you die after I carried and dragged you this close to the aid boat?" The rescuer had a severe flesh wound on his face which the medic patched up. The rescuing sergeant then insisted on returning to battle and headed back into the brush. The wounded sergeant who died had nine children.

Near dark, the brigade commander called for the troops in the field to draw back and form a defensive circle for the night. The infantry formed a half-circle inland from the shore line, with the boats forming the rear guard. Most of the VC, who had been pounded with artillery and gunship fire during the day, chose to sneak away after darkness fell. Some stayed and kept up harassing fire. Flares were continually fired throughout the night, keeping the area illuminated so any VC activity could be seen.

The boats' heavy machine guns fired irregular sporadic patterns at the opposite river bank and into the surrounding jungle during the night to discourage the VC from moving towards the troops and convoy. Around 1:00 a.m. Chaplain Johnson was awakened by a burst of M-16 fire very close by, accompanied by a sailor shouting some very eloquent Navy curses at a dead VC, into whom he had just emptied an entire magazine. The VC soldier had been trying to climb onto the boat with some sort of explosive device.

The operation was ended on Saturday, given that most of the VC forces had cleared out overnight. As the American troops swept the area, they discovered 250 heavily fortified VC bunkers dug in along the river banks for the ambush. The Navy had fired 18,000 rounds of 20 and 40 mm. shells and over 61,000 .30 and .50 caliber machine gun rounds. The Americans suffered seven dead and 133 wounded. The VC had 79 known dead and an unknown number of wounded. Chaplain Johnson noted that the U.S. press release would claim the VC casualties were heavy, and American light to moderate, and that U.S. President Johnson would keep saying that the war is going well. But was it, really? Did this actually qualify as "going well?"

In addition to the ATCs, the Navy deployed some other impressive weaponized crafts to fight in the watery, swampy terrain (See Hovercraft, *Plate CT-5*).

CT-5. Navy hovercraft capable of traveling over ground, water and swampy terrain. Photo: Charlie Taylor.

Occasionally VC soldiers were captured *(Plate CT-6)*. On one occasion, a large number, eight or nine, were captured together and had to be moved through the thick jungle, making it difficult to control them. Charlie's unit devised an excellent method for keeping them well behaved after their hands were tied behind their backs with zip ties. The VC were given a demonstration of what "Det Cord" can do. Det Cord is the rope-like detonating cord used to ignite explosive devices. Det Cord was wrapped around a tree trunk and ignited in front of the VC prisoners, who watched the cord burst into flames and cut through the tree trunk like butter.

CT-6. Captured VC soldier. Photo: Charlie Taylor.

Det Cord was then wrapped around the necks and wrists of the wide-eyed VC. They were quite cooperative after seeing that.

On November 9, 1967, Charlie won his second Bronze Star for heroism in battle, just short of two months after his first. His award citation recites that, while serving as a platoon leader on a night ambush patrol, his platoon was hit by extremely heavy rifle and machine gun fire combined with grenades and mortar rounds lobbed in, pinning his platoon down. Under this intense fire, Charlie moved about organizing his platoon into a defensive perimeter around his company headquarters, and continued to move from position to position to be sure his men had adequate cover and were well organized. He refused to seek better cover for himself, so that his men would know his leadership was always there when they needed it.

The period between Snoopy's Nose and Charlie's second Bronze Star battle proved almost as difficult as the preceding period. October of 1967 kicked off with another bloody and intense land battle. Helicopter gunships and artillery literally shredded the jungle where VC troops were concealed.

Charlie's platoon waded through a swamp towards drier ground where VC who had been firing on his platoon were holed up in a bunker inside a hooch *(Plates CT-7, 8)*. Charlie noted that hooches in combat zones always had bunkers dug into them. This bunker was so well fortified that his platoon couldn't take it out with a light anti-tank weapon (LAW)—Plan "A". Plan "B" was therefore developed. One of Charlie's soldiers approached the hooch and flattened his back against the wall, "John Wayne" style, to lob in a hand grenade. Unfortunately, the VC spotted him and shot him through the straw sides of the hooch puncturing his kidney. The platoon laid down a hail of cover fire, allowing the soldier to retreat. His wounds were successfully treated later. Plan "C" worked. A tear gas grenade dislodged the three VC from the hooch and they were eliminated. Charlie grinned as he recalled that one of his men recovered a Sony transistor radio while searching a dead VC's backpack, and used it to enjoy the 1967 World Series.

CT-7. Charlie's troops leaving jungle shredded by helicopter gunships and artillery fire after huge battle on October 5th, 1967. Troops are wading through a swamp to attack a hooch on the other side where VC were holed up and firing on them. Photo: Charlie Taylor.

CT-8. Hooch where VC were holed up firing on Charlie's unit. Photo: Charlie Taylor.

By late November of 1967, river boat patrols were replaced by traditional infantry operations over land. Charlie's unit mobilized into battle with M-113 Armored Personnel Carriers (APCs) *(Plate CT-9)*. The APCs were appreciated by Charlie for their firepower. They carried one .50 caliber machine gun at the front and two .30 caliber machine guns, one on each side. Although the APCs were designed to carry a squad of infantry troops inside (ten soldiers at full strength), the soldiers didn't ride inside. The APCs were easy targets for RPGs (rocket propelled grenades) and land mines, so the infantry troops rode on top. The APCs did carry ammunition, generally three times the standard amount given the combat conditions.

Life was not always easier between battles. Charlie did have a couple of run-ins with a sparkling-new battalion commander, one concerning the use of APCs. On the day the commander arrived, Charlie was sitting in his hooch when he heard a firefight break out at the motor pool, where some of his troops were located. Charlie happened to be sitting a little out of uniform — no shirt or hat, fatigue pants and flip-flops on his feet. His fatigue pants were, however, correctly rolled up at the bottom cuffs. The humidity and moisture were so severe that everything was always wet. The men rolled up their cuffs to avoid getting trench foot from wet feet. He ran to the motor pool dressed like that to assist and organize his troops.

Returning to his hooch, with some residual shooting going on, Charlie encountered the sparkling, spit-shined new commander, a lieutenant colonel, fresh from the States, accompanied by a major and a sergeant-major, walking down the road. The new commander barked at Charlie, "Who's in charge here?" Shirtless and flip-flopped, Charlie saluted and introduced himself as the officer in charge. The new commander was expecting maybe West Point attire in a jungle combat zone. He barked again, "How am I supposed to know who you are dressed like that?" Charlie politely explained, "Sir, my men know me and follow my orders."

On another occasion, the new commander wanted Charlie and his men to ride inside the APCs when out on patrol, despite the added risk and danger. Charlie didn't bother to debate the issue with him. He went over the commander's head to a full colonel. Charlie heard no more of such nonsense after that.

CT-9. Land mine meets APC. This mine blew the APC sideways off the road it was traveling. Photo: Charlie Taylor.

One day at the Officers' Club, Charlie spotted a group of new lieutenants, fresh from the States. He heard one of them comment, "It can't be too bad where I'm going. There's a bowling alley down there." Charlie had to break the bad news to him that "bowling alley" was the nickname for a combat zone that was always full of booby traps and that virtually every patrol that went in there came back with casualties. The American soldiers were the bowling pins that always got knocked over.

Walking point on patrols was the most dangerous position in the formation. The point man went forward alone, in front of the rest of the soldiers, sometimes quite far in front, to scout out what lay ahead. He would be the first one shot at, the first to walk into an ambush, mine, or trip-wire grenade trap. If the patrol went into a village, he would be the first to walk into a hooch and trigger any booby-traps left for the Americans. Patrols would often walk into villages where they would find cook fires and food cooking in pots, but nobody around. *(See Plate CT-10)*. Those were often booby-trapped. Point man duty was spread around so that the same soldier did not bear that risk every time a patrol went out.

CT-10. Patrol entering deserted village. Two cone-shaped stacks of harvested rice are at center. A hooch is barely visible on the right. Photo: Charlie Taylor.

On a mission in the mangrove swamp in the Rung Sat Secret Zone, the dense triple-canopy jungle growth reduced visibility to 10-15 yards. Charlie's patrol was surprised and startled when they came upon the edge of a VC base camp that was totally concealed by the jungle and literally invisible to helicopters flying overhead. His point man was killed by a booby-trapped 105 mm. artillery round. After the platoon regrouped, Charlie asked one of his squad leaders, a buck sergeant, to walk the point. He said, "No sir," knowing that the VC were very close at hand, and that the platoon couldn't call in helicopter gun ship support because the choppers couldn't see anything or anyone through the thick jungle canopy. It was no surprise that the sergeant refused.

Charlie could have told him that it was a direct order and that refusal would get him a court martial. But that was not Charlie's leadership style. Instead of confronting the sergeant, Charlie went quietly to the front and walked point himself. He confided that he was petrified, given the obvious immediate danger involved. But after that, he had no further resistance from his soldiers.

Friction between soldiers was not unusual under the extreme stress of combat. One day one of Charlie's soldiers burst breathlessly into Charlie's hooch and loudly exclaimed, "Sir, they're going to shoot the first sergeant!" Charlie always listened to what his lower ranking soldiers had to say. He cautiously approached the scene, and indeed, another soldier was holding a gun on the first sergeant. Charlie quickly ran a mental checklist and decided to keep a low profile to avoid escalation. He stood back and observed. The first sergeant was trying to talk his adversary down calmly, so Charlie thought it best to see if things would de-escalate. They eventually did. Sadly, after Charlie returned home and the war dragged on, instances of violence between soldiers and their superiors escalated as our government half-heartedly supported our troops, and green, inexperienced junior officers poured into Vietnam to replace the spiraling numbers of war casualties.

Artillery bases were set up as and where needed to rain supporting fire on VC positions in the jungle *(See Plate CT-11)*. Firing coordinates were radioed in by forward observers in the underbrush. A base might stay in the same location for several days, often exposed in the open. Action was not continuous. Although defensive perimeters were set up, after long periods of inaction and no enemy contact, there was a tendency to become lax about security. The VC took advantage of obvious letdowns, attacking the artillery bases when they occurred.

CT-11. Artillery base firing support into the jungle, seen in the distance. Photo: Charlie Taylor.

While America was suffering through the 1968 presidential and other political campaigns at home, Charlie would earn two Purple Hearts for combat wounds, as well as a promotion to first lieutenant and company commander.

Valentine's Day of that year did not bring cards, candy or flowers to Charlie's unit. His company commander was badly injured while traveling along Highway 4 in a track-driven command vehicle. He was so severely hurt that he was sent back to the U.S. for the remainder of the war. Charlie was ordered to assume command of the company and to retrieve the damaged command vehicle. He helicoptered from his base camp to pick up a tank retriever. While he was headed to his unit's field position to recover the command track, the VC detonated a huge remotely-controlled land mine (called a command-detonated mine) under his tank retriever. Charlie was hit with shrapnel and gravel up the right side of his body.

The lenses in his glasses blew out, which somewhat protected his eyes. He was airlifted to a MASH (Mobile Army Surgical Hospital) unit where he was stabilized, then on to the 24th Evacuation Unit Hospital in Saigon for ten days. Then he returned to serve as XO (Executive Officer) of his company. Charlie was awarded his first Purple Heart for this mission, and later received a 10% disability rating for his injuries.

Two months later, along the same stretch of Highway 4, Charlie was in a jeep heading to the daily battalion briefing several miles up the road. Coming back around dusk, the VC detonated another mine a fraction of a second too soon. The jeep was not directly hit, but it crashed into the crater left by the explosion at 35-40 miles per hour. Charlie was a split second away from death. Although injured, he went back to work the next day. After flirting with death, he had one of those enlightening moments when he realized he was commanding a mechanized infantry company and had access to heavily-armored tracked combat vehicles. The next night, Charlie and his artillery captain took two of them up the road for the briefing. Again, the VC detonated another command mine under one of the tracks, blowing it off the road and into water. Fortunately, Charlie was in the other. The road was heavily traveled all day. The VC simply sat by, waiting for whatever they considered the best target of opportunity.

One of Charlie's men had his foot caught between the road wheel and the track. He was in danger of drowning. The only way to free him was gut-wrenching. They had to cut off his foot, so he could be taken out by a medical evacuation helicopter. That night, Charlie told the battalion colonel what had happened on the highway two nights in a row and requested helicopter transportation to the briefings for himself and the artillery captain. The colonel agreed, and provided it for the remainder of Charlie's time. Charlie was awarded his second Purple Heart for his injuries in the jeep explosion.

Even our greatest generals have to come up through the ranks. Tommy Ray Franks was one of the more unusual high-ranking command generals in our armed services. He wasn't a graduate of West Point, the Citadel, or VMI like most of them. He went through Officer Candidate School as an enlisted man and earned his way to the top. Before retiring in 2003 as a 4-Star General (or simply "General"), he rose to Commander of the U.S. Central Command, in charge of U.S. operations in a 25-country region, including the Middle East. He was in charge of the U.S. attack on the Taliban in Afghanistan after 9-11, and led the Iraq invasion in 2003 and the overthrow of Saddam Hussein. Franks was frequently in the news during his latter years in service. But before he became famous, Franks served as a forward artillery observer in Vietnam when he was a 2nd lieutenant under 1st Lt. Charlie.

Daily life for soldiers in Vietnam was slightly different than it was, and is, for us in the States. We have locks on our doors to protect us from the bad guys. Most of us don't get shot at in our homes. Window screens keep bugs out, and air conditioning keeps us comfortable when it gets hot. Charlie's unit lived behind an elegant subdivision wall made of sand bags and oil drums to keep them from getting shot *(Plate CT-12)*. Bugs and heat weren't considered a big deal. Nor were snakes. Once in a while, enemy mortar attacks would blow holes through the thin corrugated metal roofs that barely kept the rain out *(Plate CT-13)*. And we worry about the slightest little leaks in our roofs. We walk on carpet and tile floors. Theirs were dirt and mud.

CT-12. Charlie Taylor's "subdivision wall." VC were on the other side of the wall. U.S. artillery was 75 yards forward from where this picture was taken. Photo: Charlie Taylor.

U.S. artillery emplacements were about 75 yards beyond the point where picture CT-12 was taken. Sometimes firefights took place at night. Charlie learned to tune out and sleep through his unit's artillery fire. However, he was keenly tuned in to the distinctive "thunk" sound made by a VC mortar shell when it was dropped into a firing tube as far as 1,000 yards away, and would awaken and hit cover when he heard that sound. A VC hooch not far from Charlie's "subdivision wall" was hit and destroyed by U.S. artillery during one night battle (Plate CT-14). Charlie finished his tour in Vietnam and returned to the States in June of 1968, heading " back to the world." He was never out of danger until he reached the safer environs of Saigon. On the way to the Saigon Air Base in an APC, he came under fire and his APC returned fire on the VC *(Plate CT-16).*

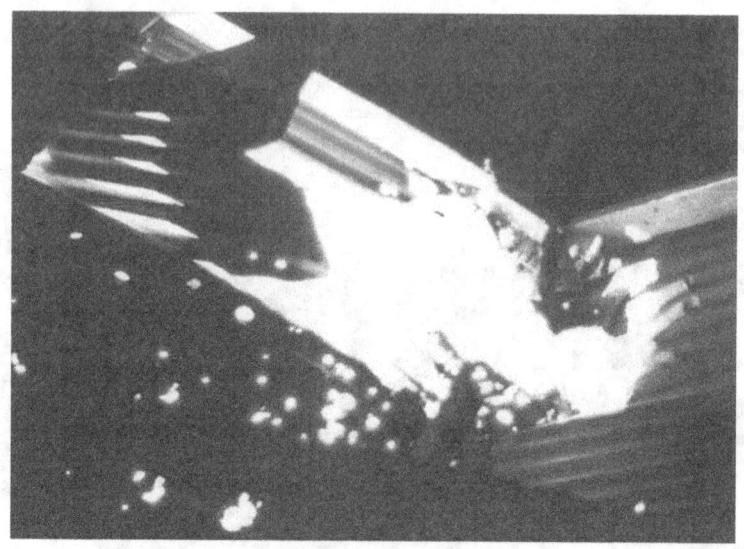

CT-13. Roof damage to living quarters caused by enemy shelling. The small holes were burned through the metal by hot mortar shrapnel. Photo: Charlie Taylor.

CT-14. Burning VC hooch just outside of Charlie's "subdivision wall" hit by U.S. artillery during a night firefight. Photo: Charlie Taylor.

Many subdivision communities in the U.S. have gated entries with welcoming signs. If lots are still available, the signs might offer information about them and the amenities included. Vietnam was introduced to this custom courtesy of our Navy's ironic sense of humor *(Plate CT-15)*.

CT-15. Welcome sign to Charlie's first base camp at Dontam, shared with the Navy. The buildings had only canvas roofs. Photo: Charlie Taylor.

CT-16. VC attack on Charlie's APC on the way to Saigon to fly home. The smoke is from returned fire by Charlie's APC hitting the VC position. A fitting parting shot to a grueling year. Photo: Charlie Taylor.

Charlie finished out his time in the service Stateside, assigned to a Special Processing Detachment that dealt with courts martials and soldiers who had gone AWOL (Absent Without Official Leave), which offense could range from overstaying a leave to outright desertion. He was released from active duty in December of 1968.

Postmortem to Vietnam

Wounds to the soul are the hardest to heal. Sometimes they are permanent. Charlie made two trips to confront and exorcise the lingering anguish wrought by the year of carnage he had survived. The first took place after 1987 when he went alone to visit the Vietnam Veterans' Memorial in Washington, D.C.

The Memorial is a wall inscribed with the names of over 58,000 soldiers killed in that conflict (see *Plate CT-17*, photo of half-size replica of the Memorial located at the LBJ Presidential Library). Charlie noted that he was afraid to go, but two other Vietnam veterans suggested that he needed to go. He waited until after dark, around 10:00 pm. for the crowds to dissipate, hoping he would be alone there. There were still some visitors lingering.

CT-17. Replica of the Vietnam Veterans' Memorial located at the LBJ Presidential Library. Photo: public domain. Source: Wikimedia Commons.

Locating the names of his men on the wall was crushing. He found the names of thirty eight men with whom he had served, including that of his company commander. Charlie relates that he found a place along the wall away from the other visitors where he broke down in tears. On the airplane back to Arizona, he read through a book entitled *Shrapnel of the Heart* containing memories and stories provided by families and friends of some who died in the war, including two of Charlie's men. The experience again left him in tears, which he quietly shed without concern amidst the other passengers.

A final trip to bring closure was made in 2011, this time to confront the dragon itself. Charlie and three other veterans, members of his battalion, together with their wives, made the trip back to the Saigon area to "lay some demons to rest." Charlie felt that it would be "really hard and spooky to go back," thinking he would "be watching for booby traps, snipers, and more importantly potential ambush sites." One of the men had grid coordinates of several of the bigger battles they had fought. They set out to "revisit the battles."

As the cliché says, "you can't go back." Charlie found that, "the Viet Nam of [his] memory does not exist. There were no more palm frond hooches, but rather every one now lives in masonry structures. The cities that [they] fought in during the TET Offensive in early '68 had grown so much that [they] could hardly recognize them. My Tho, on the Mekong River, grew from 50 or 60 thousand to over 500,000 today. Saigon grew from a little over 1 million to 8 million now." Areas along Highway 4 where Charlie was wounded and received both of his Purple Hearts that were once "out in the middle of nowhere, with only a distant hooch or so in view, the rest [being] rice paddies and wood lines," were now built up with businesses and houses. The long stretch of highway was freshly paved, sporting guard rails along the sides, rather than the broken-up war-torn road cratered with mine explosions of so long ago.

Of all the battle sites revisited, only Snoopy's Nose remained relatively "wild and remote." U.S. military equipment from the war such as APCs are on display in Saigon, a poke in the eye to those veterans who make the journey back. (See Ron Byrne, Jr.'s story. Ron's flight helmet is on display in a war museum somewhere in Vietnam). So, it was only befitting that Charlie and his fellow soldiers repay the favor by posting a sticker with his Company's logo, Bandido Charlie, at the Snoopy's Nose battle site *(Plates CT-18, 19)*. The road where the sticker is posted is now frequented by young folk afoot and on bicycles, who were not even born when the carnage along that stretch of river occurred (see *Plates CT-20, 21)*.

CT-18. "C" Company Mortarman Wayne Parrish placing the Charlie Bandido unit sticker on a utility pole, as close as the returning soldiers could reckon to the site of Snoopy's Nose. Photo: Charlie Taylor.

Charlie reports that his group never felt any animosity from the people. But they found few older people to ask questions of. It appeared that "the majority of the population [was] under 25." Although many U.S. Veterans struggle with the effects of Agent Orange (the chemical sprayed by airplanes to defoliate areas of dense jungle), Charlie wonders about the effect of that chemical on the people who lived there.

CT-19. Wayne Parrish (left) and Charlie in 2011 at the Snoopy's Nose site memorializing their unit with its logo and sticker. Photo: Charlie Taylor's travel group.

CT-20. Vietnamese children riding bicycles along the banks of the river where Snoopy's Nose was fought, certainly unaware of that horrific battle. Adults, left to right: Glenda Parrish, Wayne's wife; Diana Taylor, Charlie's wife; Wayne Parrish reaching his hand out to a child. The lady in the lower right-hand corner whose back is to the camera was someone's wife with the group, name not recalled. Photo: Charlie Taylor.

CT-21. River banks at Snoopy's Nose battle site, 2011. The building is new since the war, but the area remains heavily vegetated. Photo: Charlie Taylor.

Although going back was difficult, in the end it proved to be worthwhile. Perhaps all of the changes the years brought to Vietnam helped to erase the memories of many painful events. Charlie's strong faith in the Lord sustained him in Vietnam, and continues to be a source of comfort in dealing with the lingering trauma from the war. Charlie and his wife enjoy life in Prescott, Arizona where Charlie runs a financial planning business. He is active in his church and civic groups. We owe a great deal to Charlie and the other veterans of that war who put themselves on the line for freedom's sake, and who continue to pay the price so many years after the war ended.

Post-Traumatic Stress Disorder (PTSD)

The lingering psychological effects of the Vietnam War on its veterans, known collectively in the singular as Post-Traumatic Stress Disorder (PTSD) are an ongoing problem that persists 40+ years after the last shots were fired.

Ignoring it does a major disservice to those who continue to suffer from it. Not only does it affect them, but it also haunts many veterans from our recent conflicts and wars in the Middle East. It affects our neighbors, friends, family members and loved ones. You may never know that someone who crosses your path or enters your life suffers from PTSD. They carry their burdens in silence. Most do not want to re-live or discuss what happened to them. We need to be sensitive to, and thankful for, those veterans around us who prefer to not talk about their service experiences.

Chaplain Johnson paints a poignant and piercing comparison of our domestic fatal tragedies with what the combat soldiers faced in Vietnam. When the U.S. experiences the horror of a school shooting, the entire country shares the shock and grief. Friends, family, and entire communities come together and are at hand to comfort those affected. Grief counselors are provided to the students who witness the tragedy. Long-term help and support is provided. Strangers and citizens across the country share and mourn together with the survivors, and offer their prayers, comfort and support. Funerals, services, memorials, and ceremonies properly honor those who die in these tragedies. We do our best to provide time off for healing and closure. And fortunately, such events are widespread and not daily occurrences.

The combat soldiers in Vietnam were by and large barely out of high school, about the same age as many of the students victimized by school shootings. On an almost daily basis they watched their friends being killed, maimed and blown apart. Their family and friends were thousands of miles away, unavailable to help them cope.

They had no grief counselors. They had to clean up the bloody mess, suck it up, and go out the next day and do it all over again. Bodies of yesterday's friends were thrown into bags and hauled away in helicopters by strangers. Aside from the memorial service held by the battalions in Vietnam, when the veterans returned stateside, there were no services, no funerals, no honors for their fellow soldiers, no efforts by a community or their own country to bring healing or closure. Their exposure to carnage went on for an entire year. When they returned home they were reviled and rejected by much of our country. Imagine if we treated the witnesses and survivors of our school shootings like this. Imagine if they had to just clean it up and get on with the next day. Imagine if there were several domestic school shootings each week. How would our country's psyche hold up? At some point, our troops in Vietnam realized that those in their government who were running the war considered them expendable. Their government was not really fighting to win. If they survived, after living through hell, they came home to an unfeeling, uncaring country that had been told repeatedly by the media that the soldiers were baby-killing barbarians. The public had been conditioned by the media to mock and despise them. Our treatment of our Vietnam veterans was and is a national disgrace.

Coming home was not an end to the nightmare of combat, only the beginning of a new one. There was nobody to talk to or with whom to unload the horrors of war. Friends and family could not handle or did not want to hear what Vietnam was really like. Social conversations were insanely trivial compared to the trauma the veterans carried and desperately needed to, but could not, talk about.

Nobody could grasp the fact that the young football player/class clown/party buddy/happy-go-lucky classmate or friend who had left a couple of years prior wasn't the same person. They could not be expected to just return home as if they had been on a tropical vacation. They had been through a year-long orgy of death and killing that would mar anyone forever. This experience was one of Charlie's greater difficulties in adjusting to civilian life, even though he lived in a mostly conservative community and had the prayers and support of his church while he was deployed and after he returned. He wondered out loud what it was like for the veterans who returned to places where there was public scorn instead of community support.

While not all who suffer PTSD have all of the lingering after-affects, the total range of them is mind boggling. In no particular order they include nightmares, flashbacks, insomnia, survivor's guilt, depression, anger, despair, drinking, troubled relationships, workplace difficulties, withdrawal, emotional numbness, fear…..and the list goes on and on. Some nightmares still occur, and recur, after forty years as veterans relive the moment they were shot over and over, awakening in terror, thrashing and screaming. Loud noises, helicopters, any sounds that lodge themselves in the mind of a veteran can trigger a memory of war and cause a reaction. Watching movies with war scenes is exceptionally difficult or impossible without reaction. Even something as seemingly innocuous as the sight and smell of Vietnamese food can be traumatic. For those who fought from the river boats (the Riverine forces), the inescapable smell of diesel fuel and exhaust which is all around us can trigger the deep-seated thought that combat danger is imminent. Pent up anger and rage can boil over into violence. Family relationships can be damaged or fractured.

Some find that the only people they can talk to and open up with are fellow Vietnam veterans.

Even still, those who are able to locate and attempt to reunite with those with whom they served may find their former fellows in arms unwilling to talk or perhaps even to have anything to do with them. Quite understandably, they just want to try to forget. Such are the prices our combat veterans pay. We owe them a debt that can't be paid.

Chapter VII:
THE ROYAL RABBITS OF KOREA

Some war stories have a lighter side. This anecdote unexpectedly came out of nowhere when the book was mostly finished. It didn't really fit well anywhere, but was too entertaining to not include.

After an overnight stay in a cringeworthy budget motel in New Mexico in February of 2019, my wife and I bravely decided to take advantage of the "free" breakfast provided by the motel. Our immunizations were up to date, so the risk seemed minimal. The featured entrée was do-it-yourself waffles made with a grayish liquid substance dispensed from a container that appeared to have been last washed in 1981.

There were only three small tables in the eating area, two of which were taken. We sat next to a veteran who looked to be in his 80s, wearing a baseball cap with the markings of his former military unit. Unfortunately, I didn't get his name. For the purposes of this story, though, I'll call him Arnold. We all stared out the window at the freezing rain that had plagued us all night, and didn't seem inclined to stop any time soon. I commented to Arnold that it was a pretty lousy day to be traveling.

He had driven from the Northeastern U.S., on his way to Arizona to escape the record-breaking polar vortex gripping that region which had already killed several people. News broadcasts reported wind chills reaching forty to fifty degrees below zero in some locations. Despite his age, he was still living life on his own terms. Speaking of lousy weather, I mentioned that I had been stationed for a time at Fort Leonard Wood, Missouri, which was known as "Little Korea" to the troops there because of the miserable humid weather that made the bitter cold winters feel like those in the East Asian region. As it turned out, Arnold had experienced the real thing, having been stationed at an air base in Korea, back in the 1960s.

Of course, he had a war story to tell.

The local rabbits inhabiting the base area were exceptionally prolific. They showed no fear of the vehicles and aircraft on the runways, making themselves quite at home, and not caring a whit that they were creating a hazard. One day, Arnold was instructed by a superior to clear the rabbits from the runways. Being respectful of his assignment and the need to do a thorough job of it, he proceeded to the base armory to check out a .45 caliber pistol and some ammunition.

He was quite successful in his efforts, perhaps too much so. As he was seeking more rabbits to eliminate, his mission was halted by a contingent of superiors who informed him that he had violated some sort of restriction which was unknown to him. Apparently there were rules of engagement for the rabbits which he had broken. Such was the gravity of these rules that a court martial was threatened, and he was taken into custody. Explaining that he was following a direct order which gave no direction or limitation other than to get rid of the rabbits did not carry the day.

One of his captors recognized the injustice of the situation. There might be a way around all of this, he realized, if a certain colonel got involved. The colonel was summoned. Arnold was questioned by the colonel, again mounting his defense that he was following a direct order which came with absolutely no directions as to how to carry it out. Apparently the colonel also saw the unfairness of the situation.

But, there had to be some consequences for violating whatever the rule was. The charges couldn't simply be dropped. In the end, rather than a court martial, a notation was made in Arnold's personnel record that he had been required to attend a "consultation" with a senior officer. The honor of the military and the rabbits was vindicated, and Arnold was free to go.

An Air Force veteran neighbor of mine who was stationed in Korea in the 1970s suggested a possible explanation for what happened. All of the wildlife in Korea is considered the property of the Province Chief (similar to a State Governor in the U.S.) and can't be harmed unless the Chief allows it. So, killing the rabbits would have been a serious affront to their Korean hosts, unbeknownst to poor Arnold, who was just following orders. In my neighbor's case, the wildlife danger was more severe: pheasants that got sucked into jet engines. The official solution for the pheasants approved by the neighbor's Korean Province Chief was a once-per-year pheasant hunt, which involved everyone on the base who had, or could aim, or might once have seen, a shotgun, forming a wall moving back and forth through the base to shoot pheasants. He noted that the Korean cooks really knew how to prepare pheasants.

Chapter VIII:
A SNAPSHOT OF THE KOREAN WAR

The Korean war has really never ended. A cease fire, truce, or armistice, call it what you will—was agreed upon in 1953. But the sides remain eyeball to eyeball. In recent years, North Korea has developed nuclear weapons and missiles with which to deliver them. Today, it is a brutal, repressive Communist dictatorship whose leader has recklessly threatened to unleash nuclear weapons against the U.S. How did all of this evolve?

In the final days of WWII, the Soviet Union agreed to join the war effort against Japan, which occupied Korea, in addition to several other nations, by military force. After Japan's formal surrender in 1945, Soviet forces began to enter the northern portion of Korea to displace the occupying Japanese forces. It seemed like a good idea at the time for the U.S. to go along with this plan. American forces arrived in Inchon in September of 1945 to accept the Japanese surrender of the southern portion of Korea. Attempts to form stable governments in Korea were thwarted by competing factions, including some home-grown Communists, all of whom refused to agree on proposed solutions. In the end, Korea was divided into North Korea, a Communist state influenced by the Soviet Union, and South Korea, a democratic state influenced by the United States. Korea itself is a peninsula. North Korea shares its northern border with China. South Korea is surrounded by water, save for its land border with North Korea (map, *Plate K-1*).

From 1945 to 1949, a civil war raged in China between Communists and free democratic factions, in which Communist forces ultimately prevailed. The island of Formosa, (now known as Taiwan), originally part of China, was not conquered militarily, and the free democratic faction of China's civil war fled there, remaining free of Communist rule since then. In 1949, mainland China became a Communist country which, in addition to the Soviet Union, threatens to expand Communism through military and political actions. North Korea eventually became a client state (some even say "puppet") of China, and remains so today.

In 1949 and 1950, political forces in China, the Soviet Union, and North Korea felt that North Korea, with military help from Russia and China, could conquer South Korea and make it into a Communist state. Those leaders concluded they had superior military strength, and felt that the U.S. would not intervene for various reasons, including, (a) their conclusion that South Korea was not that important to the U.S.; (b) the fact that the U.S. had not intervened to assist the free democratic forces in China's civil war; and, (c) their assumption that the U.S. would not risk turning a regional incursion into a major confrontation. On June 25, 1950, North Korea invaded South Korea. However, the North Korean and Communist collaborators had badly miscalculated.

The U.S. did intervene, as did other nations, as part of a UN task force to counter the invasion, with the U.S. providing perhaps 90% of the soldiers and war materials for the effort.

After back and forth fighting for three years, in July of 1953, an armistice was signed, creating a demilitarized zone (DMZ) between the two countries. North Korea remained a Communist country, while South Korea remained a free democratic country. America suffered over 33,000 battle deaths in that war.

K-1. Map of Korean Peninsula. University of Texas legacy library.

Chapter IX:
LT. COL. ELVIN (AL) BAKER 1932 —

Preface

Al Baker's journey highlights the extraordinary extent of the training our military invests in its pilots in order to ensure they are superior in combat. It brings to life the remarkable evolution of the Army from a ground infantry-based fighting force to the helicopter-centric force of today, including both how the evolution occurred, and how military politics might have scuttled the evolution altogether. Along the way, we can re-live some of the mishaps and hi-jinks that flavored Al's military life. His story provides insight into how the many seemingly haphazard, and occasionally conflicting, moving parts of the military and government sometimes come together to achieve a positive outcome.

As a youth, Al Baker heard the siren song that calls some of us to break the bonds of Earth and soar above it. He dreamed of becoming an airline pilot. The U.S. Army made at least part of that dream come true. Al was born in Lima, Ohio in 1932, the oldest of eight children. He spent his early years on a farm, attended Lafayette High School in Lafayette, Ohio, and married his first wife in 1952 at age 19. Six months later, the Army gave him a belated wedding present by drafting him, along with seventeen other local youths, all of whom achieved a moment of fame in the local newspaper *(Plate AB-1)*. The Korean War was underway, and the army wanted more soldiers.

AB-1. *Al Baker and his co-draftees, August, 1952. Lima, Ohio newspaper, name unknown.*

After basic, advanced artillery, and leadership training at Camp Chaffee, Arkansas, Al attended Officer Candidate School at Fort Sill, Oklahoma, where he graduated as a 2nd lieutenant skilled in 105 mm. howitzer fire direction survey and forward observer functions, using a slide rule to calculate artillery trajectories. Although ground-based artillery was Al's official military occupational specialty, he spent a great deal of time in the air. To his delight, his dreams of flying materialized at Gary AFB in San Marcos, Texas, with basic flight training in the L-19 Trainer, later re-designated as an "O-1," *(Plate AB-2)*. The L-19 was a Cessna 170, modified with a bigger engine and tandem seats. Why was an artillery officer training to fly? Artillery units used pilots as spotters and to direct artillery fire.

AB-2. Cessna L-19 Trainer. Army Air Force photo.

After flight training, Al returned to Fort Sill for more advanced training. Then it was on to Ansbach, Germany, to Al's first duty station assignment. From 1954 to 1956, Al remained at that artillery headquarters unit, situated 25 miles from Nuremburg, Germany. During that rotation, he was promoted to First Lieutenant. Although the Korean War was over, Al stuck with the military. He was realizing his dream of flying. As a well-qualified pilot, Al flew a variety of assignments as directed by the unit commander, a colonel, who shall remain unnamed since some of his escapades appear later in Al's story.

In 1956, Al was transferred to the 7th Corp Artillery Headquarters in Germany. He continued to fly when and where needed in an L-19, transporting personnel and often delivering money for payroll to Grafenwoehr near the border with the East Germany.

AB-3. Army poster recruiting pilots from within its own ranks. Al Baker collection.

In 1957 Al was sent back to Fort Sill for a field artillery refresher course. He was continually caught in a tug of war between artillery, who wanted to keep him out of airplanes, and the commanders of the various units to which he was assigned, who always needed pilots. In fact, the Army was not shy about cannibalizing young officers from their original units to become pilots (see recruiting poster, *Plate AB-3*). At that time, there was no official aviation branch in the Army.

In Al's case, the overall need for pilots won out. In December of 1957, Al was sent to Fort Rucker, Alabama, as an instructor for the L-19. He also trained flying the Cessna LC-126, and the DeHaviland L-20 Beaver *(Plate AB-4)*. In 1958 Al received additional instrument flight training in Augusta, Georgia at an Army-contracted civilian school flying the new V-tail Beechcraft Bonanza. Returning to Fort Rucker, Al trained other pilots in instrument flight. By the time of his next assignment, he was rated as an instrument pilot as well as an instructor pilot in all rated aircraft.

AB-4. DeHaviland L-20 Beaver. U.S. Army photo.

Helicopter school training followed in the Hiller H-23D *(Plate AB-5)*. 1960 found Al in Korea where he was surprised to find that the colonel for whom he had previously flown in Germany was now a brigadier general and the commander of his unit. The general was quite pleased to have Al back and made him his operations officer and weekend pilot. Al's unit was the first one in Korea to receive the UH-1A "Huey" helicopters. Later models (UH-1 B, C, D, and H) saw significant action in the Vietnam War. (See *Plate AB-6*, Hueys engaged in Airmobile training for ROTC cadets at Indiantown Gap, Pennsylvania, circa 1971).

AB-5. Hiller H-23D training helicopter. U.S. Army photo.

AB-6. Hueys engaged in ROTC Airmobile Training, Fort Rucker, Alabama, c. 1971. U.S. Army photo.

Al flew some interesting "missions" in Korea. It seems the general had an American girlfriend in Seoul, Korea. Al was dispatched to fly her up from Seoul on weekends for "official" functions with the general. Al also regularly brought up groups of girls for parties at the officers' club. Keeping up morale was important. Al became known as the "Chaplain" among the pilots: sober when a pilot was needed, and always true to his spouse.

The Bell H-13 helicopters *(Plate AB-7)* were regular workhorses for the units. But, they were not particularly reliable in cold weather, and Korea has plenty of that. The engines had to be kept warm or they wouldn't start. At the home airfield, a portable gasoline-fired heater was used to warm the engines. When away from the home airfield, pilots would start and warm up the engines every thirty minutes to keep them usable.

In addition to being balky in cold weather, the H-13 had another problem. The gas tank, originally made like a tractor gas tank, was mounted above the engine (see Plate AB-7). In the event of a crash that ruptured the gas tank, fuel would pour out onto the hot engine causing a fire or explosion.

Later models relocated the gas tanks to safer placements.

On one particularly cold night in 1961, with the general in one helicopter and Al flying his aide in another, the helicopters reached their frosty destination without incident. But when the general's pilot tried to start his helicopter to warm it up, the aluminum throttle shear pin broke, leaving the helicopter with no rpm control. The general's pilot asked Al for help. Al went looking for one of the airfield guards, and asked him for a hammer and the location of some nails poking out of a wall. The guard produced a hammer and directed Al to one of the hangars, where Al pulled a nail out of the wall and substituted it for the broken throttle shear pin. He then switched helicopters with the general's pilot. Al's helicopter with the makeshift shear pin and the general's aide on board made it back to base safely, and the aide was none the wiser. Al did remark that if the general had been Al's passenger he wouldn't have flown that helicopter back to base. Apparently aides are more easily replaced than generals.

AB-7. Bell H-13 helicopter with dangerous high-mount gas tank. U.S. Army photo.

Late 1961 found Al back at Fort Bliss, Texas, enrolled in air defense courses. As the weapons of war evolved, Al was now learning about Nike, Hercules, and Hawk missiles, as well as nuclear weapons deployment. In 1962, Al was pulled into two significant military events, one of which nearly plunged the world into a nuclear war. A brief pullback to 1960 sets the stage. In 1960, America was giddy over the election of John F. Kennedy as its new President. Youthful, charismatic and energetic, the pundits were sure he would lead the country into a new "Camelot." Instead, his tenure was marred by some of our most painful memories.

The Cold War with the Soviet Union was in full bloom, with fears of nuclear war pervasive. (The Cold War ran from 1947 to 1989/1991. See *Appendix E* for a summary and significant incidents). In 1960, the Soviets shot down an American high-altitude spy plane, the U-2, which was supposedly immune to being shot down, and captured its pilot. It was an enormously embarrassing incident. In 1961, the U.S. mounted a failed invasion of Cuba, a client state of the Soviet Union, in an attempt to overthrow Communist Dictator Fidel Castro, who had seized power in 1959. Another embarrassment was suffered by the U.S.

Soviet Premier Nikita Kruschev concluded that Kennedy was weak and ineffective. In 1962, with Soviet backing, construction was begun in Cuba, a mere 90 miles from the U.S., of missile bases capable of launching ICBM nuclear missiles. Missiles were loaded onto ships in the Soviet Union bound for deployment in Cuba.

In response, the U.S. imposed a naval blockade to stop the Soviet ships. The two sides stood eyeball to eyeball, threatening war. The Soviets eventually turned their ships around. I recall watching this showdown unfold on TV as a teenager with a very sick feeling in my stomach. The confrontation was dubbed "The Cuban Missile Crisis."

The Cuban Missile Crisis pulled Army pilots, including Al, from their regular duty stations to Fort Campbell, Kentucky, to support the 101st Airborne Division. The Army was still short on pilots, and nobody was certain where the Cuba situation was headed. Had the Cuba crisis escalated, Al and the other pilots rated to fly the Huey helicopters would have delivered troops to the soil of Cuba for a ground war. The parachute would soon be replaced by the helicopter as the preferred mode of aerial delivery for ground troops. This major shift in operations would see its full expression bloom in the Vietnam War. Although the media made little mention of it, an armored division (a division in the Army is typically 10,000 to 20,000 soldiers) including tanks and other armor was mobilized and sent towards Miami for deployment to Cuba in case a ground war erupted.

Later in 1962, Al was ordered to Fort Bragg, North Carolina, to participate in one of the most significant exercises ever conducted by the Army: the Howze Board. *(Plate AB-8)*. En route to Ft. Bragg, Al joined an Air Cavalry unit as scout platoon leader with armed H-13 helicopters. The Howze Board set the stage for a major tactical shift for the Army.

AB-8. Al Baker's Howze Board orders. Al Baker collection.

The Howze Board

How did the helicopter become a primary weapon of an Army that had always fought on the ground? The Howze Board tells the story.

In late 1961, the Air Force seemed to believe it "owned" anything that flew in combat. The Army, meanwhile, felt it knew best its own needs and requirements. This led to tensions between the two military branches that, along with the escalating conflict in Vietnam, prompted Secretary of Defense Robert McNamara to review the Army's plans for aviation. He concluded that perhaps the Army's plan should be more aggressive, and ordered the formation of a board to review Army plans for the use of aircraft, with an emphasis on helicopters. The board was directed to discard old, possibly outmoded, concepts and policies, and to consider shifting from ground-based to airborne systems. McNamara took the unusual step of naming the board members he wanted appointed, and also directed that live field exercises be conducted to test the effectiveness of recommendations. General Hamilton Howze was named to head the board (hence its nickname), and was given wide discretion to deal with both military and civilian agencies to carry out the board's functions.

One hundred twenty five helicopters and twenty five airplanes engaged in forty field tests, compiling over eleven thousand hours of flying. Exercises included swamp warfare in Georgia, counter-guerrilla exercises in Virginia, and a withdrawal under pressure in the Fort Bragg area. Smaller unit exercises and war games evaluated tactical mobility, firepower, reconnaissance, and logistics. One exercise examined the role an airmobile division could play resisting an invasion of Iran by the Soviet Union. (Again we see the irony of the shifting alliances of countries. The U.S. once had an alliance of sorts with Iran and the Soviets were the common enemy. At this writing, after the Islamic revolution in Iran in the 1970s, Iran is now best buddies with the Soviets and an enemy of America).

The conclusions of the Howze Board dramatically reshaped the Army that had fought in WWII. Several new aerial brigades or battalions were proposed: air ambulance, air assault, air cavalry combat, and aerial rocket artillery. A significant number of attack helicopters were designated.

Many of the proposals were implemented. Thousands of helicopters were ultimately added to the Army's airborne fleet, giving it additional aircraft and valuable resources needed to fight in the evolving theatres of war. The extensive use of helicopters in Vietnam proved the wisdom of the Howze Board's recommendations. On August 1, 1965, the 1st Cavalry Division (Airmobile) was sent to Vietnam, the forerunner of a large buildup of American forces.

Helicopter units have since evolved and developed further, serving important roles in the Middle East in Operation Desert Storm in 1991 and Kuwait in 1993, as well as Somalia and Bosnia in 1999, and Operation Iraqi Freedom in 2003. They remain an integral resource in the Army's arsenal.

Al was ordered to temporary duty for six months (TDY-Temporary Duty Yonder) at Fort Bragg, North Carolina, to participate in the Howze Board exercises. He served as scout platoon leader in an Air Cavalry Unit, flying H-13 helicopters. Caribous, Chinooks, H-34s and Hueys also participated. The H-13s were badly abused. Machine guns were mounted on them, and they were flown overweight, and underpowered. Pilots were told to ignore, or scrape off, the red-lines on instruments marking operating limits, and to fly beyond those limits. If any casualties occurred from breaching the limits (Al was not aware of any), they were considered by the upper brass as acceptable losses. As a civilian comparison, if you consistently drive a car hard and fast beyond the red line on the tachometer, you would eventually blow the engine. The H-13 looked menacing with machine guns, but it was clearly not suited as a full-time combat helicopter.

The war games were not without incident. Many exercises took place on civilian farms and ranches. Al watched a Caribou that was approaching a pasture to land clip a power line with its rudder, landing with the rudder torn off and hanging from the airplane by its rudder cables. Nobody was injured, but some poor farmer was probably without power until the power lines could be repaired.

On civilian property near Fort Bragg, an H-13 with a pilot and an observer on board was preparing to take off when a Huey that had picked up troops at the top of a hill lost power and suddenly "skied" down the hill on its landing skids towards the sitting H-13. As Al looked on in horror, the rotating top rotor blade on the Huey sliced into the canopy bubble of the H-13, barely missing the H-13 pilot's face. At the last second, the Huey pilot flipped the Huey over on its side, causing its moving rotors to smash into the ground, averting a worse outcome. After witnessing the accident, Al headed for the wrecked Huey, using a fire extinguisher to spray areas that were fire hazards, and getting the damaged doors open to extricate the men inside. Others warned Al to stay back because of fire danger, but he ignored them and proceeded to help. The only injury was to a first sergeant in the Huey who had cut his forehead on the dome light (which had a glass, rather than plastic, dome cover).

At Fort Stewart, Georgia, during the war games, an 82nd Airborne unit "captured" a warrant officer from Al's scout platoon, an H-13 pilot who was bivouacked for the night in the swampy woods. The 82nd's "prisoner" was made to stand on his feet in the swamp all night, with water up to his chest, snakes and other swamp dwellers notwithstanding. Al devised an excellent plan to avoid capture: he slept in a Huey at night, with the doors tied shut.

Howze Board maneuvers continued for about six months, ranging from Charlottesville, Virginia to Savannah, Georgia, continuing to frequently operate from civilian farms and ranches. The exercises proved the need for the Army to acquire more, newer, bigger and better helicopters to increase mobility and firepower. With the exception of the Hueys, which were first test-flown in 1956, it was realized that most of the helicopter types being utilized by the Army were too large, underpowered, or complex for practical use in modern combat. With this information, Howze laid the groundwork for the development of the first generation of Cobra and Apache armed helicopters, *(Plate AB-9*—Boeing Apache AH-64-current version) as well as the formation of the First Air Cavalry Division.

AB-9. Boeing AH-64 Apache Longbow. Photo: U.S. Air Force 2013.

Al moved around to other bases in the coming years, receiving a promotion to major in 1964.

The aircraft maintenance school at Fort Eustis, Virginia needed some experienced pilots to light a fire under lackadaisical mechanics. Al was a perfect choice. He made some test flights in a Sikorsky H-19, the Army's first true transport helicopter, which saw action beginning in the Korean War, and opened the door to further integration of helicopters in the Army's operational profile. While stationed in Germany, Al flew a close descendant of the H-19, a Sikorsky H-34 *(Plate AB-10)*.

AB-10. *Sikorsky H-34. U.S. Army photo.*

Not all transfer orders received by an officer are welcomed. But during a stint in Germany as the airfield commander of the 8th Division Artillery, on June 2, 1965, Al received orders to "visit" Paris, France officially *(Plate AB-11)*, as support for the Paris Air Show. Al was there three weeks to guard the display of an armed H-13, perhaps the only dignified assignment left for that helicopter to profess to be an armed combat aircraft, following the Howze Board tests. Al served as a security guard and was responsible for insuring that the guns were locked up each night. Russian military aircraft were also on display. Some of the Russians who were at the show were asking questions, saying that they had heard the American helicopters in Vietnam were experiencing erosion of their rotor blades from the beach sand. Of course the Americans denied that there was any such problem. Although Al didn't get to see the Eiffel Tower when he toured Paris, he was able to fend off the advances of one of Paris' famous hookers. He also was able to spend some time at a similar air show in Belgium. After Al returned to Germany, he received some less leisure-friendly orders: five days notice to report to Fort Campbell, Kentucky – and to leave dependents at home. Al was being prepared to deploy to Vietnam.

AB-11. *Al's TDY Orders for the Paris Air Show. Al Baker collection.*

At Fort Campbell, Al was tasked with helping to organize an Air Mobile Assault Company, utilizing Hueys—UH-1Bs as armed gunships, and UH-1Ds as troop transports. A twenty-one day trip on a troop ship brought him to Cam Ranh Bay in Vietnam. The helicopters were brought over by aircraft carrier.

Hueys saw their first combat deployment in Vietnam. They were the first turbine powered helicopters to go into production in 1960. Seven thousand of them saw service in Vietnam. By the time production ended in 1987, sixteen thousand Hueys had been produced.

As Executive Officer of the company, Al spent the next year building a staging area for the helicopters about five miles inland at a special forces camp. From there, the unit deployed to various forward operating bases. Al participated in the first battalion-size night combat assault. 48 to 50 Hueys departed at 2:00 a.m. Their lights were taped over to prevent them from being targeted. This also meant that the aircraft couldn't see one another, although they needed to fly in formation. There was no prior training for this night mission. It flew without any moonlight or ambient light. After some truly frightening flight time, with Hueys losing their tail lights, Al realized that disaster was imminent. He suggested to the flight leader that they switch to bright navigation. The flight leader concurred and ordered, "nav lights to bright," enabling the helicopters to fix each other's locations. Although they were now exposed, they didn't draw any ground fire.

The next day Al went in to pick up the pilot of a downed medivac (medical evacuation) helicopter. The downed pilot had his camera along, and rather than strapping in to his seat in the rescue helicopter, he moved around excitedly, leaning out to take pictures. Al finally had to order him into a seat.

Al's primary task at his base camp was to clear away brush to construct a staging area for helicopters and their crews. He had funds to hire as many as 1,000 locals, who were paid $1.00 per day to clear away brush with machetes and sickles. This was an uneasy undertaking, as it was not always possible to tell enemy locals from those who posed no threat. Al hired primarily old men, women, and fairly young kids. He didn't hire young men to avoid enemy infiltration.

In 1966, after a year in Vietnam, Al returned to Fort Rucker, where he served as the chief of the Survival Committee, teaching pilots survival skills to use in the event their aircraft were downed. Pilots were taught escape and evasion tactics, and learned to eat delicacies such as snakes and fried grasshoppers, and to cook live chickens and vegetables. In 1968, Al was sent TDY to the University of Omaha in Omaha, Nebraska (renamed the University of Nebraska at Omaha around that time), finishing a degree in Political Science with an Economics major in 1969. As proof that we truly live in a small world, I graduated the same year from that same school with an undergraduate Psychology degree. But I never met Al.

Al finished his service career as an ROTC instructor at the University of Akron in Akron, Ohio, from 1969 to 1972, during the turbulent years of Vietnam War protests. The war's unpopularity with much of the civilian population was fertile breeding ground for anti-war protests and marches, some fueled by the left, many violent, on college campuses. ROTC buildings and programs were regular targets. Popular music was rife with protest songs. On the campus of Kent State University, not far from Akron, one of the worst tragedies of the protest movement occurred. The national guard had been called in to help control a student riot. In the escalation that ensued, a young national guard troop overreacted, shooting and killing a student. The incident inflamed an already volatile public.

In this climate, Al would march his cadets about the school campus for drill practice, often followed by groups of students chanting things like, "1-2-3-4, we don't want your f—ing war".

Al retired from the service in 1972 as a lieutenant colonel and a Master Army Aviator, awarded the Legion of Merit and other medals during his career. He flew at least 40 different kinds of military and civilian aircraft. His childhood dream of being an airline pilot unfolded in spectacular fashion.

Before retiring in Prescott, Arizona in 1994, where he had previously honeymooned with his present wife, Becky, Al's civilian pursuits landed him in a job with an entrepreneur who would become a luminary in the automotive world, and who would die a tragic death. Have you ever had a car with a sunroof? Al may have had a hand in that.

With aviation jobs in scarce supply, Al went to work for American Sunroof Corp. (also known as ASC) in Southgate, Michigan. After seven months he was transferred to Atlanta, Georgia, as a Vice President and General Manager to open a new operation that would serve the Ford Motor Company, working there from 1973 to 1979. ASC was founded by a German immigrant, Heinz Prechter, whose own story is worthy of mention.

Heinz Prechter

We can all thank Heinz Prechter for the sunroofs in our cars. In 1963, he came to the U.S. from Germany as a 21-year old exchange student. The next year, working out of a rented garage in Los Angeles, he began installing car sunroofs, which were largely unknown in the U.S. at that time. His startup capital of $764.00 produced a sewing machine salvaged from a junkyard, some tools, and an old door made into a workbench. At the time of his death in 2001 he owned a conglomerate of automotive, newspaper, real estate and investment companies with 60 facilities and 5,300 employees worldwide in the U.S., Canada, Germany and Korea.

Before Prechter entered the business, sunroofs were only available as aftermarket installations (after the car had been sold) that tended to leak and rust out. Prechter's sunroofs were installed for the automakers in his factories. In 1967, he moved his business to the Detroit, Michigan area to be closer to automakers. He installed sunroofs for General Motors, Chrysler, Ford, Toyota, and other companies to their specifications. Prechter is considered largely responsible for popularizing sunroofs in America. He also developed the glass moonroof. After pressure from auto manufacturers, he and his engineers developed a sunroof package that car makers could install on their own assembly lines, avoiding a great deal of disassembly and reassembly, as well as significantly reducing costs.

Prechter became a highly visible public persona, fundraising for both Bush presidents, as well as becoming a friend of that family. Civic activities and other fund raising endeavors were part of his life. He was a strong supporter of, and contributor to, candidates for public office, including various Republicans, and at least one Democrat.

Al's wife Becky was Prechter's office manager when Prechter hired Al. As Prechter's involvement in politics and public life grew, she helped him soften his very direct and sometimes gruff persona.

Prechter suffered from depression for many years. Tragically he took his own life in 2001, survived by his wife and two children, and his remarkable legacy. At the time of his death *The Detroit News and Free Press* ran a lengthy article outlining his life and considerable contributions to the local community. Beyond that well-deserved local recognition, his passing seems to have garnered little other attention.

Al and Becky retired to a mountaintop home in Prescott, Arizona which they built themselves with the help of a few others. Al is active in a local military pilot's group and enjoys working on his cars and trucks, and fixing anything that is broken. I'm grateful to Al for his long years of military service, and for sharing his eventful life and experiences.

Chapter X:
RADIOMAN 1st CLASS ALBERT ANTHONY VILLAR 1912–1983

Preface

Albert is a descendant of Cuban immigrants who settled in Key West, Florida. He endured the Great Depression, and rejoined the Navy shortly after the attack on Pearl Harbor, culminating his service at the end of WWII in the Philippines. His story takes us inside the final days of the Pacific war and Japan's surrender through a fascinating set of documents and pictures he brought home after the war, some of which were forbidden, but which we are now grateful he preserved. Through his experiences, we can catch a glimpse of life aboard his attack-transport ship, and witness the devastating conditions he encountered in post-war Manila. As he was the first soldier in his theater to receive word of Japan's surrender, we can also join his emotional realization that he and his shipmates would return home alive.

What do Ernest Hemmingway (1899-1961), Jimmy Buffet (*Margaritaville)*, and Albert Anthony Villar have in common? The first two put the small island of Key West, Florida, on the "A" list of places to visit, but well before they christened the island an iconic, funky destination, the Villar family was busy doing the ground work to make Key West a thriving community. Mr Villar's parents came to the U.S. from Cuba. They owned a stationery store in Key West *(Plate AV-1)*, which still stands on the main drag, presently occupied as a shoe store. Mr. Villar was born in Key West in 1912. He worked as a surveyor's assistant in the Civilian Conservation Corps during the Great Depression, moving for a time to work in Arizona.

AV-1. Villar family stationery store, Key West, Florida. Photo: RM Villar.

The Civilian Conservation Corps (CCC)

Millions of Americans lost their jobs in The Great Depression. In response, the Federal Government created the Civilian Conservation Corp (CCC), a public works relief program. From 1933 to 1942 the CCC employed some three million men in projects ranging from re-forestation of national parks to repairing and improving those parks and national monuments. The government created a similar program, the Works Progress Administration (WPA), in 1935 to improve and construct public buildings and roads. Many schools, bridges, roads and public buildings constructed under that program still stand. The onset of WWII re-energized the American economy and created military jobs for thousands upon thousands of soldiers, allowing those programs to be phased out.

The depression drove many citizens to hold multiple jobs. Like so many others, in addition to his work with the CCC, Mr. Villar acquired a second job, enlisting in the U.S. Navy Reserves in the early 1930s. He attained the Navy rating of Radioman (RM) before he was discharged on September 24, 1935 when his term of enlistment ended.

Building on the skills he learned in the Navy, RM Villar transitioned to civilian amateur radio operation after he left the Navy and returned home to Key West. He likely did not suspect that the military would one day recall him to use those skills again. But WWII reawakend America's work force as it recalled its veterans.

On December 7, 1941, the day of the Japanese sneak attack on the American Naval Base at Pearl Harbor in Hawaii, my brother in law Al (Albert's son) vividly recalls Military Police going through their neighborhood in Key West rounding up soldiers to return them to their bases. At that time, Key West was home to a major Naval base, with submarines, destroyers, patrol craft, PBY flying boats, and a supply depot. In addition, Boca Chica Naval Air Station also called Key West its home. The Naval base is now gone (Al thinks condominiums were built where it used to be), but the Naval Air Station is still there.

Key West is a compact and cozy island, only four miles long and a mile wide. During those years, everything big that happened there affected everyone. Al recalls the day a PBY airplane crashed into an ammunition depot, setting off a huge explosion that shook the entire island. Old ships towed into the sea around the island ended their lives as practice targets for the Navy. Al and his friends relaxed on the beach, awestruck by the huge fireworks displays put on by the big naval guns, enhanced by the sight and smell of exploded gunpowder drifting over them. Twilight gunnery practice provided evening entertainment, as tracer bullets from the ships swarmed towards canvas targets towed behind airplanes. Al always wondered what the pilots of the tow-planes were thinking as a bunch of guys in their late teens and early twenties were learning to shoot anti-aircraft guns by aiming towards their airplanes.

On December 8, 1941, RM Villar received a telegram *(Plate AV-2)* urging civilian amateur radio operators to enlist in the military. Radio operators were badly needed for the war effort.

```
ZCVS V WLM QST DE WLM
NR 49 WLM CK 230 AARS Washington, DC 6.00PM Dec. 8, 1941.
TO ALL CA SIGNALS AND ARMY RADIO AMATEURS -
ALL AMATEUR RADIO OPERATIONS INCLUDING THE ARMY AMATEUR RADIO SYSTEM ARE
SUSPENDED FOR THE PRESENT STOP CIVILIAN DEFENSE AGENCIES REQUIRING USE
OF AMATEUR RADIO FACILITIES SHOULD MAKE SUCH REQUESTS TO DEFENSE COM-
MUNICATIONS BOARD FOR CONSIDERATION STOP THE WAR DEPARTMENT TODAY ISSUED
AN APPEAL FOR RADIO OPERATORS STOP MEMBERS OF THE ARMY AMATEUR RADIO
SYSTEM AND OTHER AMATEUR RADIO OPERATORS WHO ARE ELIGIBLE FOR MILITARY
SERVICE ARE NEEDED AT ONCE FOR THE SIGNAL CORPS STOP AMATEUR RADIO
OPERATORS WHO ARE BETWEEN THE AGE OF 18 AND 35 UNMARRIED AND IN GOOD
PHYSICAL CONDITION ARE URGED TO VOLUNTEER THEIR SERVICES AT ONCE -
DURING THIS NATIONAL EMERGENCY STOP RADIO AMATEURS QUALIFIED FOR ACTIVE
SERVICE SHOULD APPLY AT ONCE TO THE NEAREST ARMY RECRUITING STATION OR
TO THE SIGNAL OFFICER AT THE HEADQUARTERS OF THE RESPECTIVE CORPS AREAS
FOR FURTHER INFORMATION AND ENLISTMENT STOP AMATEUR RADIO OPERATORS WHO
BECAUSE OF MARITAL STATUS AGE SLIGHT PHYSICAL DEFECTS OR OTHER REASONS
MAY MAKE THEM INELIGIBLE FOR ACTIVE MILITARY SERVICE ALSO ARE NEEDED IN
A CIVILIAN CAPACITY IN ARMY RADIO STATIONS AT CORPS AREA AND OTHER HEAD
QUARTERS STOP THESE CIVILIAN RADIO OPERATORS WOULD RELEASE THE PRESENT
ENLISTED MEN FOR MILITARY DUTIES STOP INTERESTED MEN SHOULD APPLY BY
MAIL OR IN PERSON DIRECTLY TO THE CORPS AREA SIGNAL OFFICER AT THE
HEADQUARTERS OF THEIR RESPECTIVE CORPS AREA FOR FURTHER DETAILS IN THIS
CONNECTION -
          COLTON ACTING CHIEF SIGNAL OFFICER

                                           7.30PM
```

AV-2. Telegram seeking military enlistment of civilian amateur radio operators. Villar collection.

Civilian radio operators already knew how to operate equipment and send and receive messages in Morse Code. The military needed those skills, and those civilians who had them were ready to go to work without needing that training. RM Villar re-enlisted in the Navy on December 29, 1941, taking his own telegraph key with him. (Radio operators tend to prefer the familiar feel and characteristics of their personal keys.)

His first duty post was Jacksonville, Florida, listening on sonar devices for German submarines. Early in the war, German submarines lurking off the Florida coast did considerable damage to American ships operating there. In 1943, Albert rotated to the Pacific theatre of war, where he would ultimately call the *U.S.S. Barnstable (Plate AV-3)* home as a radio operator, attaining the rank of radioman first class by the time his service ended.

U.S.S. Barnstable

The *Barnstable (Plate AV-3)* appears to have started life as a merchant ship. But like the Transformers we watch turn into fearsome warmongering robots in the movies, it was turned into a formidable military ship, serving in limited but significant duty. Commissioned in October, 1943, and fitted out as an Attack Transport at Commercial Iron Works, Portland, Oregon, it was re-commissioned in full as the *U.S.S. Barnstable (APA-93)* on May 22, 1944. The *Barnstable* saw action in the capture of the southern Palau Islands September-October, 1944; landings in Leyte in October and November, 1944; Luzon-Lingayen Gulf Landings, January, 1945; and the assault and occupation of Okinawa Gunto in April of 1945. Crewed by 99 officers and 593 enlisted personnel, it carried 24 landing craft of varying types to deliver its cargo of 1,475 combat troops to the beaches of their combat zones. The *Barnstable* wasn't just a floating bus. It carried a full complement of anti-aircraft and large caliber guns.

AV-3. U.S.S. Barnstable. Photo: U.S. Navy.

The assault on Okinawa, Japan, in April, 1945, was a titanic battle. RM Villar learned after the war that his brother, Seaman Second Class Kali Villar, participated in that battle as a sailor aboard the Destroyer Escort *U.S.S. Feiberling*. The *Feiberling* somehow survived a Kamikaze attack in massive Kamikaze raids on the American fleet on April 6.

Kamikazes

The tide of the war was turning against Japan. In desperation, the Japanese were crashing their fighter planes, known as Kamikazes, into U.S. ships. Although the Japanese bombs and bullets might miss their targets, it was difficult to shoot down a Kamikaze before it did its damage. The Kamikaze pilots were willing to commit suicide for their Emperor. They considered it an honor to die that way.

By August of 1945, the *Barnstable* had joined the flotilla of naval vessels positioned in the harbor of Manila, in the Philippine Islands, as the Allied forces worked their way towards Japan, recapturing the Pacific islands the Japanese had previously conquered and occupied.

Although Germany had already surrendered, the war with Japan had no end in sight. On August 12, RM Villar was on duty in the radio room of the *Barnstable (Plate AV-4)*, when he received what was likely the best news of his life: the telegram announcing Japan's surrender *(Plate AV-5, below)*.

AV-4. RM Villar at his radio room station aboard the U.S.S. Barnstable. Photo: RM Villar.

AV-5. Telegram announcing Japan's surrender, August 12, 1945. Villar collection.

Our soldiers and sailors in the Pacific continued to fight and die for months after Germany surrendered. Given Japan's intransigence, the war-weary U.S. troops who doggedly continued to battle the Japanese in the sweltering Pacific tropics likely lived with the lingering doubt that the war with Japan would ever end. It must have been frustrating to fight on against an intractable enemy while the thousands of troops in Europe and North Africa were returning home.

On August 12, 1945, as RM Villar sat on duty in the radio room of the Barnstable, he watched the teletype spit out that telegram. Imagine being the first soldier in the Pacific Theatre to receive the news that the enemy who had bombed and shot at you for so long, and had vowed to never surrender, had in fact surrendered—that you would be going home soon, alive, together with your shipmates who made it.

Is it possible to feel the exact same emotions as he did? How long did he sit and stare at that telegram, reading it over and over, before the reality sank in? Who was the first person aboard the ship that he delivered it to? Did he shout for joy? Did he hug the nearest sailor? Perhaps only those who have fought in and survived war can truly relate to those feelings. The rest of us can simply be thankful for those, living and dead, who suffered through our past wars to protect the freedoms we enjoy (and often take for granted) today.

Three days later, the Emperor of Japan announced the surrender of Japan to his nation by radio address. All of the telegrams received by the *Barnstable* were printed out in multiple copies for distribution to various officers on the ship. The copy of the surrender telegram RM Villar brought home was supposed to have been destroyed. A valuable piece of history has been preserved thanks to his recognition of its historic value and the risk he took in bringing it home.

The documents and pictures RM Villar took which he brought home from the war open a window into his wartime experiences *(Plates AV-2 through AV-25)*. His memorabilia fall into three perhaps arbitrary categories: documents portraying life aboard the *Barnstable*; pictures of the devastation that the fine old buildings in Manila suffered in the war; and photographs of events associated with the surrender of Japan.

Life Aboard the U.S.S. Barnstable

In July of 1945, the *Barnstable* was steaming towards Manila. The ship's daily newspaper for July 4, 1945, the "Press News," *(Plate AV-6)* updated the crew on the Allied war effort. Germany's prior surrender had led to an international effort to restore order to a war-torn Europe. B-29 bombers, known as "superfortresses," based in the Mariana Islands, continued to pound Japan, while Australian troops fought on in Borneo. British troops were engaged in retaking Burma. The U.S. was busy mopping up the last remaining Japanese resistance in the Philippines.

"During This Trip" *(Plate AV-7)* outlines the leisure activities and facilities available aboard ship, cautioning that the "Press News" should not be sent off the ship since it is not censored. The Navy officers scored the better entertainment, being offered the more "cultured" movie *King Kong*. Enlisted men were downgraded to something called *Sarong Girl*.

U.S.S. BARNSTABLE
PRESS NEWS

Capt. V. R. Roane
Commanding

Lieut. C. F. Tomlin
Executive Officer

4 July 1945

B-29s MAKE 7TH ATTACK IN 8 DAYS!

In a predawn raid early this morning 4 fleets of Superforts celebrated the 4th of July with fireworks over 4 Jap cities. 3,000 tons of fire bomb pyrotechnics were dropped dropped on secondary cities on Shikoku and Honshu. This morning's raid was the first ever made on a Shikoku objective. All 4 cities were important shipping centers. 450 American planes participated. This is the 7th raid in the last 8 days for the Marianas based Superforts. In that period they have dropped 14,500 tons of bombs. A total of 117 square miles of industrial Japan is now considered burned out.

On Borneo the Aussies have advanced 3 miles to take a town and an airfield only 6 miles from Balikpapan. Engineers are already at work restoring the airfield which will put Java, the heart of the Dutch East Indies, within fighter plane range for the first time in 3 years. An advance Aussie column is said to be only 3/4 of a mile from the huge oil refineries. A 6 mile long beachhead has been won. The sons of heaven are withdrawing from burning Balikpapan to ridges surrounding the city where they will have to be dug out methodically.

American patrols continued to strike Formosa, the China Coast and Indo-China railways. Army planes destroyed 4 ships in Macassar Straits, while Navy planes sank 6 ships in wide sweeps. Marine fighters knocked down 8 Jap planes over southern Kyushu and continued neutralization of the by passed Marshalls and Carolines. 1500 natives were evacuated from enemy held central Pacific islands during June.

The 14th AAF yesterday shot up 3 enemy headquarters near Changsha, and continued support of all Chungking troops.

In Burma British troops waded thru waist deep mud and water to take a new town, while other Nips walked into an Allied trap and were ambushed.

Mopping up continued in the Philippines amid torrential rains.

UNITED STATES IS FIRST NATION TO GET CHARTER.

With Pres. Truman's presentation of the new world charter to the Senate on Monday, the United States became the first nation to undertake formal consideration. It now appears that Australia will be the second.

Sec. of State Byrnes has been sworn in. The ceremony took place in the White House with most of the Senate, State Dept Staff and White House Staff present. He has already announced that there will be "no basic change in the foreign policy already laid down by my predecessors."

Edward Stettinius, preparing to enter upon his new job as United States representative on the World Security Council, has taken offices in the White House.

Artemus Gates has been sworn in as Under Secretary of the Navy, succeeding Ralph Bard, resigned. Harry Hopkins has also retired from all government service. His last job was a special mission to Moscow for Pres. Truman.

The Allied Control Council for the Axis territory is to start work immediately. One of its first jobs will be to supervise a free election in Poland.

Elements of the U.S. occupational forces entered Berlin on Tuesday and were directed to the southwest sector by Red Army troops. The British are expected to enter today.

Among the outfits soon to return from Europe to the States are the 104th Glider Division and the 45th Infantry. They will be redeployed to the Pacific.

AV-6. The "Press News," the official newspaper of the U.S.S. Barnstable. Villar collection.

"DURING-THIS-TRIP"

MOVIES: Movie programs will be presented the first night for Navy personnel and the second night for Army men. Enlisted men will see shows at 1845 in the Mess Hall. Entrance will be by ladders forward of #3 hatch. No smoking. Navy officers will see shows in the Wardroom; Army officers in the Troop Officers Mess. Tonight Navy will see "SARONG GIRL" with Ann Corio. Navy officers will be shown "KINGKONG."

ORCHESTRAS: Tonight's orchestra program will include:
THE 415th ARMY SERVICE FORCES SWING BAND of 15 pieces in a half hour program for Navy men before the movie in the Mess Hall. The band is under the general direction of Warrant W.S. Jones, and is led by Jimmy Coe, former alto sax player with Tiny Bradshaw.
THE 2nd FILIPINO BATTALION HAWAIAN ORCHESTRA will play for the Navy officers in the Wardroom before the movie.
Tomorrow and on succeeding days at 1400 near #2 hatch the 415th ARMY SERVICE FORCES CONCERT BAND under the direction of Warrant W.S. Jones will give an open air concert. Formerly known as the "Quartermaster Caravan," these boys have toured New Guinea for the past 22 months. It is the only all colored band in the Pacific theater.

LIBRARY: The Library, located on the main deck, port side, aft, will be open commencing tomorrow on the following schedule: 1000-1200 All naval personnel and Army officers; 1200-1700 Troops. Only 1 book at a time. Also free cigarettes, smoking tobacco, games, V-mail, ink, etc.

RELIGIOUS SERVICES: Army Catholic Chaplain Regalado will say Mass each afternoon at 1530 on the shady side of #2 hatch, and will hold service Sunday morning. Confessions will be heard each evening beginning tomorrow at 1830 in the Library.
Chaplain Allen, Navy, Protestant, will conduct the regular Friday night session of the Barnstable Bible Class and will hold a joint Army-Navy Protestant Service Sunday morning. Both chaplains will be available for consultation at all times; and can be contacted thru the Library. New Testaments, Links, Missals, etc. are available in the rack outside the Library door.

OTHER INFORMATION: Maps are posted on the bulkhead, main deck aft near the dental office and opposite the Troop Officers Mess.
The ship's destination is Manila. Orientation information will be given over the speaker when we pass thru the Philippine Islands. The ship is cruising on a prescribed zig-zag course.

GETTING ACQUAINTED: Army men interested in boxing Navy amateurs are asked to submit their names to any of the Navy Masters-at-Arms at once.
Photographs taken at the recent "crossing the line" ceremonies will not be displayed until after the present Army contingent has left the ship.
The Barnstable "NEWS" will appear each evening and will be distributed at chow. It will not pass censorship, and no attempt should be made to send copies off the ship.

Since the present passenger list is composed of many miscellaneous units, no attempt will be made to enumerate them. But for the benefit of the Army the following information is presented: The USS BARNSTABLE was built in S.San Francisco, Calif. as a cargoman, and converted to an attack transport at Portland, Ore. It was commissioned on May 22, 1944 and has taken part in the assault runs on Palau, Leyte, Luzon and Okinawa, and has also made numerous reenforcement trips. The Commanding Officer is Capt. V.R.Roane, USN, and the Executive Officer is Lieut. C.F.Tomlin, USNR. It is the flagship of Commodore Philip P. Welsh, USN, Commander of Transport Division #38, who is aboard with his staff.

AV-7. "During This Trip" announces shipboard leisure activities aboard the U.S.S. Barnstable. Villar collection.

The Surrender of Japan

Although the formal instrument for the surrender of Japan *(Plate AV-8)* was signed on the U.S. battleship Missouri in Tokyo Harbor on September 2, 1945, well before that date, critical compromises of the initial U.S. demands were hammered out by American and Japanese delegates in Manila, the headquarters of the U.S. forces in the Pacific theatre. Those modifications resolved significant obstacles and paved the way for the formal surrender ceremonies. Actual fighting continued in isolated areas beyond September 2, until Japanese forces could be informed of (and/or convinced of) Japan's surrender. The story of Maj. Gen. Pierpont Hamilton, the soldier who authored the Instrument of Surrender, appears earlier in this book.

U.S. President Harry S. Truman appointed U.S. General Douglas MacArthur as Supreme Commander for the Allied Powers to implement Japan's surrender and its subsequent occupation by U.S. forces. MacArthur notified the Japanese government of his appointment and ordered the immediate termination of Japan's hostilities. He also directed that Japan send to Manila a competent representative authorized to receive in the name of Japan "certain requirements for carrying into effect the terms of surrender." MacArthur's specific instructions dictated that the Japanese representatives embark from Japan in a Douglas DC-3 aircraft painted white and marked with green crosses, to a given destination where they would land and then be transferred to a U.S. plane for further transport to Manila.

A sixteen-man Japanese delegation, headed by Lt. General Torashiro Kawabe, left Japan on August 19th, arriving at Nichols Field south of Manila about 6:00 p.m. that day. A group of U.S. linguist officers led by General MacArthur's wartime director of intelligence, General Willoughby, met the Japanese delegation upon its landing. Less than three hours later, the Japanese delegation began conferences in U.S. General Chamberlin's office in the Manila City Hall, with members of General MacArthur's staff, including translators.

INSTRUMENT OF SURRENDER

We, acting by command of and in behalf of the Emperor of Japan, the Japanese Government and the Japanese Imperial General Headquarters, hereby accept the provisions set forth in the declaration issued by the heads of the Governments of the United States, China and Great Britain on 26 July 1945, at Potsdam, and subsequently adhered to by the Union of Soviet Socialist Republics, which four powers are hereafter referred to as the Allied Powers.

We hereby proclaim the unconditional surrender to the Allied Powers of the Japanese Imperial General Headquarters and of all Japanese armed forces and all armed forces under Japanese control wherever situated.

We hereby command all Japanese forces wherever situated and the Japanese people to cease hostilities forthwith, to preserve and save from damage all ships, aircraft, and military and civil property and to comply with all requirements which may be imposed by the Supreme Commander for the Allied Powers or by agencies of the Japanese Government at his direction.

We hereby command the Japanese Imperial General Headquarters to issue at once orders to the Commanders of all Japanese forces and all forces under Japanese control wherever situated to surrender unconditionally themselves and all forces under their control.

We hereby command all civil, military and naval officials to obey and enforce all proclamations, orders and directives deemed by the Supreme Commander for the Allied Powers to be proper to effectuate this surrender and issued by him or under his authority and we direct all such officials to remain at their posts and to continue to perform their non-combatant duties unless specifically relieved by him or under his authority.

We hereby undertake for the Emperor, the Japanese Government and their successors to carry out the provisions of the Potsdam Declaration in good faith, and to issue whatever orders and take whatever action may be required by the Supreme Commander for the Allied Powers or by any other designated representative of the Allied Powers for the purpose of giving effect to that Declaration.

We hereby command the Japanese Imperial Government and the Japanese Imperial General Headquarters at once to liberate all allied prisoners of war and civilian internees now under Japanese control and to provide for their protection, care, maintenance and immediate transportation to places as directed.

The authority of the Emperor and the Japanese Government to rule the state shall be subject to the Supreme Commander for the Allied Powers who will take such steps as he deems proper to effectuate these terms of surrender.

AV-8. The formal Instrument of Surrender signed by Japan.

Signed at TOKYO BAY, JAPAN at 0904 I
on the SECOND day of SEPTEMBER, 1945

重光 葵

By Command and in behalf of the Emperor of Japan
and the Japanese Government.

梅津美治郎

By Command and in behalf of the Japanese
Imperial General Headquarters

Accepted at TOKYO BAY, JAPAN at 0908 I
on the SECOND day of SEPTEMBER, 1945,
for the United States, Republic of China, United Kingdom and the
Union of Soviet Socialist Republics, and in the interests of the other
United Nations at war with Japan.

Douglas MacArthur
Supreme Commander for the Allied Powers.

C. W. Nimitz
United States Representative

徐永昌
Republic of China Representative

Bruce Fraser
United Kingdom Representative

Derevyanko
Union of Soviet Socialist Republics
Representative

T. A. Blamey
Commonwealth of Australia Representative

L. Moore Cosgrave
Dominion of Canada Representative

Leclerc
Provisional Government of the French
Republic Representative

Helfrich
Kingdom of the Netherlands Representative

Leonard M. Isitt
Dominion of New Zealand Representative

AV-8. Page 2.

The meetings forged on through the entire night and into the next day. Among the changes made to initial U.S. demands, the disarmament of the Japanese local troops in occupied Japan would be conducted gradually rather than all at once, and conducted by Japanese rather than Americans (but to be overseen by Americans). The respective delegates successfully negotiated other differences which arose, and the Japanese delegation left about 1:00 p.m. on August 20th.

RM Villar photographed the arrival of the Japanese delegation in Manila on August 19th, as well as that delegation meeting with American officers *(Plates AV-9, 10)*. The size difference between the American General in Plate AV-10 (not identified by name) and the Japanese delegates is remarkable.

AV-9. Japan's surrender delegation arriving in Manila. Photo: RM Villar.

The ability of the Japanese and American delegates in Manila to resolve such difficulties as arose, in a remarkably short time, laid the foundation for a smooth transition of power. The American forces who would occupy Japan would be overwhelmingly outnumbered by the Japanese themselves who had just surrendered their entire homeland to an enemy, an act of shame in a culture which held honor and avoidance of shame as some of its highest values. The U.S. was the first foreign power to ever occupy Japan. The potential for catastrophe was exceptionally high, but the occupation was successfully conducted. The U.S. occupation ended in 1952 when Japan was granted independence. While U.S. troops brought home a great many photos taken during the war, some subjects were forbidden. One of them was Japanese prisoners. Nevertheless, photos of off-limits subjects made their way home with the thousands of returning troops, including RM Villar.

Plate AV-11 depicts the U.S. flag flying over the flag of Japan on what was likely a captured Japanese P.T. boat. A U.S. soldier, name unknown, is shown on deck with captured weapons.

AV-10. Japan's surrender delegation meeting with U.S. delegates in Manila. Photo: RM Villar.

AV-11. Top: Captured Japanese PT Boat, de-flagged; bottom: U.S. soldier with captured weapons from boat. Photos: RM Villar.

Plates AV-12, AV-13, and *AV-14* depict captured Japanese soldiers. Photos of prisoners were officially forbidden, but prisoners were part of the reality of this war. It is not known why some of the prisoners wore what look like white bathrobes.

AV-12. Japanese prisoners of war, Manila, Philippines. Photo: RM Villar.

AV-13. Japanese prisoners of War, Manila, Philippines. Photo: RM Villar.

AV-14. Japanese prisoners of war, Manila, Philippines. Photo: RM Villar.

Plate AV-15 shows a white ship with what appear to be prominent crosses extending vertically above the decks. RM Villar's son Al thought it might be a hospital ship. It has similar configuration and coloration as the ship shown close up in *Plates AV-13* and *14*, so perhaps it was being used to transport prisoners.

AV-15. Hospital ship with incoming Japanese prisoners of war, Manila, Philippines. Photo: RM Villar.

Plate AV-16 shows an American ship photographed by RM Villar, name unknown, being sunk during action.

AV-16. American ship being sunk in combat, Pacific theater of war. Photo: RM Villar.

Life in Manila, 1945

In 1898, after some 300 years of Spanish colonial rule, the Philippines territory was ceded to the U.S. in the Spanish American War. The relatively successful and modernizing nation was on its way to independence when Japan invaded and took control in 1942. Full independence came in 1946.

The ravages of war left Manila in shambles. In peacetime, young Navy sailors aboard the *Barnstable* and other ships could enjoy shore leave in far off exotic ports like Manila. But liberty in Manila at the end of WWII held nothing but reminders of the depravity and destruction of the savage war that had torn it, and its people, apart.

Plate AV-17, next page, warns the sailors who chose to take liberty in Manila of the dangers that awaited them: few safe restaurants, food and water contamination, deadly alcoholic beverages, and badly infected local girls.

```
From:       Executive Officer.
To:         All Hands.
Subject:    General information for Personnel on liberty in Manila.

    1.    The price levels in the Manila area have not been stabilized as yet
and there are only a limited number of things which can be obtained at reasonable
prices.

    2.    Native food should not be eaten at any time. There are some rest-
aurants in the city which have been inspected by the Army Medical authorities and
all of these will display a placard indicating that they have been so inspected.

    3.    Men going ashore should carry ships water in canteens. The number
of restaurants serving food are limited and feed very few men in addition to
their present load. Liberty should be planned with this in mind.

    4.    The venereal disease rate is exceedingly high and men should be
provided with preventatives before going ashore. Army Prophylactic Stations are
located in various districts of the city.

        (a) 85% to 90% of "pick-up" girls are infected.

        (b) There is a 125% infection among the prostitutes, many having 2 or 3 in-
fectious veneral diseases.

        (c) Leprosy is a known disease among the prostitutes, its presence having
been proven by Army survey.

    5.    Men should be cautioned about the consumption of local alcoholic
beverages. Some of these have contained wood alcohol, ether, and poison, resulting
in death. False seals and labels are frequent, and old bottles are refilled with
illegal liquor.
                                                        C. F. TOMLIN.
```

AV-17. U.S.S. Barnstable ship bulletin warning sailors of dangers to avoid while ashore in Manila. Villar collection.

When RM Villar went ashore to escape the ship's confinement, he found what was likely the only safe diversion in Manila, watching a local game cock fight *(Plate AV-18).*

AV-18. Local game cock fight, Manila. Photo: RM Villar.

Before the war, Manila was replete with beautifully ornate buildings, but the war devastated this once great city. Some who have seen it before and after the war claim that its attempted reconstruction has fallen far short of its former pre-war glory.

Plate AV-19: American soldiers entering Intramuros, Manila, March, 1945.

AV-19. American soldiers entering Intramuros, Manila, March, 1945. Original photo: U.S. Army.

Intramuros, also known as the walled city, is a ¼ mile square historic area with buildings that dated back to Spanish colonial times. It was utterly destroyed in the Battle of Manila which took place in February through March of 1945. Over 100,000 civilians were killed. Of the more than 35,000 U.S. troops who fought in the battle, over half were killed. The Japanese were ultimately defeated, but at such a terrible cost. An aerial view of the destruction is shown in *Plate AV-20*.

AV-20. Aerial view of destruction of the Walled City, Manila, May, 1945. Photo: U.S. Army, Surgeon General's files and records.

Plate AV-21. Escolata Street, Manila. Escolata reigned supreme as the trendiest, most fashionable street in Manila from the 1920s through the devastation that occurred during the terrible fighting in March of 1945 that destroyed so much of the city. Art Deco style buildings flourished along the street, which some compared to New York City's Broadway. Many of Manila's first's debuted on Escolata: the first ice cream parlor, the first American department store, and the first savings bank. An incredible ornate Art Deco movie theatre was ruined in the fighting and never brought back to its original glory. Efforts to rebuild the street to its prewar eminence have been partially successful, but have fallen short of fully restoring what was once a glamorous international urban venue. A few other photos of the damage in Manila follow, subjects as captioned.

AV-21. Escolata Street, Manila. Photo: RM Villar.

AV-22. Quiapo Church. Photo: RM Villar.

AV-23. City Hall. Photo: RM Villar.

AV-24. Legislative Building. Photo: RM Villar.

One might think that the Navy would give its sailors a bit of a break from military routine in light of Japan's surrender, but the "Plan of the Day" dated August 24, 1945, *(Plate AV-25)* dispels that notion. Nothing much changes in the military from day to day, whether at war or during peacetimes.

```
                        PLAN OF THE DAY

FRIDAY                                          24 AUGUST 1945

DUTY HEAD OF DEPT.                              STAFF DUTY OFFICER.
T. SUMMERS.                                     Ens. SMITH

0000   Daily routine in port and to include the following:
0530   Call Duty Police Petty Officer - Duty Police Petty Officer to call Division
       Petty Officer.
0600   REVEILLE.
0620   TURN TO - A CLEAN SWEEP DOWN OF ALL DECKS AND LADDERS.
0645   UNIFORM OF THE DAY - UNDRESS WHITES FOR LIBERTY PARTY; CLEAN DUNGAREES (AND
       HATS) FOR RECREATION PARTY AND DUTY SECTIONS.
0645   MESS GEAR.
0700   BREAKFAST.
0800   TURN TO - Continue chipping, wire brushing, chromating and painting over
       side as directed by the 1st Lieutenant.
       TEST GENERAL AND CHEMICAL ALARMS - Test bull horns.
       MUSTER ON STATIONS.
       Turn in in-port watch lists.
1130   MESS COOKS MUSTER IN THE MESS HALL.
       SWEEP DOWN ALL DECKS AND LADDERS.
1145   MESS GEAR.
1200   DINNER
1230   Liberty and Recreation to commence for the 3rd section. Liberty to expire
       on the Fleet Landing Dock at 1700.
1300   TURN TO - Continue Ship's Work.
1315   Below Decks Inspection.
1600   MESS COOKS MUSTER IN THE MESS HALL.
1630   SWEEP DOWN ALL DECKS AND LADDERS.
1645   MESS GEAR
1700   SUPPER.
1800   SWEEP DOWN ALL WEATHER DECKS - EMPTY ALL TRASH CANS.
       BIBLE CLASS ON THE FORECASTLE HEAD.
                                                J. K. Braddy
                                                J. K. BRADDY,
                                                Executive Officer.

       Duty Boats and crews will be furnished as follows:
              1st Division - 1 VP and crew.
              2nd Division - 2 VP's and crews.
              3rd Division - 1 VP and crew.
              2nd Division - 1 LCM crew for liberty.

Note:  At 1530 a concert program and at 1830 a swing program will be given by the
       5th ARMY SERVICE FORCES BAND.

           OVER                 OVER                 OVER
```

AV-25. U.S.S. Barnstable Plan of the Day for August 24, 1945. Up at 6:00 a.m., sweep the decks, eat, sweep the decks... life goes on. Villar collection.

RM Villar earned several medals and citations for his service, including the Asiatic Pacific Campaign, Philippine Liberation Ribbon, Philippine Republic Presidential Unit awarded the Barnstable, Good Conduct Medal, World War II Victory Medal, and the American Campaign Medal. The reverse side of his Certificate of Discharge *(Plate AV-26)* provides an eye-opening picture of how far the value of our currency has fallen since that time. How could someone survive today with a monthly salary of $125.40?

After his discharge, RM Villar received a letter from Navy Secretary James Forrestal thanking him for his service *(Plate AV-27)*. Although such letters are frequently sent to honorably discharged veterans, this one is somewhat different from those of post-war years in that it proudly recites the wartime accomplishments of our Navy, which were indeed epic. The letter says it all; we are the beneficiaries today of the sacrifices of our veterans, living and dead, made in order to preserve our freedom.

AV-26. RM Villar's Certificate of Honorable Discharge. Villar Collection.

AUTH: AlNav 252-45

Enlisted as _____ (Rate) _____ (Date)

At _____ for _____ years

Born _____ (Date) _____ at _____

Qualifications _____

_____ Ratings held _____

_____ Certificates _____

_____ Trade schools completed _____

_____ Special duties for which qualified _____

Service (vessels and stations served on) or (served satisfactorily on active duty from

_____ 29 December 1941 _____ to _____ 6 October 1945 _____)

For convenience, a Certificate of Eligibility No. 494505 has been issued by the Veterans Administration to be used for the future request of Guaranty or Insurance Loans under Title III of the Servicemen's Readjustment Act of 1944, as amended, that may be available to the person to w

Rating at discharge RM2c, 12 October 1943 (Permanent) 4-6-77-36 (Service Number)

Character of service excellent.   Final average _____

_____, U. S. N.
and Executive Officer.

Height _____ ft. 64 in. Weight 131 lbs. Eyes Brown
Hair Reg   Complexion Dark
Personal marks, etc., Tattoo on right arm, Tattoo on left arm, on back also.

Is physically qualified for discharge. Requires neither treatment nor hospitalization.
I certify that this is the actual print of the right index finger of the man herein mentioned.

B. R. E. Jackson, U. S. N.
and Medical Officer.

Monthly rate of pay when discharged $125.40.
I hereby certify that the within named man has been furnished travel allowance at the rate of
.05 cents per mile from Jacksonville, Florida to Miami, Florida
and paid $ 81.73 (Amount) in full to date of discharge.
                                28 December 1943
Total net service for pay purposes 6 years _____ months _____ days.
                                PAID $100.00 MOP 6 October 1945
                                520012 E. L. Tucker

Albert Anthony O'Bear
(Signature of man)

_____, U. S. N.
E. L. TUCKER, Lt. (jg) (SC)   and Disbursing Officer.

AV-26. pg. 2.

THE SECRETARY OF THE NAVY
WASHINGTON

October 25, 1945

My dear Mr. Villar:

    I have addressed this letter to reach you after all the formalities of your separation from active service are completed. I have done so because, without formality but as clearly as I know how to say it, I want the Navy's pride in you, which it is my privilege to express, to reach into your civil life and to remain with you always.

    You have served in the greatest Navy in the world.

    It crushed two enemy fleets at once, receiving their surrenders only four months apart.

    It brought our land-based airpower within bombing range of the enemy, and set our ground armies on the beachheads of final victory.

    It performed the multitude of tasks necessary to support these military operations.

    No other Navy at any time has done so much. For your part in these achievements you deserve to be proud as long as you live. The Nation which you served at a time of crisis will remember you with gratitude.

    The best wishes of the Navy go with you into civilian life. Good luck!

Sincerely yours,

James Forrestal
James Forrestal

Mr. Albert Anthony Villar
877 S.W. 2nd St.
Miami, Florida

AV-27. RM Villar's letter of thanks from the Secretary of the Navy. Villar collection.

Chapter XI:
WILLEM ("BILL") DE LANNOY, JR. 1932 —

Preface

Bill and his Dutch-Indonesian family were fortunate to survive imprisonment in Japanese prison camps in WWII. But by then, Bill's struggles were only beginning. In order to escape persecution and possible execution after the war, he journeyed to Holland, only to face ethnic discrimination and an uphill battle to attain a decent standard of living. Emigrating to the U.S. opened new doors. His pursuit of the American dream led to a career in nuclear engineering, but at the cost of his first marriage and family.

Struggling to rebuild their lives as a blended family, Bill and his second wife reached the bottom of their own physical and emotional resources. Friends led them to a church where they chose to turn their lives over to Jesus as their Lord and Savior in 1977. Full of renewed purpose, they began a forty-year journey as missionaries venturing into life-threatening countries throughout Eastern Europe, Asia and Africa, braving dangers ranging from hostile Communist governments to witch doctors. Their story highlights the limits even the strongest among us face when we try to conquer overwhelming adversity by our own resources, and will inspire and encourage anyone who is seeking to discover meaning, purpose and peace in their life.

I now invite you to venture beyond the boundaries of war to experience an extraordinary lifetime journey from darkness to light, spanning the globe into Asia, Europe, America and Africa. Cross the threshold of the material world into realms that are unseen, but every bit as real.

The stage for the first act of Bill's story was set some four hundred years ago when Holland colonized the island nation of Indonesia.

Indonesia

A chain of more than 13,000 islands stretches 3,100 miles from East to West, and 1,000 miles from North to South. 1,000 of those islands are inhabited. This is Indonesia, the world's largest island nation, located primarily in Southeast Asia (see Map, *Plate BD-1*). Populated by over 261 million people, hundreds of different native ethnic and language groups live within its 735,000 square miles. It also holds the largest Muslim population of any country in the world.

During the European colonial era, the trading giant Dutch East India Company colonized Indonesia starting in 1603, taking hold of its valuable spices and natural resources. The nation became known as the Dutch East Indies, a name that persisted into the mid-twentieth century.

After the company's bankruptcy in 1800, Holland took control of the islands around 1826 following a war with the natives, imposing a period of forced labor and indentured servitude.

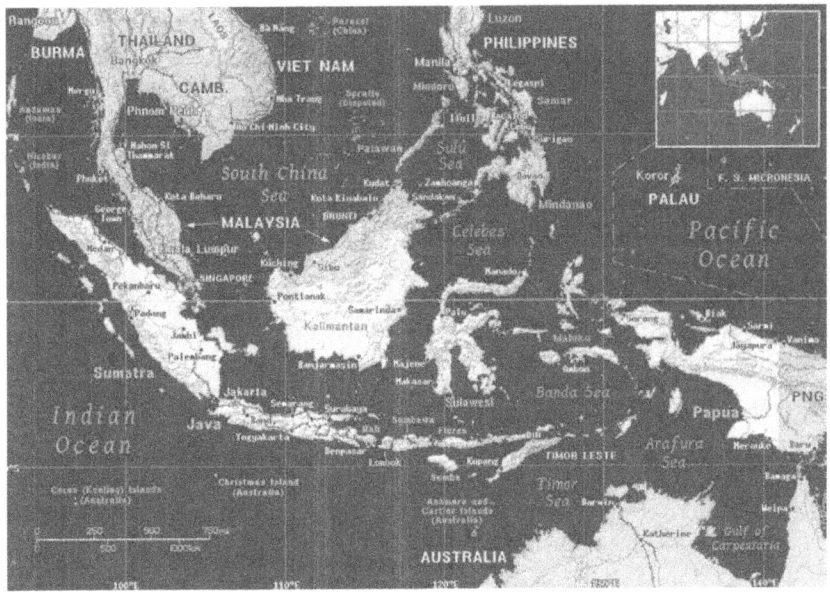

BD-1. Indonesia. PAT Public Domain Maps.

Dutch rule was loosened a bit in the early 1900s, but it persisted until Japan invaded and took control of Indonesia during WWII.

The Japanese occupation began in March of 1942 and continued until the end of WWII in September of 1945. Allied forces and Dutch troops were unable to resist the Japanese invasion.

Holland had been overrun by Germany, and was unable to provide any military assistance to its colony. Japan's conquest was completed quickly.

Until the invasion by Japan in 1942, the Dutch had kept a firm hand on various Indonesian nationalist groups opposed to continuing Dutch rule. At first many Indonesians welcomed the invading Japanese as the means to overthrow the Dutch. After Japan's invasion, many Dutch were killed by native Indonesians lashing out against their colonial rulers. The Japanese eventually sent some 100,000 European civilians and a large number of Chinese civilians who were living in Indonesia to Japanese prison camps, as well as an estimated 80,000 Dutch, British, Australian and U.S. troops. Between 13% and 30% of the imprisoned troops died in the camps.

The Japanese sought to take advantage of the anti-Dutch sentiment to make their conquest more palatable. Although some Indonesians fared well under Japanese occupation, many were subjected to forced labor, torture, sex slavery, and execution. It is estimated that four million people died in Indonesia because of the Japanese occupation. Some 2.4 million people died from famine in Java, the most populous island.

Following Japan's surrender in 1945, Indonesia engaged in an armed, as well as diplomatic, battle against the Dutch for independence, which finally came in 1949. Today, Indonesia remains a sovereign, self-governing nation.

The DeLannoy Family

The DeLannoy family was of mixed Dutch and Indonesian ethnic heritage. In 1942, the father, Willem Sr., an officer in the Dutch Army, lived in Magelang on the island of Java with his five children. The children's mother, who had been a teacher, died at a young age, around 41, in 1938. The family lived a comfortable life in a nice house with three Indonesian servants, two of whom had permanent living quarters in the family home. The DeLannoys owned their own car, and enjoyed the services of maids and a part-time gardener. The family spoke Dutch and had Dutch nationality. The local indigenous people, on the other hand, spoke Sundanese.

Willem J. DeLannoy, Jr., (known as "Bill" to his friends), was born in 1932 in Bandung, a mountainous region of West Java. Bill had two sisters, Puck and Dee, and two older brothers Harry and Emile, as well as various aunts and uncles. Magelang in central Java, where the family later moved, was encircled by five active volcanoes. The area has a history of mixed traditions infused with

Hinduism, Buddhism, Confucianism, Islam, and various other non-deity cults and religions. Superstitions and fears of spirits and evil forces were widespread. Various places, such as one large tree that always seemed to be dark underneath, were avoided for fear of the evil spirits thought to live there.

Bill had just entered first grade in the private school he attended when his mother died. Lessons were taught in Dutch by formally dressed teachers. Bill's 3rd grade class is shown in *Plate BD-2*. Bill is the last child on the right, second row from the front.

BD-2. Bill DeLannoy's third grade class, Magelang, Java, Indonesia. DeLannoy family photo.

As the 1930s came to a close, rumors of war in Europe had everyone, adults and children alike, on edge. In 1939, the world's fears materialized when Germany invaded Poland, igniting WWII. During the next three years, as matters in Europe and the Pacific worsened, Bill and his fellow schoolmates were told by teachers and parents not to worry. Even though the Netherlands, (mother Holland) was being overrun by Germany, there were impenetrable obstacles protecting the Indonesian Islands from Japanese invasion.

Pearl Harbor was a solid fortress of the U.S. Singapore was protected by the Prince of Wales Naval Task Force. The formidable Dutch Naval Task Force commanded by Vice-Admiral Doorman stood in the way. And, as icing on the defensive cake, Japanese pilots were no match for the Allied pilots because Japanese children were all carried on their mothers' backs when they were little, and thus had a poorly developed sense of equilibrium.

Despite this false sense of security, children were taught the meaning of air-raid and all-clear sirens. They carried identity cards and supplements such as pictures showing family members and their home locations. Bill's family had its own air raid shelter in the back yard, complete with an emergency generator, open to all, whether Dutch or Indonesian.

As the specter of a Japanese invasion loomed larger, Bill's father was mobilized to an Army unit and called away to a location in West Java about three days travel from his home. Willem, Sr. gave his service pistol to Bill's oldest brother, Harry, and his curved army battle sword to older brother Emile, assuring everyone he would be back soon. The Allies would quickly dispatch Japan. They would not see him again until WWII ended.

Reality came swiftly. Pearl Harbor was crippled by the Japanese sneak attack on December 7, 1941. The British Prince of Wales Task Force and the Dutch Fleet under Vice-Admiral Doorman fell within a few hours of battle. The Dutch Colonial Army in Indonesia was surrounded by Japanese forces and surrendered without firing a shot. By March of 1942, the Japanese shock troops were on the way to central Java.

As news of the Japanese successes spread, law and order disintegrated. Citizens who were European but not Dutch started wearing armbands to protect themselves from Japanese aggression, or retribution from the native population. Swiss and Swedish citizens would be treated as neutrals. Bill's friend and neighbor, a high-school student named Eicke Herold, who was a German citizen, began proudly wearing a Nazi armband and a Hitler Youth Dagger bearing the inscription "Blut und Ehre," which translates in English to "Blood and Honor." Eicke knew that Germany's alliance with Japan would immunize him against any aggressive actions by the Japanese, or by the local population.

Mobs of Indonesian villagers began to attack the prosperous neighborhoods occupied by the more wealthy and despised Dutch occupiers. Inevitably, villagers armed with torches and homemade weapons marched up the one road that led into Bill's neighborhood to eliminate the people who lived there. As waves of torches approached, Bill and his siblings fearfully prepared as best they could for the attack.

There was no longer any organized presence of police or soldiers to keep the peace. The five children were home alone. Their father had left to fight the Japanese. A miracle of sorts would be needed to save them. Amazingly, the mob stopped short as it approached the neighborhood. A lone figure stood defiantly in the middle of the street—a skinny teenager wearing a swastika armband and holding a Hitler Youth Dagger in one hand, shouting, "If you want to get in here, you have to kill me first!" The mob realized that Eicke Herold had the protection of the Japanese army, and grudgingly backed off.

Throughout the occupation, Eicke continued to proudly display his armband, loudly shouting, "Heil Hitler!" Unfortunately for him, after the Japanese were defeated some three years later, and he no longer had their protection, the native Indonesian villagers came after him and killed him for saving the European neighborhood three years earlier.

When the first units of Japanese forces arrived in Magelang they restored order, eliminating the threat of looting and mob attacks by Indonesian villagers, but life otherwise began to rapidly fall apart.

Without incomes, Dutch citizens entered into a period of slowly encroaching poverty and insecurity.

The reality of Japanese occupation was driven home. New rules were established. Children were required to stop and turn to face any Japanese soldiers they encountered, and then bow down to them.

Dutch families combined households, and sold their furniture and other possessions in order to survive. The Dutch community did its best to provide food for those Dutch families who were unable to do so. With Bill's father now imprisoned by the Japanese and his salary gone, the DeLannoy children were forced to move out of their home. They pushed their car to the home of Eicke Herold's family who promised to keep it safe until the end of the war. Their valuables were entrusted to wealthy Chinese neighbor friends, who unfortunately were never seen again. Likewise, after the war was over, the family car disappeared, possibly taken by the villagers who killed Eicke Herold.

The brutality inflicted by Japanese soldiers on their prisoners of war is well documented. But there were some exceptions. One Japanese army officer brought baskets of nuts to Bill and his siblings, knowing they had little food, and perhaps also knowing they were living without their parents. Other Japanese soldiers seemed to like children, giving food to them and teaching them Japanese songs. Food lines existed for a while, but were canceled when food ran out. Bill's private school closed. He and his siblings lived for a short time with another Dutch family until the family slowly ran out of money. *Plate BD-3:* DeLannoy children, left to right: Harry, Bill, Puck, Emile, Dee.

Life in a Japanese POW Camp

With no options left, the five children were forced to relocate to an internment camp for Dutch citizens, an abandoned agricultural facility ironically named "Happy Swamp." The camp was situated in the mountains, surrounded by dense forests, about seven miles from Magelang. Families were separated. Women with small children had one area, boys thirteen and older and adult men had another, with still another for boys aged 4 to 12. It was to this area for the youngest boys that Bill was sent.

BD-3. *DeLannoy children. Left to right: Harry, Bill, Puck, Emile, Dee. DeLannoy family photo.*

The youngest boys' were housed in one large building. They slept in three-high bunk beds, close together to fight the cold night air. An official toilet was a hundred yards away. The unofficial one was right outside the building. Older boys escorted the younger ones to the official bathroom at night. It was pitch dark, and fear of evil spirits and wild animals ruled the night. Lice and bed bugs chewed on the boys constantly. They shaved their heads, hoping to avoid head lice. *Plate BD-4:* Top: camp building, 1950s; bottom: camp buildings, 1983.

Days were spent working in vegetable gardens. The youngest boys received no education, save for being taught Japanese marching and battle songs, the Japanese alphabet, and how to march. Bill concluded that the Japanese camp commander was fond of the youngest boys. They were never beaten or punished, and he would proudly show visiting officers the boys' singing and marching skills.

BD-4. "Happy Swamp" prison camp, boys' building, Java, Indonesia. Top: 1950s; Bottom: 1983. DeLannoy family photos.

Despite these small reliefs, life was brutal. There was never enough to eat; the children continually lost weight. They tried to supplement their meager rations by killing lizards, snakes and squirrels, or stealing out of the garden. At night, they would reminisce about the food they used to eat at home before the Japanese invaded. The youngest boys began losing any memories of good food, and would merely stare in awe at the older boys' food stories. One day, one of Bill's family's Indonesian servants tried to deliver food to him and his siblings at the POW camp. The family was close to their servants, and this one had tracked them down, then walked for miles, barefoot, to try to bring them some food. She was turned away. His family never saw any of their servants again.

Hunger can do terrible things to people, even children. The Japanese camp commander bought a cute puppy, which was fed more than the prisoners were. The puppy had the free run of the camp, except at night when it was brought inside. Black panthers were known to prowl around the camp at night. One day the puppy went missing. Coincidentally, at the same time Bill's oldest brother got a secret message to Bill to meet him at a particular location in the forest; his brother had found and cooked a whole pan of meat. Nobody asked what kind of meat it was. The puppy never turned up. The camp commander assumed a panther had eaten it.

Punishment for crimes by prisoners against other prisoners was left up to the prisoners themselves. The Japanese doled out punishment only for crimes committed by prisoners against the Japanese. Older adult prisoners fashioned a crude but effective form of punishment for crimes (most typically theft) called "walking through the gate." The guilty person was forced to walk as fast as they could between two parallel lines of prisoners about thirty feet long, lined up facing each other three feet apart. Prisoners on both sides were allowed to beat and kick the guilty party as hard as they could. One short, muscular tough guy who had stolen something only made it about fifteen feet before he collapsed and passed out, covered with blood.

Even the young boys were allowed to hand out punishment. A woman stole some clothing from one of the little boys and was caught. She was forced to walk through a gate of the young boys about twenty feet long. She was crying, not knowing what to expect. But the boys had already decided it wasn't proper to hit a woman. Instead, they all spat on her face as she went through. She made it through, covered with spit and humiliated. But she never stole from the young boys' camp again.

Medical care ranged from primitive to nonexistent. A disabled sergeant medic whose only medicine was a barrel of potassium permanganate antiseptic was the sole "doctor" for all three camps. Badly needed medicines for malaria, dysentery, skin diseases and malnutrition were never provided. Bill and his brothers all spent time in the makeshift sick bay for the boys, which only had space for about ten patients, for problems ranging from exhaustion from overwork to frequent malaria attacks. Malaria patients who seemed to be on the verge of death were taken out of the sick bay and laid down outside so they would not disturb or upset the other patients. Bill was brought in one day with malaria and a fever so high he was delirious. He woke up screaming from a terrible nightmare in which he was in an ocean of fire, unable to run away, and found himself outside the sick bay, alone, on the floor, where they brought the patients who seemed to be approaching death. Bill demanded to the medic to go back inside the sick bay with the regular patients.

Toward the end of the war, food shortages became acute. The boys were on starvation diets and so skinny, hungry and desperate that they could do little work. Bill decided to organize a hunger strike. Bill and two other boys who were the leaders sat down in the vegetable field and told the guard that they were on strike because they needed more food. The guard threatened to take the boys to the camp commander to be severely punished, but they were so hungry they continued to strike. The guard then marched the three of them up the hill to be punished. The boys were truly scared at this point.

The story quickly spread through the camp. Bill's sister Dee was screaming and pleading with her guard to go up the hill to plead her brother's case, but to no avail. Dee likely feared that Bill would be beaten, or worse, killed.

Bill recalls that he and the other boys felt like tiny bugs as the big doors to the commander's office opened. They were literally scared to—and of—death as they entered. Confronted by three scowling Japanese officers seated at a huge wooden table, they stared wide-eyed at three Samurai swords on the table. The boys had seen the officers slaughter wild pigs with those swords, and pictured themselves being the next victims. A huge Japanese battle flag hung on the wall behind the table. The officers looked so mean and frightening, the boys wanted to sink into the floor and disappear. The commander stood, and the guard reported that Bill and his friends were the troublemakers organizing the strike. The commander looked straight at the three boys, pointed towards them with his right hand—and started laughing loudly, saying something in Japanese while continuing to point at the three boys. The other two officers joined in the laughter. They apparently thought it was hilarious that these three tiny grasshoppers had the guts to challenge mighty Japan.

The commander seemed to have a heart for young boys. He explained that nobody, including his soldiers, had enough to eat. The commander promised that if the little boys returned to their work immediately, for one day they would get the same rations as the soldiers; and they did, for one day. No punishment was handed out. Later in life, Bill concluded that God had surely intervened to spare his life and those of the other two boys.

Camp life dragged onward, but after a time, some sort of change was in the air. The attitudes of the guards seemed different. And one day, when the boys woke up, there were no guards—anywhere. No soldiers, military trucks, or any other signs of Japanese. Smoke was pouring out of the camp office buildings on the hill (later discovered to be from the burning of the camp records of the prisoners).

Japan had surrendered; the war was over. The camp was being evacuated; all of the prisoners were forced to make the long walk to the nearest town, which was Magelang. Bill was so ill at the time that he couldn't remember how he got back to the town. He thought his friends and family must have carried him.

On their way out of Indonesia, the Japanese purported to grant independence to Indonesia from their despised Dutch colonial masters. The Indonesians were forming their own army, and attacks on the Dutch citizens seemed just a matter of time. Units of the British Colonial Army, in cooperation with the International Red Cross and Allied Forces, were sent to protect the liberated Dutch prisoners, who had been moved into buildings and areas that could be guarded and kept safe.

Bill's father had been imprisoned in another camp, out of communication with his family for the three years of Japanese occupation. During that time he had endured much, but he had survived one experience in particular which he later related to Bill. Bill's father and other Dutch Army soldiers had been forced to board a Japanese ship to be transported to Burma where they were to work on the Burma Railway. As the ship was leaving the bay at Jakarta, Indonesia, it was torpedoed by an American submarine and sunk. The Japanese did nothing to try to save their Dutch Army prisoners of war. Those who could swim to shore, including Bill's father, lived. The others drowned. The torpedo attack probably saved Bill's father's life. Thousands imprisoned by Japan who were sent to work on the Burma Railway died. When Bill's father was returned to prison camp, the Japanese taunted him, saying, "It was your allies the Americans who sunk the ship."

The Burma Railway

The Burma Railway, better known as the Death Railway, was a 258-mile stretch of rails between Ban Pong, Thailand and Thanbyuzayat, Burma, started by Japan in 1943 to supply its forces in the Burma campaign in WWII. The link completed a rail connection between Bangkok, Thailand and Rangoon, Burma.

Burma was seized by Japan from the United Kingdom in 1942. Other than a completed rail link, the only way Japan could supply its forces was by a 2,000 mile sea journey susceptible to delay and Allied attacks. Building the Burma Railway was a monumental task, passing through almost-impenetrable jungle, numerous rivers and hilly terrain. To complete the task, the Japanese used and abused workers recruited or forced to work as prisoners. Between 180,000 and 250,000 Southeast Asian civilian laborers and about 61,000 Allied prisoners of war were subjected to forced labor. Some 90,000 civilians and over 12,000 Allied prisoners died during the construction. Conditions were abhorrent, with long hours of forced labor, disease, insects and jungle animals, blistering heat and humidity, inadequate food and medicine, and for the prisoners, maltreatment and torture in addition. This was the fate that would have awaited Bill's father, had the Japanese ship not been sunk.

When Japan surrendered, Camp Cihapit in Bandung where Bill's father was confined was abandoned by the Japanese, just like Bill's camp. As with Bill's camp, units of the British Colonial Army moved in to guard the Dutch citizens from attacks by the newly-"liberated" Indonesians. Early on, there were several attacks on the camp by the Indonesian "freedom fighters," but they never made it past the camp fence, which consisted of barbed wire obstacles and a woven bamboo fence.

Bill's father left the safety of his well-protected camp to seek out his children, risking injury or death at the hands of the vengeance-seeking Indonesians who controlled the country outside of the camps. Other fathers chose to do likewise. None of them could count on cooperation from the Indonesians in their searches. They were not allowed to carry weapons, since they retained an official status as POWs.

Bill's father set out for Magelang, the last place he had seen his children, bravely and proudly wearing his now-tattered army uniform. After a harrowing three-day train journey, he arrived in Magelang and located his children. He was so skinny, and his uniform so tattered, that they didn't recognize him.

Bill's sisters remained in Magelang under the protection of the International Red Cross and British Colonial Army troops. They were quartered in a hotel occupied by prisoners liberated from the Japanese camps. Bill's father and his three sons set out to return to the camp in Bandung. The three-day journey by an old-fashioned steam train was dangerous. Bill's father was pushed, punched, insulted and threatened by Indonesian travelers, but he maintained his dignity, providing an excellent example for his sons.

Upon return to Camp Cihapit, Bill's family found that many sons of other fathers who had sought out their children had also arrived. The children were in terrible condition, physically and emotionally.

For the first time in three years, the children had access to decent medical care and food. Bill received many shots and treatments for jaundice, scabies, and other ailments, as well as clean clothes.

The camp was bordered by a buffer zone about one hundred yards wide patrolled by British troops. Bill and his brothers enjoyed climbing a tree in front of the house in which they were staying, close to the camp's protective fence, looking out into what they called "enemy territory" for action.

One day bullets began hitting the roofs of the houses near the fence. A large Indonesian force was attacking the side of the camp by their house. Bill and his brothers climbed up the tree for a better look. They saw a patrol of British troops shooting at the attackers, who were crawling towards the camp.

Bill's father came out of the house and ordered his sons out of the tree. When the boys protested, other fathers came out and threatened to pull the boys out of the tree. The boys reluctantly climbed down. The last thing the boys saw was the attackers overrunning the British positions.

The excitement of the battle immediately vanished, replaced by a gut-wrenching fear that the attackers would overrun the camp and kill everyone. Suddenly, a fighter flew into the battle, probably a British Spitfire, and began machine-gunning the attackers. Loud screams were heard, and the smell of something burning. The fighter made several passes, shooting the whole time. More screams were heard, then—silence. The attack had been repelled.

Life continued, but with an uncertain future ahead. A school was opened, which the boys started attending. Bill's father insisted that his sons enter the grade they would have been in had the war not occurred, and three years of education lost. Bill entered as a seventh-grader. With some difficulty he was able to handle the curriculum. All the students were rusty and needed catching up. Bill's sisters were eventually evacuated from Magelang to be reunited with the family in Bandung. *Plate BD-5:* Bill and his brothers, better fed and clothed at POW camp in Bandung. *Left to right:* Harry, Bill, Emile.

The camp, which had been a residential neighborhood before its conversion into a camp, was eventually turned over to Dutch control, cleaned up, and returned to its original use. Bill's father, along with Bill's brothers and sisters, were transferred to Jakarta. Flying from Bandung to Jakarta, the old Dakota transport plane carrying the family was hit by rifle fire while flying over territory controlled by the Indonesian opposition forces. Bill's father remained unconcerned, so the children did not worry either. Liberated camp prisoners, including children, carried identification cards issued by the Netherlands Department of Justice *(Plate BD-6)*.

BD-5. *Bill and his brothers, Bandung POW camp. Left to right: Harry, Bill, Emile. DeLannoy family photo.*

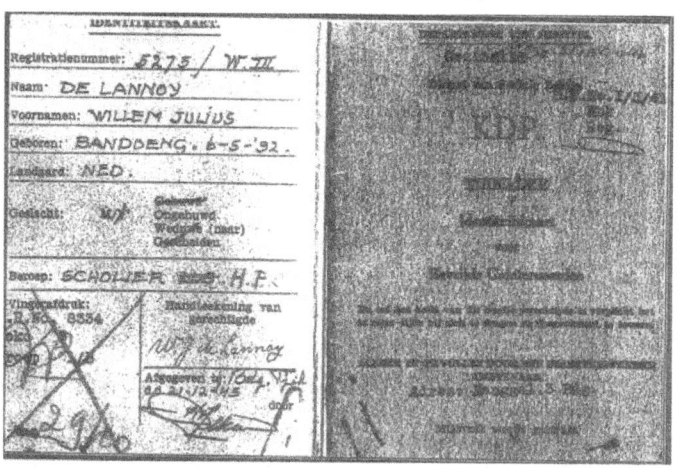

BD-6. *Bill's Dutch-Government issued I.D. card after POW camp release.*

Bill and his brothers belatedly received Red Cross food rations donated by countries such as Sweden, Switzerland and the U.S. during the war. The rations were intended to be distributed by the Red Cross to prisoners in the Japanese camps, but the Red Cross was never able to deliver them during the war. They had been stored somewhere, and ironically, distributed after the war when they were welcome but no longer desperately needed.

Bill's two friends who had joined him in the hunger strike never made it out of the camp in Magelang after the British took over security. It was rumored that they were shot by Indonesian troops while trying to retrieve supplies that had been dropped by parachute just outside the camp. The British Army had apparently sent them out to get the supplies never expecting that anyone would shoot children simply trying to retrieve them. Such was the hatred that drove the opposition. If Bill had still been in the camp, he likely would have been with his friends and shot along with them.

In Jakarta, Bill attended a Christian school with a multicultural mix of students—pure Indonesians, ethnic Chinese, Dutch-Indonesian, and pure Dutch, studied and worked together in peaceful tandem with their teachers. Bill joined the volleyball and soccer teams, and enjoyed the few brief years when his country proved that the hatred and killing could be overcome. But the prevailing politics of the adults, infused with strife and vengeance, would soon bring an end to peaceful coexistence.

Following Japan's surrender, the power vacuum in Indonesia spawned a four-year civil war from 1945 to 1949, as Holland and various competing indigenous political and religious groups fought one another for control of the country. Armed conflict raged in several regions, alongside of geopolitical battles into which various outside countries and the United Nations inserted themselves (or, some would say, meddled). International and economic pressure ultimately forced Holland to cease its efforts to regain control of Indonesia, leading to an international attempt to help formulate an independent Indonesian government. Although Holland well knew the mix of multiple incompatible religious, racial and ethnic groups that populated the country, its proposal for the new government's structure was rejected. The final solution was, some thought, the worst possible outcome. The multi-island nation would be governed from one central location in Java, by ethnic Javanese, leaving the other groups with no real voice. The phrase "Indonesia Tulen" was born, meaning pure Indonesian to the core. Thus the United Nations, with the support of other countries, including the U.S., insured the continuation of ethnic warfare and discrimination for Indonesia after four years of civil war. Although Holland was largely removed from the conflict in late 1949, internal factions continued their own power struggles well into 1950.

With the specter of the new, and many feared, ultra-nationalist government looming, many of the ethnic Chinese, European and Dutch Indonesians were urged to change their names to Indonesian names to avoid discrimination. There was a short window of time for those families to escape before the new, pure Indonesian, government took over. The ethnic Chinese had no chance to escape to China, even if they wanted to. China was in a turmoil from its own civil war between Communist and democratic factions. Dutch Indonesians were fortunate to have a choice. Those families, such as Bill's, who had members in the military, police, and Netherlands East Indies Army would suffer the worst persecution and were urged to leave. Bill and his brothers and sisters would migrate to Holland, although Bill would have been happy to remain.

A New Life in Holland

The challenges of culture shock, prejudice, and spartan living awaited Bill at the end of his month-long journey by ship to Holland in 1949. Instead of the balmy tropical climate he left behind in Jakarta, he was greeted by foggy, cold weather. The family was split up again. Bill and his brothers and sisters arrived ahead of their father. Bill and his older brother, Harry, shared one room in a small, cold house in Dordrecht owned by a young couple expecting their first child. His sisters went on to another destination. Holland was still recovering from WWII, and the young couple was poor and needed the rent money. There was little to no privacy for any of them.

Bill's classmates in high school were all "pure" Dutch. Several of his teachers resented him, either because of their political orientations or his ethnicity. The other boy students came to school in coats and ties. Bill had only his military jacket with which to ward off the cold and rainy gloom, which further marked him as an isolated outsider.

There was no social life for Bill. His one and only friend lived close by and walked to school with him each day. In fact, Bill walked everywhere. There was no place to store a bicycle at his boarding house. Entertainment consisted of watching the working riverboats, some with whole families living aboard. A few were like small floating grocery stores, supplying the larger boats passing through. Bill was fascinated by the bartering and negotiating for the sales of goods. Sometimes he fantasized about being on a boat leaving the gloom of Holland and returning to the warm, tropical country of his birth.

It seemed that change was the only constant in Bill's life. His father, who had remained behind in Indonesia for a time, had remarried and was coming to Holland. The influx of refugees from Indonesia continued to create friction, as the Netherlands struggled to recover from Nazi occupation. At the same time, many Dutch citizens were leaving Holland for places like Australia, South Africa, Canada and New Zealand because of the bleak job and housing situation.

Bill's father had lost almost everything from the Japanese invasion: his house, car, savings, and most of the family's possessions. There was no money for Bill to continue to live in Dordrecht. It seemed that Bill was doomed to move to Haarlem to live with his father and new step-mother, where his father wanted him to attend a four-year technical university and live at home. This did not fit with Bill's plans. Bill was adamant that he did NOT want to live in his father's home, and did NOT want to go to college for four years. He also was facing the mandatory Dutch military draft requiring two years of service. A male over the age of eighteen could be drafted at any time. Bill needed an escape route, and he found one. He would become a Navy pilot, a prestigious and desirable occupation. He enlisted for the initial two weeks of candidate selection, passing all of the tests except the most important one—the link trainer, in which he repeatedly crashed. Bill was offered the chance to reapply in a year. However, that attempt also failed.

Released from temporary military duty, Bill entered the work force, commencing a journey through a disjointed variety of jobs. His first foray into the working world landed him at a wholesale company for household goods in Amsterdam. The company's offices were close to the railroad station, at the edge of the red-light district where the pimps ruled the streets. Bill walked to work with a friend, another Indonesian-born man who had survived the camps and worked near where Bill did. Though it was a rough and edgy neighborhood to work in, they were never bothered. They once even heard one of the pimps say, "Leave those two boys alone, they are okay, they work and belong here."

About a year later, Bill got the call to fulfill his military duty. He was selected for reserve officer training, becoming an intelligence officer and learning basic Russian. He served for 27 months. His unit came under NATO command, moving all over Western Europe, often close to the border with Eastern Europe. *Plate BD-7:* Bill (pictured at top) and some fellow NATO Field Artillery soldiers in their Army camouflage uniforms deployed in Luneburg, Germany, in 1954.

BD-7. *Bill with fellow NATO soldiers, Luneburg, Germany, 1954. Bill DeLannoy photo.*

Winters provided the enjoyment of activities common to Northern countries like Holland. The waterways and ponds froze solid, becoming ice-skating and ice-sailing playgrounds. The Army held voluntary exercises teaching soldiers how to skate in full military gear, without using arms and hands for balance. Skating was not one of Bill's prominent skills, but he enjoyed the camaraderie the events provided. Springtime brought the blooming of the colorful flowers for which Holland is famous. Only the bulbs were harvested. There were too many flowers to be sold. Sadly, the canals were full of barge loads of flowers headed for the dump.

After mandatory military service, Bill was hired by the Government Department of Traffic and Waterways, venturing into the swamp of bureaucracy. Promotions were automatic. One simply needed to show up at work. Bill became convinced he would never become a permanent government employee. The government job tided Bill over for a few months until university started. He had decided to head back to school.

Circumstances forced Bill, belatedly, to do what he had vowed not to do: move in with his father and stepmother for several months at a time while attending school. Odd jobs filled the time during breaks and vacations. Bill became an expert at stuffing pickles into glass jars, folding women's stockings, picking strawberries and cherries, and harvesting potatoes.

Stuffing pickles paid one cent per pickle jar. There were two pickle-stuffing teams, separated in different areas: older women who were permanent workers, and part-time student workers. Bill gained such expertise that he was promoted to supervise a table of the older women. That didn't last long. Their obscene language and profanity were intolerable. Bill was relocated back to the student section at his own request.

Bill's third year in college brought some financial relief, as well as some of those invaluable life lessons learned by college students when they venture out of the college bubble. Students were required to perform hands-on work, for real wages, for a local company, and to write a report on some aspect of the company's operations. Three consecutive four-month employment periods at three different companies were required. Some of the companies paid higher wages than others, but were shunned by students. Although Bill was warned that there was usually a reason for this, he jumped, without investigating, into one of the better-paying jobs that students avoided. He needed the money. He learned why the hard way.

His first job was with a well-known brewery in Amsterdam, one of the workplaces which students avoided. Bill was assigned to an emergency repair mechanics' crew. Almost all of them were politically far left and read the local version of the Russian Communist newspaper, *Pravda*. It was here that Bill was rudely introduced to the world of class warfare. He was of a different class than the full-time workers, and was therefore headed for a better future. His language was at a different communication level, and he was resented for it.

Bill was regularly reminded that he was just a worthless college kid who knew nothing of the working world. He was often forced to start the day with a liter of cold beer, even in winter with snow on the ground. When he didn't know how to do a particular task, they sneered, "Didn't teach you that in college, did they, kid?" One day he found the handle of his hammer partially covered with human feces. Bill did not want to give up, but he needed a way to reduce the harassment. After studying the uncomfortable political discourse, he devised a way to boomerang it.

The regular workers continually criticized Bill's political beliefs and tried to market their leftist views. Bill noticed that one of his primary tormentors, Rooie Toon (Red Tony), had some differences with the others. Red Tony and one other worker were both pro-Chinese Communist. The rest were pro-Russian Communist, or Labor Party. A plan developed. Bill would ask Red Tony a political question, then walk over to a pro-Russian and innocently say, "But Red Tony says something different." The two sides slowly escalated their political differences, allowing Bill to stand aside as a neutral observer, smiling, while each side tried to sell their own version of Communism to the other. One day tempers ran so high that the pro-Russians stormed Red Tony's big tool cabinet, broke the door, and scattered the written propaganda material he kept in it. Management had to step in to restore order.

After a time, Bill was finally accepted as one of the guys. The other workers confided in him about the many tricks they played on management. (Bill didn't mention any of the tricks in the report he wrote for his school). But sadly, his satisfaction at finally winning acceptance was short lived. It was time to move on to the next job.

Ford Motor Company in Amsterdam became home for his second four-month employment term. It also paid well. Assigned to an assembly line, Bill struggled to keep up with the pace. The engineering manager, who was a fraternity brother, saw Bill having a hard time, and rescued him by transferring him to a drafting table job. It was clean, warm, and paid good money for a fairly easy job. Second lesson learned: it helps to have friends in high places.

A hard and dirty job at a steel plate factory rounded out the year. Like the brewery, the workers and their vocabulary were rough. Third lesson learned: management and office jobs are better careers than labor.

Senior year and graduation went well. Bill was ready to enter the real world and the job market.

As Bill's tenure in Holland continued on, his awareness of the political and social dynamics that influenced Dutch society grew. Multiple political parties competed for dominance, compared to the U.S. two-party system. The KVP (Catholic Party) and PVDA (Labor Party) were typically the largest, with several smaller religious parties adding to the mix. The CPN (Communist Party) gathered a large following in the late 1940s in response to the Nazi occupation of WWII. That party declined in numbers following the end of that war. Bills party, the VVD (People's Party for Freedom and Democracy), similar to the U.S. Libertarian Party, no longer exists.

Queen Beatrix was the head of state, married to Prince Bernhard von Lippe Biesterfeld. Army officers pledged their allegiance to the queen, not the country. A prime minister led a coalition of two or more parties. Left-wing parties were growing stronger, seeking government care from cradle to grave, a not unfamiliar refrain to us today. Medical care was centrally controlled. A worker calling in sick received a visit from the "sick leave" doctor, a bureaucrat, who decided whether or not the employee was sick enough to stay home. If he decided not, he would send the employee to work. The employee could appeal to his own personal doctor to make a home visit. Bill never did learn the intricate rules for what happened if the personal doctor disagreed with the bureaucrat. Employment applications required a person to state their religion, or "none." If a religion was specified, a part of the employee's salary was deducted to pay the salary and benefits for the clergy in that denomination. In this way, the clergy were paid by the government, not by the voluntary contributions of church members.

Bill's ethnic makeup made him the target of some ugly racial discrimination in the late 1940s and into the 1950s. The most egregious were the slurs thrown by people (usually children or teens) hurling insults like "pinda chinees, pinda-pinda lekka-lekka" (peanut-selling Chinese street vendor) or "zwarte aap" (black monkey) when Bill walked in public. Bill learned to ignore these. More hurtful were the slurs that slipped out of someone's mouth—a military officer saying "who is that brown dog walking into our lounge," or a college professor pointing to Bill saying, "the answer is so simple, even he knows it." The majority of pure Dutch citizens did not tolerate such behavior, and would call out the perpetrators when they witnessed it. Earning a college degree moved Bill into the upper class in Holland, but his standard of living did not advance by any large measure. Although he landed a job as a design engineer for a new startup company in Amsterdam that performed design services for the oil and power industry, the housing shortage limited him to a 15'x 10' room in a boarding house with no toilet and only a small wash basin in his room. The multiple and sizable tax deductions from his salary to fund the many government programs left him very little net take home pay from the gross salary he had initially been excited to receive. All the "free stuff" from the Government was not really free after all. He was also disappointed to find that, although his job performance was superior to other employees who started at the same time he did, everyone received the same amount of their first raise. Even getting married to his girlfriend, Cobi, did not open up any better housing opportunities. After they married, Bill and Cobi explored housing possibilities for a married couple without children, but their hopes collided with the multiple tentacles of bureaucracy. The government had a hand on everything.

Bill and Cobi ultimately found space on the third floor of a house (the attic) that was divided into three living units, with a shared bathroom for all three units. The accommodations were better than what most young couples had, given the post-war housing situation in Holland, but were nevertheless gloomy and confined.

Twenty minutes away on foot was a famous historical site — the clock shop of the ten Boom family where refugees from Nazi persecution were hidden by the family during WWII in 1943 and 1944. It remains a museum today, a reminder of the ten Boom family's brave and costly resistance to Nazi occupation.

Corrie Ten Boom

The ten Boom family was moved by its Christian faith to offer shelter to persecuted Jews and other refugees from Nazi tyranny. (Nazi Germany, which anointed itself as the master race, killed some six million Jews who were German citizens or citizens of the countries they conquered during the war, in an attempted ethnic genocide). The ten Booms are credited with saving the lives of some 800 refugees. They were eventually betrayed by someone and arrested by Nazi agents in February of 1944. Three family members were sent to prison camps, where they shared their faith with fellow prisoners. Two of the family members died in the camps; Corrie ten Boom survived. After the end of the war, she traveled to sixty countries over the course of thirty years, sharing her story and how God's love had carried the family through their ordeals.

In the midst of their seemingly hopeless housing situation, good fortune blessed Bill and Cobi. The U.S. passed legislation known as the Walter-Pastore Act, which expanded the immigration quota from Holland beyond the normal 3,000 person annual limit. Until the passage of that Act, the list of people wanting to come to the U.S. from Holland created such a long waiting period that most gave up hope. The Act granted additional quotas for Dutch citizens who were displaced from their birthplace by WWII. Bill later heard that The Act provided such generous quotas that many went unused. Churches in the U.S. were willing to sponsor displaced Dutch immigrants, assisting with housing and employment. Bill's entire family and their spouses qualified, but only Bill and his brother, Emile, and their wives, accepted. Both couples were sponsored by a Methodist church in La Habra, California. A new chapter in Bill's life began.

Coming to America
February, 1960

Bill and Cobi boarded an airplane in Holland, headed to the bright, shining promise called America. They landed in New York, with all their belongings packed into two small suitcases. Cobi was pregnant with their first son, Michael, who was due in four months. They continued on to California by train, where they planned to stay for the first few months with Bill's brother Emile and his wife, Rose, in La Habra. The sponsoring church had generously committed to provide financial, housing, and employment assistance. Although the church did not need to provide financial or housing assistance, its help with job hunting and newborn-baby advice was welcomed. Job hunting began.

A member of the sponsoring church, Bill J., a chemical research technician, had already investigated the job market ahead of Bill's arrival, and had located four companies where Bill could apply. Bill will never forget the receptionist at Ralph M. Parsons Company, their first stop. When Bill J. and Bill arrived, she looked right past Bill DeLannoy, Jr. and said to Bill J., "Sorry, we used to feel obligated to hire some of these people because we are doing projects in their countries, but we don't do that anymore." Bill J. was terribly embarrassed and apologized for the woman's degrading comments. He assured Bill that this woman was an exception, and that other large American companies are very professional and unbiased. The stop at the next large company, Fluor Corp., immediately erased that episode. Fluor hired Bill on the spot, and Bill spent almost thirty years working for Fluor and its overseas subsidiaries.

The following years unfolded as the prototypical American success story. Bill, an immigrant, came to the land of opportunity, climbed the corporate ladder, obtained an M.S. Degree in Systems Management, and moved constantly upward in engineering assignments. Cobi and Bill purchased their first home in 1964. His family, which now included a son and two daughters, accompanied him for his first overseas assignment, working for company subsidiaries in London, England; Dusseldorf, Germany; and Holland. Later project assignments included work for international oil conglomerates in the Americas, Europe, the Middle East, Southeast Asia, and South Africa. But, as is often the case, Bill's unwavering focus on his career came at a personal price. His relationship with Cobi slowly deteriorated. He hadn't realized how far until one day she surprised him by filing for divorce.

The trauma of divorce and the resulting financial consequences darkened Bill's life. Years of savings and retirement account accumulations were liquidated, to be divided between Bill and Cobi. Bill moved into a small apartment and struggled financially. Cobi remarried and moved to Minnesota with the three children, creating a void in his life left by his children's absence.

Bill also remarried. Sharon, his new wife, had three boys from a previous marriage. Bill's oldest son, Michael, moved away from Cobi to live with him and Sharon, as they all tried to overcome the pain caused by the disruption of their prior marriages. A blended family with four boys is a challenge for anyone.

As Bill recounts the story, he was a firmly committed agnostic at this point in his life. Colleagues in his workplace had tried to engage him, in past years, in discussions about God and Jesus, but he quickly dispatched them by pointing out what he considered the illogic of their beliefs. Growing up surrounded by multiple conflicting theistic and animist spiritual beliefs, suffering as a victim of prejudice and the inhumanity of war, and being of a scientific mind set, his world view left no room for such things. People, in his view, were in total control of the world and their own destinies. Darwin was right; only the fittest survive. Science explained everything. But things were about to change.

Bill was now employed by Bechtel Power, a company known for its expertise in designing and constructing nuclear power plants. A temporary field assignment took him to Calvert Cliffs, Maryland, to assist with building a new nuclear plant. The partially completed containment dome, huge and quite impressive, was visible from miles away. The governor felt that the time was right to stage a public event to promote the plant. He directed the plant workers to assemble together with dignitaries he had brought to the site for a speech. The governor heaped lavish praise on the workers for the wonderful job they were doing for his State, for their knowledge and expertise, and for the enormous amount of power their work would supply. He continued the gushing *ad nauseam*.

That night, Bill returned to the site and gazed up at the massive building. The enveloping darkness wrapped around him, still and quiet. Millions of stars glistened in the clear sky. He was alone, with only his thoughts as company. Amidst the struggles of trying to rebuild his life in his new marriage, his mind echoed the governor's platitudes earlier that day. "Indeed," he thought, "*we* really have made an impressive building." Silently and sadly, he asked himself, "So why am I not proud? Why is there no satisfaction in this?" In his emptiness, something stirred in his thoughts. His question was being answered. By some unexplained means, he perceived a very direct response, not audible as if someone was speaking, but nevertheless very clear: "Look beyond the building. Look at the stars, the moon, and the vastness around you! There you will see MY power!"

Bill was shaken and frightened. Something unknown had just shattered the reality he had constructed for himself. He weighed the past conversations with those who had tried to convince him of the reality of God. Could they be right? His shell began to crack open. Something inside him was changing. If God was real, maybe God could resolve Bill's confusion and loneliness. But, if God created the universe, Bill's entire world view based on chance evolution and mankind's supremacy would be turned upside down.

Questions abounded. Bill was opening up to the possibility, maybe even the probability, that there was a supreme being. He started asking questions of Christian colleagues. His need to know became a quest. Looking for answers, and at the urging of various diverse colleagues, he studied Mormonism, Jehovah's Witnesses, Islam, Hinduism, Buddhism, Rosicrucianism, and Christian Science while at the same time trying to focus on keeping his new family together. Meanwhile, his family struggles began to take their toll. Sharon, who had attended church as a child, felt they might find some guidance at a church. A friend suggested they try the nearby First Evangelical Free Church of Fullerton, led by well-known pastor Charles Swindoll. Hesitant but desperate, they drove up to the church on a Sunday morning. Upon noticing that most of the people walking in were carrying a book, Bill grumbled, "if they assign homework, I'm not coming back." Not only would they come back, but their lives would take a dramatic turn.

Bill's life experiences had left him with a dog-eat-dog philosophy. But now he began to hear something completely different: that God is indeed real, that He created the heavens and the earth, and that He created mankind. The dog in all of us is something called sin, a universal trait of all mankind born out of our pride, our selfishness and our refusal to follow God's directives. Our sin separates us from God. He learned that God loves all of us, and indeed he and Sharon experienced a loving atmosphere among the people at the church. The sermons and lessons in Sunday School began to take root and grow. Bill and Sharon learned that God provided a way to reconcile sinful mankind back to a relationship with Him by sending His son, Jesus Christ, to Earth to die on a cross, paying for the sins of mankind. After three days in a tomb, God raised Jesus from death, providing a path to eternal life for mankind. This forgiveness is a gift from God. In order to accept this gift, we need only declare with our mouth that Jesus is Lord, and believe in our hearts that God raised him from the dead.

Sharon tearfully considered all that she and Bill were learning. The emotions stirred up by their family situation, and their growing understanding of God, wore heavily. After a few weeks at the church, Sharon prayed to receive Jesus as her Lord and Savior in October of 1977. Bill was a bit more skeptical, and somewhat afraid to surrender his life after a lifetime of relying on his own resources to conquer the considerable hardships and adversity he had endured. But in December of that year, Bill also made that commitment. This in turn led to a life-changing refocus for both of them. In the coming years their new-found direction would lead them all over the globe, into dangerous countries and challenges,to share what they had learned about God and the gift of His Son, Jesus, to reconcile a fallen world.

Next Stop, Communist Eastern Europe

Bill and Sharon plunged headlong into what the Bible says, and how to share that with others. They attended classes at their church, enrolled in outside study programs, and answered the call to go forth into the world. Regardless of being young in their new faith, and fearful of being unqualified, they offered themselves to God to go wherever He wished, with one exception: please don't send us to Africa. Of course, God would eventually send them there—but not right away.

In 1983, Bill and Sharon embarked on a mission trip to The Peoples' Republic of Poland led by an organization named Campus Crusade for Christ (now known as "Cru"). At that time, the country was under Communist rule and occupied by Soviet Russian troops. Religious expression was severely repressed, as it is under any Communist government. Political turmoil boiled over. The "Solidarity" movement, an anti-Communist backlash, was percolating through the country. The Polish clergy had requested help and encouragement from the U.S. for the beleaguered and oppressed Polish believers, most of whom had a Roman Catholic background.

A group sponsored by Bill and Sharon's church flew to Warsaw, Poland where they split up into smaller teams of two to four people who would travel out of Warsaw to smaller towns. As the smaller groups departed, the comfort of being with a larger group in a somewhat hostile foreign country began to fade away. Eventually Bill and Sharon were the last couple standing, waiting to board their plane to Wroclaw, alone in a gloomy airport departure hall surrounded by poorly-dressed and suspicious Polish people, wondering who these interlopers were and why they were there. In the midst of their discomfort, a young man dressed like an American headed for the golf course approached them. "Hi, my name is Pete," he announced cheerfully. "Do you have $20.00 I can borrow? I need to give it to my friends who live here in Poland. I'll be back before your plane leaves and return the $20.00." Bill was taken aback, but gave Pete a $20.00 bill, thinking he would never see that money again.

Time wore on; as expected, no Pete. But just before their departure, here came Pete, running toward Bill and Sharon with a small stack of papers in his hand. "Hi guys, I'm going to the same destination as you. I have my car parked at the airport there, and I have to be out of Poland by midnight." Bill and Sharon were surprised to see him again.

The plane was a small, propeller-driven aircraft which sorely needed maintenance. Pete sat in front of Bill, both of them in aisle seats near the middle of the plane. As they sat there, two huge, heavily armed soldiers in nicely-pressed light-blue uniforms boarded the plane. One sat at the entrance, while the other sat at the exit. Pete leaned back and whispered, "Those are Zomos, the riot police; watch out for them, and don't get up out of your seat without first raising your hand until they notice you. They don't trust the passengers and are trigger happy. The Polish people hate them, and they know it. Because of this hatred they are afraid. Also, never turn your back on them."Pete handed Bill the little stack of papers he had been carrying. "Read this," he said, "it will give you an update on the political and military situation in your area." Bill was now quite curious. He asked, "Who are you Pete? Where did you come from?

Why are you here? And why the same destination?" Pete merely answered, "I work in education and come here often. I have to rush to Wroclaw in order to be out of Poland before midnight."

When the plane landed, the two Zomos stood up, the backs of their fresh blue uniforms soaked with perspiration. As tense and uncomfortable as it was for Bill and Sharon, it must have been worse for the Zomos, confined in a small space with fellow citizens who hated them.

Bill and Sharon heaved a sigh of relief when they got off the plane, as they spotted their welcoming party. Their hosts, Tadeusz and Magda, and their translator, a 19-year-old Polish girl named Gosia who was studying English, were thankfully there waiting for them. Bill looked around for Pete so he could introduce him to his hosts, but he had disappeared. Bill recounted Pete's story to Tadeusz and Magda. They remarked that they hadn't seen any other Americans get off the plane, and that the border was too far away for anyone to reach it before midnight. The mystery of Pete was never solved.

Accommodations were "cozy," as the newly-arrived Americans shared their hosts' tiny fifth-floor apartment. Although their neighbors had little themselves, they gladly donated their own food coupons so the visiting Americans would have enough to eat.

As he accompanied Gosia out and about one day, Bill got a bitter taste of life in Poland under occupation by Communist Russia. Gosia had invited him to go with her to see how they lived compared to Americans. The first stop left them standing in a long, slow line to turn in a food coupon for a small hunk of cheese. Gosia asked, "You don't have to stand in line for food, do you? And you can buy all you want." Somewhat embarrassed, Bill told her that was correct. As they continued on, they passed a line of Russian tanks parked along the street. By the time people figure out that Socialism leads to Communism, and what Communism is all about, it's too late. Sometimes, as in Poland, Communism comes in uninvited, and simply conquers by force. Communism maintains control at the point of a gun. If the oppressed people cannot fight back, they remain under domination, their freedom taken away and lost.

This is why the Second Amendment to the U.S. Constitution exists: to preserve the ability of the people to resist a takeover by a government that does not govern by the will and consent of the people. As Bill and Gosia passed by the tanks, Russian soldiers popped up out of the hatches to whistle and leer at Gosia, making lewd comments. She was quite a pretty girl. Bill's stomach churned with fear, wondering if they might climb out of their tanks and try to molest Gosia. If that happened, he wondered, how could they fight back?

Over the coming days, Bill and Sharon worked closely with Father Anthony, the leader of the local Franciscan Catholic Church, at their hosts' apartment. When Father Anthony visited, he wrote his discussion notes on his arm underneath his brown Franciscan habit. He did not carry any papers, for fear the police would stop him. Father Anthony's traditional garb included sandals. He walked through snow almost daily to reach the apartment, barefoot except for the sandals, such was his dedication.

Bill and Sharon witnessed to many local people. Several accepted Jesus as their Lord and Savior, including their translator, of whom they had grown very fond. Half-way through their assignment period, their host family was warned of upcoming student riots in Wroclaw. They were told that the military and the Zomos planned to use brutal riot suppression techniques. The Zomos had already gone into student dormitories and randomly beat up groups of students who had done nothing to provoke them. The police called this "preventive riot control," apparently their way to win the hearts and minds of the people. Bill and Sharon were advised to escape the city immediately until the troubles passed. This advice was well timed, since they were shortly due to travel to another location in Poland for an interim meeting with their U.S. team, intending to return to their hosts' home after that meeting.

They quickly gathered their things and hired a taxicab to get them out of the city, the cheapest way to get around Poland at that time. The nervous taxi driver did his best to get out of town quickly, but was slowed by military barricades and soldiers in riot gear, assisted by assault vehicles and tractors. Bill was fearful and intimidated, for the people of the city as well as for himself and Sharon. They slowly picked their way out of the city and safely headed to their next destination in Poland. After things in Wroclaw calmed down, they were able to return to their original hosts' home.

The time in Poland passed too quickly for Bill and Sharon. Leaving Poland to return to the U.S. brought tears and pain for both the Americans and their Polish friends. In just a short time, they had forged a strong heart bond. Once again, with some trepidation,

Bill and Sharon boarded a small beat-up plane at an airport near Wroclaw. As their plane rumbled down the runway, many of their Polish friends ran along the road adjacent to the runway waving goodbye, some still in tears. Bill and Sharon marveled at how they could come to love so deeply a people across the world in a foreign culture to whom they had never given any thought before this trip.

Before returning to the U.S., the entire team met in Switzerland, a safe location in a free country, to debrief and share their experiences. Virtually everyone in the group, men and women alike, shed their own tears as they shared their experiences. They were overwhelmed by the repressive, inhumane living conditions of the Polish people, compared to their own easy, pampered lives.

Bill and Sharon made two more three-week trips to Poland before 1985. (In 1989, Poland began to break free of Soviet control, achieving freedom in 1991. The last Soviet occupation troops left in 1993). When 1985 arrived, Bill and Sharon's concern for the people of Eastern Europe living under repressive Communist dictatorships had grown into a burden and a dilemma. In order to devote more time to ministering to them, Bill would have to quit his job at Northrop Electronics in California. Leaders in the Eastern European "underground churches" were seeking help from American missionaries in broadening their faith and learning day-to-day application of Biblical principles. In response, a Vienna, Austria-based organization, The Eastern European Seminary, began assembling teams of full-time lay ministers in order to meet this need. These would be dangerous assignments. They had kids to consider.

Should they jump in?

Bill and Sharon's children were now in high school. Bill's son Lance had joined the Navy.

Another huge life-changing decision faced them.

1985 – Another Giant Step

Their hearts made the decision for them: full-time ministry. The next year was spent raising funds, selling their home, downsizing into a condominium, and going through training. With support from their sponsors and the First Evangelical Free Church of Fullerton, Bill and Sharon moved with their youngest son, Chad, to Tutzing, West Germany, their stepping stone into Eastern Europe. Two of their sons remained behind, living in their condominium as they finished school.

Eastern European countries under Communist control at that time, such as Hungary, Romania, Poland, Czechoslovokia, East Germany, Yugoslovia and Bulgaria, were in need of missionaries. Bill's primary focus was Romania. Since Communism is the natural enemy of Christianity, going into any of these countries as clergy carried the risk of imprisonment and mistreatment. Bill and Sharon could not simply cross the border as itinerant preachers, with a load of Bibles. They went in as tourists. Their trips were as dangerous, and required the same secretive cautions, as those of CIA spies. If they were caught, the penalties would be severe. An early trip into Romania highlights the extent of the secrecy required.

Bill was instructed to meet up with pastors "Little John" and "Big John" who were leaders of the clandestine "Army of the Lord." In a particular city he took the train to a designated station where he had been told to walk to a certain part of the station with a specified local newspaper in his left hand. Bill was petrified at the thought of being arrested and imprisoned in a Communist country. Two people walking in the station cautiously reacted to him when they spotted his newspaper. They furtively approached Bill and told him to come with them to their car, where they talked. Bill received instructions for what to do next, and was driven in the car to a house outside of town.

Bill entered the house, in which three people awaited. A lady with a violin spoke English. She asked, "Are you Bill?" Bill answered "Yes," but that was not proof enough. Bill was asked to lead them in worship. Bill did so, which confirmed that Bill was genuine. "Welcome, Brother Bill," they said.

Things did not always go so well. On one occasion, Bill walked into a situation where an underground pastor's house was being ransacked by police. He thought quickly and casually walked away as if he were a tourist. Four men from the police contingent at the scene broke off and started following him. Unnerved and frightened, Bill wandered into several stores, and purchased some tourist-style souvenirs. His tails finally dropped off. That trip ended earlier than planned.

Bill had been warned early on to avoid talking to Romanian girls, especially attractive ones, as the government often used them as spies to ferret out missionaries and report them. On one trip, he encountered one who was unusually friendly and inquisitive, but remembering this warning, he told her little.

Clearly a new strategy was needed. Bill and Sharon formed a business and began traveling as representatives of a European company, purchasing and exchanging small Eastern European goods. The Communist authorities were hungry for Western currency, so Bill and Sharon easily obtained visas and travel became easier. *Plate BD-8: bottom picture:* underground pastors with Bill (third from left), Romania; *top picture:* underground pastors with Bill (back row, fifth from right), Indonesia.

A family tragedy struck at Christmas time in 1986. Their oldest son, Lance, had married a girl named Carla whom he had met while working as a missionary in the Philippine Islands. They were living in California, and she was expecting Bill and Sharon's first grandchild. The family was overjoyed at that good news, as well as the fact that Lance had emerged from difficult younger years as a well-grounded adult. On Christmas Eve, Bill and Sharon learned that a terrible car accident had killed Carla and their grandchild-to-be. Lance was injured but had survived. Shaken and grief-stricken, Bill and Sharon rushed to California.

BD-8. Bill with underground pastors. Top: Indonesia. Bottom: Romania. Bill DeLannoy photo.

The grieving process was difficult, especially for Lance, persisting for a very long time. All of them questioned if they could trust the God they had pledged to honor and serve. Faith that has been shaken must be rebuilt and repaired. The question of why this tragedy had happened continued to haunt all of them.

It was not easy to return to Europe. Bill and Sharon pressed on with their ministry work with great sadness and lingering questions, seeking answers and comfort in their faith. Over the next three years, time and faith slowly mended their hearts. Their team became more adept at moving about and teaching in Communist countries that were hostile to Christianity. As 1989 approached, they sensed political change brewing. Their instincts proved correct. In 1989, the infamous Berlin Wall that separated Communist East Berlin from free democratic West Berlin was torn down, a massive victory for freedom.

(Appendix F provides the history of the wall and a photographic tour of the wall, Brandenburg Gate, and other structures in Berlin from the author's trip there in 1971 while stationed in Germany).

At the same time as the wall came down, Eastern European countries were gaining independence from the Soviet Union. The "Iron Curtain" which separated the Soviet Union and its Communist satellite nations from the free world was being drawn back. Freedom was dawning. Events once thought impossible were occurring, even to the point where Easter was openly celebrated in Moscow, Russia *(Plate BD-9)*.

Bill's team had the option to move into some of the ex-Communist countries as residents to continue their work, or to return to the U.S. Bill and Sharon's son, Chad, was ready to start college. The family decided it would be best to move back home. After four years of full-time ministry, Bill plunged back into the work force.

Choosing the best available job wasn't easy. In the confusing mix of options, one seemed to continue to rise to the forefront. It offered opportunities similar to what Bill and Sharon had been doing in Eastern Europe. The country of South Africa was in need of technical workers with the education and skills that Bill possessed. A brief digression sets the stage for what Bill and Sharon were about to plunge into.

BD-9. Easter celebrated in Moscow, Russia, after the collapse of the Soviet Union. Bill DeLannoy photo.

South Africa and Apartheid

As its name implies, South Africa is the southernmost country in Africa. European traders began to settle there as early as the 1600s. As their ships rounded the southern tip of the continent, they discovered a land with agricultural potential and natural resources. British and Dutch interests established colonial presences which grew substantially in the 1800s. Friction and competition between the two countries' territories resulted in the Dutch settlers, known as Boers or Afrikaaners, moving away from the areas of British activity and founding two primarily agricultural states, Transvaal and Orange Free State, which considered themselves sovereign.

The Dutch and British lived in relative peace with one another, (although armed conflict between them and some of the indigenous tribes, notably the Zulus, was occurring) until the discovery of diamonds and gold in the Dutch enclaves in 1868. This ultimately led to two wars between the British and Dutch known as the First Boer War (1880-1881), and the Second Boer War (1899-1902). Although the British ultimately prevailed and declared South Africa their own, part of the treaty ending the war promised eventual independence to South Africa, which was granted in 1910.

When gold and diamonds were discovered, the Europeans brought in slaves and workers from other countries, including Indonesia, to work the mines. Natives of other African countries migrated there as the standard of living and opportunities were superior to those of their own countries. The country grew into a mixture of ethnic and racial groups. The white Europeans became the ruling class, having essentially colonized and developed the country, although they eventually became outnumbered by the mixed-race and indigenous black citizens.

A segregated society existed between whites and other races, which was formally institutionalized by the government in 1948 in a system known as "Apartheid." Over the ensuing years, the system drew increasing criticism from the international community which led in the late 1980s and early 1990s to multinational boycotts and embargoes, including an embargo imposed by the United Nations on several crucial products such as crude oil, in an effort to force the South African government to abandon the policy. The leader of the in-country opposition to Apartheid, Nelson Mandela, was imprisoned for his anti-apartheid activities.

World pressure was ultimately successful, and Apartheid laws were repealed in 1991. In 1994, South Africa held its first free election in which all races could participate. Nelson Mandela was elected as the country's president, having previously been released from prison.

Redistribution of property ownership was one of the major goals of the new government, but it did not proceed as rapidly as some wanted. The white population continued to own large amounts of the more desirable land. Some felt that drastic measures were needed.

In 2018, led by the majority political party, the African National Congress (ANC), steps were begun to amend the country's constitution in order to allow the government to simply confiscate white-owned property without paying anything for it. The future of these efforts is uncertain as of this writing. Regardless of whether one thinks these ends justify the means, we ought to consider the implications of any government purporting to give itself the authority to simply confiscate someone's real estate without paying a nickel for it, in order to simply give it to another person whom they feel is more deserving of it.

In October of 1989, Bill accepted a job as a Project Logistics Manager in South Africa and headed into this turmoil. He had no idea of the culture shock he would encounter, transitioning from an itinerant missionary in Europe to a privileged businessman in a segregated country.

Bill was picked up at the Johannesburg airport in a limousine and taken to his hotel, the Holiday Inn, where he was met in the lobby by a company representative, who handed Bill the keys to a company car, a stack of cash, a company identification card, credit cards, and a map of the local area. Bill was told, "You need to be at the offices at 9:00 a.m. tomorrow morning. This hotel on the map is in the 'Whites Only' area." Bill couldn't believe his ears, but decided his physical safety depended upon first focusing on a practical concern. He headed to his car to practice driving an auto that had the steering wheel on the right side of the dashboard, in a country that drove on the left-hand sides of its roads, before having to do it in rush hour traffic. The practice went reasonably well.

Bill's office building in Sandton was new and modern. It would have been equally at home in Southern California, except that in Sandton at that time there were few non-whites working inside. Outside, there were many, working in the gardens and garages.

A similar situation confronted him even in his place of worship. Bill found an excellent church to attend. The families there were welcoming and friendly, flooding him with invitations to barbecues and home visits. But the absence of non-whites in the service was troubling. Sermons frequently emphasized God's protection in uncertain circumstances. Indeed, the country was mired in unrest and an uncertain future. Bill asked his manager at work if there were any mixed-race churches in the area, but was told there was no such thing. As he learned more about the tensions that permeated the country, it seemed that each of the disparate groups with whom he came into contact had legitimate grievances. There were no clear "good guys" or "bad guys."

Driving alone on a mostly-deserted six-lane highway after a Sunday service one day, Bill was feeling unsettled and lonely. Sharon was still in the U.S., and he was troubled by the lack of churches that had mixed congregations. Then, he spotted an unusual sight: a black woman in a colorful dress holding a large bible with a cross on the cover. Bill was drawn to pull over and talk to her. She could read his emotions, and asked why he was troubled. Bill explained his desire to find a mixed race church. She directed him to one close by, and said she was headed there on foot, and would see him again. Following her directions, Bill found the church that day, and started attending the next week. It was what he was looking for. On the day he found the church, and each visit after that, he looked in vain for the woman who had directed him there. After a time, he mentioned the encounter to the pastors. They said there was nobody by that description who went there. Furthermore, there were no tribal colors that matched the dress she was wearing. With memories of the mysterious Pete likely resonating in his mind, Bill was left to draw his own conclusions.

When Sharon finally arrived to join Bill in South Africa, he was overjoyed to have her there. They remained quartered at the Holiday Inn. Sharon needed to adjust to the unfamiliar and very different culture. She was warned not to venture into the black townships because of the racial tensions and unrest. It was quite dangerous, so she was told. But Sharon's love for people and her desire to share God's word would not be deterred. She met a German lady at the hotel who wanted to get out among the people as well. They found a black taxi driver who would take them into the nearby Soweto Township, one of the more dangerous areas. The taxi driver took care of them as they ventured into Soweto a few times. No problems were encountered.

Eventually, Bill's employer provided a house for Bill and Sharon. It was huge, with a twelve foot high fence and wall around it topped by barbed wire and broken glass. A swimming pool adorned the yard, along with beautiful landscaping. Sharon was concerned about the challenge of keeping up the enormous house and yard, but those concerns were unfounded. They would have two maids and a gardener. For security, they would be provided two guard dogs. But once again, Sharon was warned not to go into the streets to talk to people because of the danger. She would be a prisoner in a palace.

Bill and Sharon asked to simply remain at the Holiday Inn, where Sharon could continue to enjoy the friends she had met. The company agreed. They returned to the U.S. in 1990 amidst fears that civil war could erupt in South Africa. The friction between whites, coloreds, black tribes, and other groups of different races was strong. Bill notes that the country's churches remained in prayer that war would not break out. Although tensions remained, war was averted.

Ministry work was now a central focus of their lives. They continued studying, learning more about the Bible and how to reach out to people. In 1992, they embarked to Haarlem, Holland for a two-year stay.

In Holland, they lived close to the ten Boom family clock shop which had become a museum. Some sixteen years earlier, Bill and Sharon had learned Corrie ten Boom's story, told in her book entitled *The Hiding Place*, and summarized earlier in this book. Corrie was a friend of one of the pastors of their church in California. Sharon found work as a guide at the museum, bringing full circle Bill's close proximity to the museum in his earlier years of living in Holland, and their introduction to the ten Boom story at their California church. In 1994 they returned to the house they had maintained as their home base in Lake Forest, California.

1998 brought a two-week return trip to South Africa. By this time, Bill and Sharon had joined Cru full time. Their earlier time there had shown first-hand how mixed races could come together and reconcile under the common bonds of faith and worship. Cru was using a multi-language DVD of the life of Jesus, known as the Jesus Film, as a ministry tool. (It has now been translated into more than 1,500 global languages.) Together with members of local white churches, their group ventured into black townships to show the film and reach out to black churches.

The trip was going well until a heated labor dispute erupted between the bus drivers' union and the taxi drivers. The dispute was not racially charged, as both groups were black. Bill's Cru team was warned that the police did not have the resources to protect them any longer. The police had to devote their limited manpower to the labor unrest. The Cru team decided to stay, and encountered no problems.

Bill retired in 2000, but remained available for engineering consulting work and assignments from time to time. From 2000 to 2004 he and Sharon were heavily involved with Cru and the Jesus Film Project. They continued their ministry work with other organizations after that. When Bill accepted overseas engineering assignments, he always sought opportunities to reach out to local people. From 2000 onward, the years brought too many overseas trips to recount. But some produced sharp memories.

Four more trips were made to the same area in South Africa between 2004 and 2010, focusing on teaching AIDS/HIV prevention to teenagers in public schools. American teens, including three of Bill and Sharon's grandchildren, went along with the traveling groups. The American teens were better able to connect with the South African teens than the adults.

Trips to Indonesia, China, and Africa after 2000 took Bill into darkness and danger.

East Timor, Indonesia

Although Indonesia came under the rule of a central government following its independence after WWII, the island of Timor remained an outlier. While the Western portion under Dutch rule had obtained independence, the Eastern portion, East Timor, was originally a Portugese colony in the 1700s and retained its own culture apart from Indonesia at large, as well as an independent streak. In particular, East Timor was Christian to a great degree while Indonesia had evolved into the largest Muslim country in the world. In 1999 and into 2000, a successful vote in East Timor for independence erupted into a bloodbath, with armed Muslim Indonesian Army troops and anti-independence militias supported by the Indonesian army attacking and killing the East Timorese civilians. Catholic churches were destroyed. The world community finally woke up and United Nations troops, primarily from Uganda and neighboring Australia, *(Plate BD-10)* were sent in to attempt to protect the civilians.

Into this war zone, Cru sent Bill and another missionary to assess the physical damage from the fighting and the needs of any remaining churches. So little information was leaking out that there was scant knowledge of what was going on. They did know that there were no lodging accommodations available and that it was dangerous at night. Their best bet would be to try to find places to sleep close to where the Australian troops, who wore light blue berets, were stationed.

BD-10. United Nations forces sent into East Timor to protect civilians from genocide. Bill DeLannoy photos.

Bill and his co-worker, Bob, landed in a small plane with a lump of fear in their throats. When they stepped off the plane, they encountered a young man from Thailand who recognized them as visitors. He offered them hotel rooms on a cruise ship which his company had bought and towed into the harbor there the previous day *(Plate BD-11)*. With only one way on and off the ship, just one Australian soldier was needed to guard the gangplank. Over the next days, Bill and Bob were elated to find several local pastors who were grateful for the materials and help that Bill and Bob had brought. Bill noted that God had provided a safe place for them to stay ahead of their arrival.

BD-11. Cruise ship converted to a hotel, East Timor, Indonesia, during U.N. intervention. Bill DeLannoy photo.

During the same time period, Bill made trips into Tanzania and the Island of Madagascar to show the Jesus Film in Muslim villages. Rather than complete hostility, the film teams encountered many who welcomed them and willingly watched the film *(Plate BD-12)*.

A Trip to Mainland China

Although it has been a Communist country since 1949, largely hostile to and repressive of Christianity, windows of opportunity open and close from time to time in China on no particular schedule or predictability. Shifting political winds bring periods of some relaxation of oppression, and times of outright crackdowns, including arrests and imprisonment. Local officials' attitudes may vary from region to region. Bill and Sharon joined a group of eight other people with the Southern Baptist Overseas Missions organization which was sending teams into "smaller" (one to two million population) cities. They went in with no set plans, but looked for God to open doors for them.

Bill and Sharon's team landed in a city with a large nursing university. They met with the city and government officials in charge of tourism and learned that they would love to have American tourists teach students about American customs and holidays, on one condition—there was to be no proselytizing of any religion. However, the team could answer any questions the students would raise. Bill was assigned to a class of 30 to 40 girls. He had no planned presentation, thinking Independence Day or Thanksgiving would be good topics. But the eager, bright-eyed students provided the opportunity to discuss far more. A tiny, slender girl asked right away what was Bill's favorite book and why, opening the door wide to talk about the Bible. The entire team shared similar experiences.

Sharon and the other girls on the team formed such a bond with the nursing students that the students showed up every morning outside the team's hotel to talk about anything, but mostly to just hang out together. A follow-up trip to the same city in early December of the following year presented the opportunity to organize an official American birthday party, complete with cake and presents for all the guests—including the chief government tourist official and his family. Of course the One whose birth was celebrated was

Jesus. *Plate BD-13: top:* two group members with Chinese police and officials; *bottom:* nursing students with two group members.

A later solo trip into China highlighted the darker side of its religious intolerance. Because of his previous experience with secret churches in Communist Eastern Europe, Bill was talked into taking a trip alone into a major city in Szechuan province to teach an unregistered (underground) church about applying what the Bible teaches to their daily lives, and how to teach other people about its principles.

Bill was the only obviously non-Chinese person to get off his airplane after a long, long flight. He was therefore easily recognized at the airport by his driver. On the way to where Bill would be staying, the driver traveled a route for over an hour that circled, doubled back, and made no sense — except to be sure they weren't being tailed. Bill was quartered in a gated apartment complex, guarded by a bored middle-aged guard who sat in a little guardhouse that barely kept away the rain and snow.

Bill's apartment was large and very quiet, complete with three weeks worth of food and drink and a big television, programmed full of sports channels. An older lady caretaker was introduced the next day who became his "mother hen," constantly checking to be sure he had enough food and other necessities.

The next night, Bill began teaching members of the secret church in his apartment, giving them practical methods for studying together and ways to reach out to local residents. He was surprised to learn that there were seventeen underground churches in the city. The members were not free to openly worship for fear of arrest and reprisal. Their faith came at a significant price. Toward the end of his stay, however, Bill confronted another adversary that was more frightening than the local authorities.

Several people in the group told Bill they were so frightened of three Taoist temples located on the main road that they would take large detours around them every day. They had to pass by them on their way to work or college. Several said they could actually feel evil emanating from the temples when they were near them. Bill knew nothing about Taoism, but hastily, without thinking or investigating, agreed to go see the place. He shared with the group the Bible verse that reminds us that God is greater than the prince of evil who is in the world. The group did not know how to apply that to this situation.

Bill had not thought through a solution before he spoke, and quickly realized he was going to have to physically confront whatever it was they were afraid of.

BD-12. *Bill with local residents, Tanzania and Madagascar. Bill DeLannoy photos.*

BD-13. China. Top: two group members with police and local officials; bottom: nursing students with group members. Bill DeLannoy photos.

Taoism

Like Bill, I knew nothing of Taoism. After some research, I concluded that it would be difficult to summarize. Not only is it complex, but descriptions varied enough from source to source that its overall essence seemed elusive. A few recurring aspects are noted in this summary. Some of Taoism's elements are compared and contrasted to the Bible to put Bill's experiences into that framework. There is no aim here to be critical or judgmental. The reader is encouraged to explore the many religions which surround us with an open mind and to seek out where truth lies.

Taoism has ancient roots dating back over 2,000 years. It is one of five officially recognized religions in China. Its aim appears to be for followers to become one with the unplanned rhythms of the universe, to "go with the flow." A BBC source advised that Taoists believe that the constantly evolving and changing universe springs from the Tao, or Dao, which impersonally guides the way. Practices include rites of purification, meditation, and offerings or sacrifices to deities. There is no supreme god, but rather multiple deities, none of whom are eternal or omnipotent. The deities are emanations of celestial energy. Seventeen primary deities were named: three Pure Ones, eight Immortals, and six others who bore individual names and traits.

There is no central theological text such as the Bible or Koran. Rather, a variety of literature, stories, and honored writers contribute to its themes. The stories include renditions of encounters with spirits, immortals and gods. Some rituals involve mediums and trances.

The Bible confirms the existence of a spiritual realm. However, there are spiritual forces who are not our best friends forever. We read that mankind's struggle is not against flesh and blood, but against the rulers, the authorities, and the powers of this dark world, and against the spiritual forces of evil in the heavenly realms (see Ephesians 6:11). The Bible warns people to avoid spiritualists, mediums, and trying to communicate with the dead or the spirit realm at large (a far different activity than prayer to God Himself). It further warns against the practice of worshiping man-made idols, and multiple gods; there is but one God.

Against this background, Bill recounts his experience. A group of about 30 of the Chinese Christians took Bill to the temples, but they were afraid to approach too closely. Bill was also frightened. He could see fires and sacrifices in the temples from far away. Bill and the group began praying. He asked for volunteers to go into the temples with him. Only one boy volunteered, and he was clearly terrified. The rest stayed outside and continued praying. As they headed for the first temple, Bill assured the group that God would deliver them back safely. But he felt the same emotions as the students were feeling.

The first temple was frightening. Bigger than life red and black demonic-looking statues surrounded them. They passed through the first temple and headed to the second one. It was far more threatening. Red and yellow smoke and a sulfur-like smell infused the entire temple. Bill felt an ice cold shiver crawling up and down his spine. He almost panicked, as he knew from experience that a strong presence of evil could cause that sensation, but his faith in God's promise to stand with him stabilized him. The student held on to Bill for dear life, as they passed through and pressed on to the third temple.

The last temple was the worst. A huge mother demon-like figure with her three sons, twice the size of humans, glared malevolently at all who entered. The statue was standing up and leaning forward as if it would reach out and grab people. A Chinese woman came in and laid her baby on the ground in front of the statue, speaking Chinese. After staying there a time, Bill retraced his steps to exit back through the second and first temple with the student still clinging to him. The oppression and darkness were palpable.

Rejoining their group was a relief. The student who went in with Bill was a hero to the group, but he remained humble. What hit home to the group was God's power to overcome even the darkest of evil. After that experience, the students lost their fear of passing by the temples, and quit taking detours around them.

A Return to South Africa

South Africa re-entered the picture in 2017. Building on Bill's previous trip in 2010, this venture would again highlight the ability of faith-based events to overcome the racial and ethnic divisions that have plagued that country for so long. Beacon of Hope International and Cru sponsored a group to travel there to present the AIDS prevention curriculum that had been widely successful since its 2004 introduction in South Africa and some nearby countries. The teaching group included Bill and five others from the U.S., two local Cru representatives who lived in-country, a local black pastor, and a representative from the U.S. Embassy. (The ethnicity of the pastor and others is mentioned by Bill only because mixed-race cooperation is not yet commonplace in South Africa).

After his arrival, Bill was struck by signs promoting abortions *(Plate BD-14)* for an almost-free price. Bill inquired of the local contacts how abortions could be performed so cheaply and was told that the U.S. had been subsidizing the procedures. He also learned that the aborted fetuses were not given a burial but simply thrown into the trash. The presence of the Embassy representative was to advise and confirm that the U.S was no longer subsidizing the abortions as of 2016.

The first venue for the teaching group was a retreat center where the audience was mostly teachers who were being trained to present the curriculum to students, primarily teenagers. The curriculum had evolved, with government approval, to include a Bible-based approach to abstinence and sexuality. It was learned early on that teens simply were not able to resist the desires of youth with an effort towards abstinence on their own without the help of a higher power. The second venue was altogether different.

BD-14. *Sign advertising low-cost abortions, South Africa. Bill DeLannoy photo.*

After the first venue, the teaching group traveled to a black village compound *(Plate BD-15)* where the black pastor led a church. Bill was startled to find that one white family also lived in the village. Requests for teaching the AIDS curriculum had come to the pastor from all around the area—including from six local witch doctors who had asked permission to attend. Given Bill's years of experience with the racial and ethnic strife in the country, he was astonished at the makeup of those who came to learn. He had never seen all of these groups come together for any purpose in all the years he had traveled to South Africa. In addition to the witch doctors, whites, blacks, coloreds, and even Indians (from the country of India) were present.

When it came time for Bill's presentation, he noticed that the six witch doctors were seated in the front row. He was nervous, as well as frightened, not knowing what was going through their minds, or what they might do. A previous encounter with witch doctors on one of his trips to South Africa between 2004 and 2010 had him on edge.

On that previous trip, Bill had been teaching AIDS prevention in an area where witch doctors practiced their craft. He mentioned to the local Cru representative that he had been experiencing sinus headaches, which he never had. The Cru representative asked him if he had purchased, or been given, any trinkets. When Bill answered in the negative, the Cru representative asked Bill to check his pockets, which were quite deep. Bill did so, and was surprised to fish out a small talisman, which someone had slipped into his pocket without his knowledge. It was a wood carving made in the shape of an animal, perhaps a monkey. Bill was going to simply discard it, but the Cru representative told him there was a specific way they needed to handle this. Bill had to give the talisman to the Cru representative and ask him to take it, which Bill did. The Cru representative then cast the talisman into a fire and burned it. The headaches went away.

BD-15. *Village compound, South Africa. Bill DeLannoy photo.*

With this incident in mind, Bill began his presentation with foreboding. In addition to his presentation regarding AIDS, Bill had added some new material for this group. He spoke of the reality of a spirit world, in addition to the material world we experience through our five senses. Bill knew that the witch doctors were familiar with such a spirit world. They regularly made forays into it when they practiced their arts, probably not knowing the dangers of the malevolent spirits that dwell there. Some of the others in the audience seemed to take this information as being heard for the first time.

In order to illustrate the dual nature of our physical and spiritual beings while we are alive, Bill picked up a white robe and a red robe, one in each hand, and brought them together to represent our combined physical nature (the white robe) and spirit nature (the red robe). At death, the physical nature (white robe) dies and falls to the floor, but the spirit (red robe) continues on to one of two places for eternity: for the followers of Jesus Christ, a place of peace and beauty at rest with God; for those who refused to follow, a place of pain and torment. Bill noticed that many in the audience reacted strongly to this.

Bill's presentation and trip concluded without incident. After he returned home, he learned that seven more witch doctors had sneaked into the presentation, dispersed throughout the audience. All thirteen of them had decided to accept Jesus as their Lord and Savior after Bill had returned to the U.S.

Those who attended the classes were given diplomas recognizing their attendance *(Plate BD-16)*, which they were quite proud to receive.

As of December of 2018, 184,000 students throughout Africa have been trained in the AIDS Prevention Program which began in 2004. It is so effective that it was adopted by the South Africa Department of Education.

Bill and his wife Sharon continue to reside in Prescott, Arizona where they are active in study and social groups and continue to seek out opportunities to share their faith with others. Although his life has been remarkable, Bill remains quite humble. He emphasizes that his story is not about him, but rather about God's hand in his life, and how his decision to accept Jesus as his Lord and Savior transformed him and can transform anyone who accepts God's invitation to make the same decision.

BD-16. Village residents with their AIDS Prevention Course diplomas. Bill DeLannoy photo.

If anyone reading Bill's story feels led to make this same decision, a simple prayer from your heart such as this one is all that is needed to take that step: *Lord Jesus, I want you to come into my life. Thank you for dying on the cross for my sins. I receive you as my Lord and Savior. Thank you for forgiving my sins and giving me eternal life. Please make me the kind of person you want me to be.*

Chapter XII:
BEGINNINGS AND ENDINGS

We end with two letters to my parents which sparked an early interest in preserving wartime artifacts. The letters were discovered while sorting through the boxes of papers my parents left behind after they passed away. My parents came through the Great Depression of the late 1920s and 1930s, and they never threw away anything, (even home utility bills from the 1940s). Fortunately, among the things that may not have been so important, these two gems were saved. They intersect with the stories that have been recounted in this book in ways large and small.

After David Hamilton paved the way for the invasion of France, Private Grube began slogging his way across its muddy battlefields. While Major Gould's letter from his B-29 unit was making its way across the ocean to my father on the other side of the globe, a bomber from that unit was dropping the atomic bomb on Hiroshima, Japan, that ended WWII. Six days after the first atomic bomb was dropped on Japan, RM Villar received the telegram announcing Japan's surrender.

If you are sensitive to less-than-flattering depictions of the French, you may wish to skip over the second paragraph of Private Grube's letter.

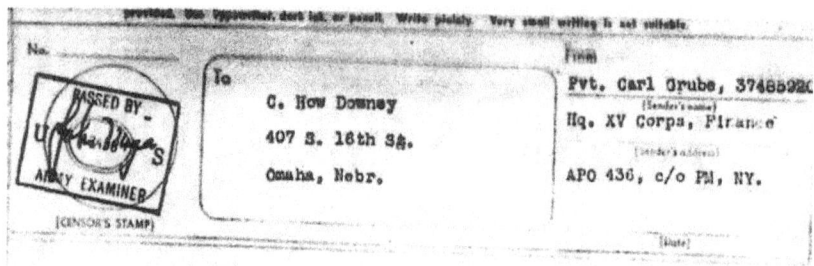

Plate 1. Wartime letter from Private Carl Grube, dated October 21, 1944. Downey family collection.

V-Mail

Long before we had email we had V-Mail. Private Grube's letter shows how America coped with the thousands of tons of letters sent by and to the hundreds of thousands of our troops deployed overseas. It was sent by V-Mail, or Victory Mail. The staggering volume and weight of those letters was reduced to a manageable level by this process, which was first developed in England. Soldiers typed or hand-wrote letters on specially designed correspondence which combined a letter and envelope into one piece. After the letters were written, they were censored in order to delete any information that could be used by an enemy, then photographed and microfilmed to reduce them to thumb-nail size.

Without V-Mail, thirty seven mail bags weighing a total of 2,575 pounds were needed to carry 150,000 normal one-page letters. V-Mail reduced this volume and weight to a single mail sack weighing 45 pounds. Upon arrival of the V-Mail in the U.S., postal officials enlarged the microfilmed letters and sent them on to their destinations. The actual dimensions of Private Grube's V-Mail letter received by my father are 4" x 5".

The Army censor's approval stamp appears in the upper left corner. Note that Carl's location is not disclosed as anywhere other than "SOMEWHERE IN FRANCE." One can imagine him in some bombed-out building in a muddy French village, wishing he was back home. Likewise, the letter doesn't reveal much about what was going on, although the fact that he was still a private after several years of war hints that he may not have found great favor with his superiors. Censorship severely limited the contents of letters for security's sake, but at least the letters were an indication that the soldiers were still alive, which was of great comfort to their families and friends.

The second letter found in my parents' papers has a historic connection which was likely unexpected when it was written. This letter foreshadows the telegram announcing Japan's surrender which was supposed to have been destroyed, but was instead brought home by RM Villar, whose story appears earlier in this book.

TINIAN, M.I.
4 August 1945

Dear Mort,

    The letter that I have been promising to write you for 1o these many months is finally in production. I have thousands of very dandy excuses buy somehow they dont even sound good to me. Assuming that I have been forgiven I will continue the letter.

    Speaking of production I hear that Downeys Inc. are putting out a new model Downey this year. Congradulations and it only goes to prove that there is life in us old duffers yet.

    Since I have left the states I have been in more places that I ever want to see again. I have used up more of your taxes wandering around than you can afford to pay. My mail has been having a tough time keeping up to me and in some cases I have been three weeks without a letter which I didn't like worth a darn.

    To show you how confused I am I will give you a short blow by blow description of my travels. When I arrived in Oahu I was in the process of transfering to the Air Corps when the powers thought that I should go out to Okinawa and make the world safe for Democrats and even tho I explained that I was a Republican nothing would do but that I get on a plane and fly out. When I arrived it was raining and the mud was --- deep and everyone was throwing shells and bullets around. My first impression was very unfavorable. Then that night the Japs came in and dropped some bombs and landed some airborne troops. This made me sure my first impression was right. I was then assigned to a combat group that was backing up the infantry. After being shelled, bombed, and shot at I concluded that I was in a very dangerous occupation and that it if wasn't careful my friend Mort wouldn't consider me a good risk for insurance.

    The situation did get better and around the first of July it became pretty routine with just a few Japs wandering around but not causing too much trouble. I was just about to take command of a combat battalion when the air corps threw their rank and I was pulled into the air corps, bless them!!!

    At the present time I am the Wing Staff Engineer, very fancy dont you think?, and have the job of keeping the construction going and the things that are constructed from going to hell. This is a B-29 outfit that is engaged in giving the little brown brothers a bad case of the hotfoot. I am strictly one of the ground force and since I have not lost anything over Japan I have no intension

of going over Japan to look for it. The only thing I do along
the flying line is to go the Guam and Siapan once ia a while on
business and look at the before and after photographs and
note that the bombs are causing a sever housing sitaation in
Japan. They must be getting very tired of it by now.

The outlook is very encouraging and it doen't look like
the end is very far off. This is sure a damn long war tho
and I for one want to get balk in a tweed suit.

The stimulant situation is very much better than in Okinawa.
There we would get s little medicinal alcohol and mix it with
grapefruit juice which was not the best in the world but lots
better than nothing. Here we can buy whiskey, one bottle per week,
(Old Taylor $1.75/fifth) and six bottles of beer per week.

Josephine and the family are coming back to Omaha this month
and will probably get home around the 24th or 25th to take up
business in the old stand. I would like to arrive there at the
same time but Uncle probably wont see eye to eye along those lines.

I guess this is all for now but give my best to June and
the family, the Macs, Mrs. Ban and drop me a line when you can.

As always,

Plate 2. Letter from Major George T. Gould dated August 4, 1945.

Major George T. Gould 0295251
Hq. 58th Bomb. Wing
APO 247
c/o P.M. San Francisco, Calif.

Mr. C. How Downey
5612 Woolworth St.
Omaha, Nebraska

Plate 3. Envelope for Major Gould's letter.

As Carl Grube slogged his way through France, on the other side of the world, George Gould waded through jungle sweat and humidity in the tropical islands of the Pacific theatre of war. Life as a major was probably treating George better than was Carl's life as a private. Note the date and posting of Major Gould's letter: Tinian, Mariana Islands, August 4, 1945. Two days after George sent his letter to my father, the U.S. B-29 Bomber named *Enola Gay* flew out of the Tinian northern airfield to drop the first U.S. atomic bomb on Hiroshima, Japan. If Major Gould knew that his B-29 units were about to strike a colossal final blow that would likely end the war with Japan, his letter conceals it well. Perhaps Major Gould knew what was coming, but knew well the sensitive nature of the mission and so kept it well under wraps. Perhaps more likely is that the secrecy surrounding *Enola Gay's* mission was so tight that few of the soldiers working the B-29 units knew what was about to take place. On August 9, 1945, the second U.S. atomic bomb was dropped on Nagasaki, Japan, bringing Japan to its knees. Japan's Emperor Hirohito announced the surrender of Japan to its citizens by radio address on August 15th.

Contrasting Major Gould's letter with Private Grube's letter, and the manner of their sending, (V-Mail vs. U.S. Postal Service), one might suspect that Major Gould's letter was sent free of any screening by military censors. One can only speculate why Major Gould chose to reveal so much of what he and his fellow troops were doing in his letter. Germany had already surrendered. Perhaps the feeling that Japan was about to fall one way or the other led to a looser attitude towards the flow of information from soldiers to those back in the states.

Appendix A: Bob Hoover

When Hoover signed off on David Hamilton's C-47 engine changeout, David could likely have scarcely imagined that he was in the presence of a future flying legend. After David left for his unit in England, Hoover was sent to his fighter squadron. Hoover's malfunctioning Mark V Spitfire was shot down by a German Focke-Wulf FW-190 off the coast of Southern France on February 9, 1944, during his 59th mission. Captured and taken prisoner, he would languish for sixteen months in a German prison camp in Barth, Germany before a fight among other prisoners provided a diversion that allowed him to scale a barbed-wire fence and escape. In a twist of irony, he managed to steal an unguarded FW-190 and fly it, slowly and carefully, to recently-liberated Holland.

After the war, Hoover flew as a test pilot at Wilbur Wright Field in Dayton, Ohio (now a part of Wright-Patterson AFB) where he befriended famous test pilot Chuck Yeager. Yeager was so impressed with Hoover's skills that he chose Hoover to be his backup pilot in the Bell Aircraft X-1, *(Plate BH-1)*, an experimental rocket-propelled airplane in which Yeager was the first pilot to break the sound barrier in level flight. In 1947, Yeager's X-1 reached 700 miles per hour, with Hoover flying chase in a Lockheed P-80 Shooting Star. The X-1 was carried aloft underneath a B-29, and then dropped from the B-29's belly to execute its flight.

The Sound Barrier – Flying Faster than the Speed of Sound

When an airplane breaks the sound barrier, people on the ground below it get to share the event. I lived in Omaha, Nebraska not far from Offut Air Force Base in Bellevue, Nebraska during the 1950s and '60s. When military jets broke the sound barrier in flight, a sonic boom would explode like a huge cannon being fired, the windows in the house would rattle, and knick-knacks on shelves would vibrate out of place (sometimes onto the floor). The rest of the experience was like a science experiment showing the difference between the speed of sound and the speed of light.

Looking up into the sky, the jet would appear ghostly silent without any sound accompanying it. When it was almost out of sight, here would come the sound of its engines trailing behind it, but with no plane "attached." The sound was flying all alone by itself, almost surreal. This is because light travels that much faster than sound.

After a time, people complained about the sonic booms over residential areas and the jets slowed down — or did it somewhere out on the plains to hassle the cows instead.

BH-1. Bell X-1 in flight. Photos: NASA.

Hoover enjoyed a distinguished flight career, advancing forward as a test/demonstration pilot in various civilian aircraft, and later training military pilots to dive bomb with the F-86 Sabre Jet during the Korean War. After that war he flew a variety of military planes, demonstrating their capabilities to U.S. military units.

In the early 1960s, Hoover began flying aerobatics at air shows around the country. He set transcontinental, time-to-climb and speed records, and counted among his friends over the years Orville Wright, World War I ace pilot Eddie Rickenbacker, Charles Lindbergh (the first pilot to fly solo and non-stop across the Atlantic Ocean in 1927), Jimmy Doolittle (the Congressional-Medal-of-Honor-winner, air pioneer, and officer who led the aircraft-carrier based B-25 raid on Tokyo, Japan shortly after U.S. entry into WWII), U.S. astronaut Neil Armstrong, and Russian cosmonaut Yuri Gagarin. One of Hoover's most famous stunts involved shutting off both engines of the Aero Commander Shrike Commander (a twin-engine business aircraft) he flew, executing a loop and an eight-point hesitation slow roll, then landing with the engines still shut off. Hoover flew air shows until 1999, passing away in 2016 at the age of 94 after his remarkable career. A 2014 documentary film entitled *Flying the Feathered Edge: The Bob Hoover Project* honored his life and legacy. In addition to his numerous military decorations, he was named the third greatest aviator in history in the Centennial of Flight Edition of *Air & Space/ Smithsonian*. David's C-47 engine approval was in very good hands.

Appendix B: William Linzee Prescott

Linzee was one of those every-day people David frequently encountered who would go on to exceptional achievements in the future. Linzee participated in the D-Day parachute drop as part of the 82nd. Five or six days later, he was hiding in the basement of a French house with a few other outnumbered soldiers as masses of German troops swarmed through the buildings. Unfortunately, they were captured. Linzee spent ten months in a German Prisoner of War (POW) camp. While in the camp, he sketched some of his German captors with charcoal he somehow managed to acquire. After the war, he painted several murals, one of which is displayed at the West Point Military Academy in New York *(Plate WP-1)*.

WP-1. *Mural of D-Day invasion painted by Linzee displayed at West Point Military Academy. Source: photo believed to be from The Army Digest. Published reproduction is from wlprescott. blogspot.com which features many of Linzee's fine works.*

Linzee was sent to Vietnam during that war as the first civilian painter with the Army Combat Artist Program. At the time of his death in 1981, he was working on a book of Vietnam drawings that was never completed. The drawings were infused with the dark aura of that war. Many of his works can be found on the internet at the above website.

Appendix C: David Niven

Niven was a famous English actor who appeared in nearly 100 films during his career, usually wearing his trademark jaunty mustache. After a stint in the British armed forces before WWII, Niven migrated to Hollywood where he appeared in several movies in the 1930s. When war broke out, Niven returned to England, re-enlisting as a second lieutenant in the British forces. He also appeared in a couple of films promoting England's war effort before D-Day. At age 34, he participated in the D-Day invasion. Inserting into the battlefields of France a few days after June 6th with the Phantom Signals Unit, he located and reported enemy positions and informed rear commanders of changing battle lines.

After the war, Niven returned to Hollywood, appearing in numerous films. Better-known appearances include *The Pink Panther* with Peter Sellers in 1963, a classic comedy well worth watching.

Appendix D: Why Do Pilots Wear Silk Scarves?

David Hamilton explains: It's not to look jaunty and cool, although it does. Anyone who has worn a scarf around their neck in winter knows how effectively they keep the body warm. WWI pilots flew open cockpit airplanes and needed scarves for warmth. WWII airplanes got brutally cold as well. High altitude alone is frigid, even in summer. Many bombers flew with open machine gun bays on their sides. Warplanes are not insulated, sealed or heated like airliners. In addition to the cold, pilots are constantly turning their heads from side to side looking look for other planes. Silk scarves don't chafe your neck when your head swivels like other materials do. So, they are first of all practical. Jaunty and cool as well.

Appendix E: the Cold War and Significant Incidents – 1950s and 1960s

The only difference between "Cold War" and war itself is this: in a cold war, no bullets, bombs, rockets, missiles or other weapons or munitions are fired by the adversaries against one another, in this case the U.S. on the side of freedom and the Soviet Union pushing for the global spread of Communism. But the goal of defeating the enemy remains the same. Rather than shooting at each other, proxy wars, military coups, economic warfare, political warfare, geopolitical realignments of allied countries, massive military buildups and arms races, and anything else short of bullets is fair game.

The Korean War might be considered a proxy war. Although soldiers from the Soviet Union and Communist China weren't shooting at U.S. troops, the Communist countries were supplying North Korea with training and weapons, and the goal was a Communist takeover of democratic South Korea. Likewise, the Vietnam War could be considered a proxy war. The same dynamics applied in the war of Communist North Vietnam vs. democratic South Vietnam.

The Cold War is typically considered to have been "fought" between 1947 and either 1989 when Communism fell in Eastern Europe, or 1991 when the Soviet Union collapsed.

However, it is plainly obvious that the ideological war between socialism/communism and freedom has never ended. The end of WWII simply set the stage for the start of a different sort of war.

Towards the end of WWII, German scientists had developed operational rocket missiles as well as jet aircraft. The Messerschmitt

Me-262 *(Plate CW-1)*, a jet fighter, saw some combat starting in July of 1944, and was formidable against Allied bomber formations. Fortunately, few of them ever got off the ground. However, rockets designated as V-1s and V-2s bombarded London, England. Until the introduction of the jets and rockets, the most powerful and sophisticated airborne weapons were propeller-driven airplanes. Germany had many other advanced aircraft on the drawing board, but the tide of war had turned against Germany by that time, and it was unable to mobilize any significant threat with its missiles and jets. If Germany had been able to deploy those weapons earlier in the war, some think Germany might have won. But, as they say, the genie was out of the bottle.

CW-1. Messerschmitt Me-262A Schwalbe jet fighter. Photo: U.S. Air Force.

After Germany's surrender, U.S. and Soviet forces competed to capture the German scientists responsible for this frightening new technology, and each country was able to spirit away some of them. In the next two decades, the free democracy of the U.S. and the Communist dictatorship of the Soviet Union battled for political influence and geopolitical domination, with the Soviet Union succeeding in converting some countries into Communist dictatorships. In 1959, Soviet-backed Communist dictator Fidel Castro took over the once-prosperous and successful island nation of Cuba, turning it into an impoverished third-world country. People fled the country in droves, with most settling in the Miami, Florida area. Cuba has never returned to the prosperity it once knew.

More urgently, both the U.S. and the Soviets had nuclear capability. In 1953, two Americans, Julius and Ethel Rosenburg, were executed for treason for selling American nuclear secrets to the Soviets which enabled them to develop their own atomic bomb. An arms race ensued with each country developing and improving their own nuclear weapons and ballistic missiles capable of delivering nuclear weapons thousands of miles. Jet fighters and bombers were developed and improved, with U.S. and Soviet-made jet fighters engaging each other in air combat as early as the Korean War.

Americans were convinced the Soviet Union was going to attack with nuclear weapons, and the Soviets apparently were convinced the U.S. was going to do the same. In grade school in the 1950s, I recall having air raid drills where the teachers would tell everyone to immediately get under their desk and hide their heads (as if that would have offered any protection from a nuclear blast.) Air raid sirens were regularly tested. If you have ever heard the grim sound of those sirens, it's something you don't forget. Our primitive little black and white television regularly showed public service ads entitled "Take Cover" depicting the mushroom cloud created by a nuclear blast, *(Plate CW-2)* with the announcer urgently intoning, "If you see a bright flash of light, take cover at once!"

The race to conquer space, utilizing superior missile and rocket technology, took an ominous turn in 1957 when the Soviet Union launched Sputnik, the first human-made satellite to orbit the Earth. After the Sputnik launch, the fear of the Soviets taking control of space and having superior military missiles reached a fever pitch in the U.S.

CW-2. Mushroom cloud created by an atomic bomb. Photo: U.S. government archives.

In order to monitor Soviet military activities, long before the era of spy satellites, the U.S. developed a spy plane known as the U-2 which could take pictures while flying at incredible altitudes over the Soviet Union beyond the reach of their fighters and anti-aircraft missiles — or so it was thought. Inevitably, in 1960 they shot one down, capturing the pilot, Francis Gary Powers, and creating a major diplomatic and military embarrassment.

Another diplomatic and military embarrassment occurred in 1961. The U.S. mounted an invasion of Cuba. Known as the Bay of Pigs invasion, it was an attempt to free Cuba from Castro's dictatorship.

Unfortunately, it was unsuccessful. The invasion involved Cuban ex-patriots who had fled the island following the Communist revolution. (One of our neighbors in Colorado in the 1980s was a lady whose parents had sent her and her brother out of Cuba alone in 1959 as young children, knowing that Castro's dictatorship would bring ruin to the country. She and her brother were raised in a U.S. orphanage, as their parents could not escape. Parents sending their children out of Cuba alone to escape Castro was not uncommon then).

In 1962, the world came to the brink of a nuclear war between the U.S. and the Soviets.

Following the failed Bay of Pigs invasion, Soviet Premier Nikita Kruschev concluded, for a number of reasons, that U.S. President Kennedy was weak and ineffective. Cuba, with Kruschev's backing, began building launch facilities for nuclear missiles in Cuba, only 90 miles from the U.S. Missiles were loaded onto ships in the Soviet Union, bound for Cuba. The U.S. imposed a naval blockade, giving the Soviets a red line to turn back or be fired upon. I can recall as a teenager watching t.v. news pictures of the Soviet ships approaching the blockade red line with a very sick feeling in my stomach. Nuclear war was that close. Ultimately, the Soviet ships turned back and disaster was averted.

President Kennedy was assassinated in 1963. Some feel that whatever cohesiveness America enjoyed up to that time began to erode with that tragedy.

Appendix F: the Berlin Wall: a Cold War Memoir

After WWII, Germany was divided into two essentially separate countries by the principal Allied powers. East Germany became a Communist country which was for all practical purposes a puppet satellite of the Soviet Union, while West Germany became a free democratic country aligned with the U.S.

The principal city of Berlin, located within East Germany, was also divided into an Eastern/Communist sector and a Western/free sector. For a time, citizens of each country, and residents of Berlin, could pass somewhat freely between the two countries and sectors. Over time, large numbers of residents of East Germany and Eastern European countries controlled by Communists began to flee those stifling dictatorships. Hundreds of thousands escaped from, and through, East Germany to West Germany, including large numbers of highly educated professional people—doctors, scientists, teachers, lawyers and the like. East Germany eventually closed its border with West Germany, preventing the continuing exodus of Eastern Bloc citizens. However, Berlin remained as a point where people could still occasionally escape to the West.

In 1961, Soviet Premier Nikita Kruschev decided that U.S. President John Kennedy was young, weak and inexperienced following the failed Bay of Pigs invasion of Cuba. Concluding that Kennedy would do nothing, Kruschev and fellow East German Communists sought to seal off the escape route through Berlin, and commenced building a wall that year between the East and West sectors. Upon completion, the wall was some 87 miles long. There were actually two walls or sets of barriers, with guard towers and a wide, open, killing zone in between. Anyone trying to escape East Berlin who was able to get over or through the first wall would be trapped between the first and second wall, and could be easily shot by the East German troops in the guard towers. In fact, several people were killed trying to escape.

The wall stood as a monument to yet another failed Communist state until 1989 when it was finally torn down as a result of political pressure and the unsustainable expense to the Soviet Union of maintaining its satellite countries. While stationed in Germany in the Army in 1971, I traveled to West Berlin with some fellow soldiers and our wives.

The U.S. military ran a regularly-scheduled overnight troop train through East Germany to West Berlin, which we were allowed to use. Under the terms of an agreement with East Germany, it was permitted to stop at certain points for the engineer to perform a train check. The train stopped at all of those points and the engineer got off and made a walk-around inspection, whether or not there was a problem, in order to maintain the right to continue to do so. At each stop, armed East German soldiers were present. We stood at the open train windows and looked out at them, trying to picture what their lives must be like. They seemed very young, probably in their teens. I wondered what would precipitate them using their weapons. Eventually we smiled and waved at each other. One of them flashed a peace sign at us to break the tension, perhaps wanting to signal that not every East German liked the way the world was being run at that time.

The Berlin wall was a principal attraction for visitors, a grim reminder of what Communism leads to. We could look past the gated checkpoints into East Berlin. Although some U.S. soldiers were allowed to travel into East Berlin with passports, those from the

NATO unit I was stationed with were not allowed to do so. Given the tensions at the time, I was glad to have an excuse to not play tourist in a Communist enclave.

While West Berlin was a prosperous, flourishing city with a free economy, East Berlin's buildings were badly run down. No human activity could be seen in the buildings closest to the wall. It was chilling to see the East German soldiers in the guard towers that rose above the walls with their machine guns slung around their necks. As the guards watched us with binoculars, I actually felt sorry for them, being stuck in a country with a system of government so twisted that it would shoot its own citizens if they tried to leave. One wall section I observed was made of concrete about eight to ten feet high with broken glass embedded at the top of the wall to deter anyone from climbing over it.

Several of the pictures I took in West Berlin in 1971 illustrate the situation: *Plates BW-1–BW-5* show various views of the wall. The killing zone and guard towers are visible in some. Viewing platforms were built at occasional locations on the Western side to allow one to climb up to the top of the wall, and look over it into East Berlin. Lawful passage into and out of East Berlin was only permitted through controlled and guarded checkpoints. West German guards were stationed at the Western checkpoint, and East German guards at the Eastern checkpoint. Documents permitting passage into and out of the Eastern and Western sectors were checked at each guard station.

Signs in multiple languages gave warning at the approach to the Western checkpoint that you, the traveler, were about to venture from freedom to Communism. Checkpoint Charlie was an iconic symbol of the fact that those who live under Communist regimes are essentially prisoners of their own governments.

BW-1. Berlin Wall, 1971. Author's photo.

BW-2. Berlin Wall, 1971. Author's photo.

BW-3. Berlin Wall, 1971. Author's photo.

BW-4. Berlin Wall, 1971. Author's photo.

BW-5. Three women sitting at the Berlin Wall, 1971; a curiosity. Author's photo.

Plate BW-5: three older ladies who had brought chairs to sit and talk at the base of the wall on the Western side. We speculated that perhaps they had loved ones who were trapped behind the wall, or who were killed trying to escape. It was a curious moment worth a picture.

Plate BW-6: the ruins of a church tower bombed during WWII, left standing as a reminder of the war. Next to it stands a newly-constructed modern church tower, symbolizing the rebirth of West Berlin and its new beginning after the war.

BW-6. WWII church ruins, West Berlin, next to new church tower, 1971. Author's photo.

Plate BW-7: ruins from WWII bombings that were still standing in 1971. I can't recall whether these buildings were in West or East Berlin, but likely they were on the Western side since the wall is not visible in the foreground.

BW-7. WWII ruins, West Berlin, 1971. Author's photo.

BW-8. Brandenburg Gate, East Berlin, 1971. Author's photo.

Plate BW-8: Brandenburg Gate. Perhaps no structure in Berlin is more iconic than the gate. Built between 1788 and 1791, and located in former East Berlin, it has been the backdrop for multiple political events. Before the Berlin Wall was built, free passage between East and West Berlin was possible over the road that passed through the gate. The road is named Unter Den Linden, (under the Linden), for the many Linden trees planted along its roadside.

The road and the gate were sealed off by the wall on August 14, 1961 and remained closed until December 22, 1989, when the gate was reopened in conjunction with the tearing down of the wall. After the wall was built, U.S. and West German politicians gave speeches in front of the gate decrying the destruction of freedom represented by the wall. On June 12, 1987, U.S. President Ronald Reagan gave his famous speech there in which he challenged Mikhail Gorbachev, General Secretary of the Communist Party of the Soviet Union, to "tear down this wall," chiding Gorbachev for his hypocritical rhetoric in claiming he favored freedom and world unity.

This picture shows the gate well worn with age. The dark splotch at its top center could be powder residue from an artillery shell burst close to the top, or simply weathering. Today, the gate stands beautifully restored and remains a popular tourist attraction and public gathering plaza. It is worth the time to search the internet for a picture of the gate as it stands today in pristine condition. The contrast between 1971 and now is quite amazing.

Acknowledgements

My sincere thanks to noted author and lecturer Tammy Kling who first encouraged me to pursue writing, and to her staff at OnFire Books, who contributed their editing expertise, polishing my rough draft and eliminating several "rabbit trails." I am certainly grateful for the help and support of Harley Patrick and Hellgate Press, for undertaking to bring my endeavor to life. Special thanks go to my dear wife Pat who provided support and patience during the months I spent with my nose buried in a computer.

This book would not have been possible without the generous cooperation and time graciously offered by Al Villar, Elvin (Al) Baker, David Hamilton, Ronald E. (Ron) Byrne, Jr., Charles (Charlie) Taylor, James D. Johnson, and Bill DeLannoy, all of whom patiently endured my interviews and many questions, shared painful memories, and contributed their awesome historic pictures, memorabilia and documents. Chaplain Johnson kindly granted me permission to refer to his personal notes describing the Battle of Snoopy's Nose in Vietnam, as well as his book entitled *Combat Trauma-A Personal Look at Long Term Consequences* (Rowman & Littlefield Publishers, Inc.,© 2010).

All Americans should be thankful for soldiers like Lt. Col. Elvin (Al) Baker, lst Lt. Charles (Charlie) Taylor, Lt. Col. David Hamilton, Col. Ronald (Ron) E. Byrne, Jr., and Chaplain Lt. Col. James D. Johnson who selflessly served to preserve and defend our freedom. We should likewise never forget those who have passed away who also freely served and sacrificed, including Maj. Gen. Pierpont Morgan Hamilton, Marise Campbell, and RM Albert Anthony Villar. Some of our popular sayings are written in blood: Freedom is not Free.

Photo and other credits, where known, are supplied. We are all benefited by the generous efforts of those persons and organizations who donate their time to preserve and post photographs and information to the public domain on the internet, all of which serve to preserve history which would otherwise fade away.

Bibliography

A P.O.W.'s Story: 2801 Days in Hanoi, Col. Larry Guarino, 1990, Ballantine Books.

Combat Trauma: A Personal Look at Long Term Consequences, Lt. Col. James D. Johnson, 2010, Rowman & Littlefield Publishers, Inc.

Shrapnel In The Heart, Laura Palmer, 1987, Random House, Inc.

pownetwork.org, sourcing in part from *We Came Home,* c. 1977, Captain and Mrs. Frederick A. Wyatt (USNR Ret.), Barbara Powers Wyatt, Editor, P.O.W. Publications, 10250 Moorpark St., Toluca Lake, CA 91602, and from other sources.

Ron Byrne and Larry Guarino appear in at least one video of the Hanoi March available on the internet.

About the Author

What's your memory of history? Serving as a soldier, or being caught up as a civilian, during the turbulent times of WWII, the Korean War, and Vietnam, left indelible impressions on those who fought and suffered through those events. As the survivors who endured those wars gradually pass away with advancing age, their stories, struggles and triumphs are forever lost to us.

Author, speaker and historian James Downey set out to preserve some of the rapidly-vanishing valor and courage exemplified by the veterans who sacrificed to preserve our freedom, as well as civilians who endured to triumph over the brutality of war. His third book, BROTHERS IN ARMS, brings together eight different stories from Army, Navy and Air Force veterans, and civilians as well, spanning our last three major wars, that capture the best of the human spirit and the incalculable cost of our freedom.

James received a B.S. Degree in Psychology from the University of Nebraska-Omaha in 1969. He deployed to Germany in the U.S. Army, serving at Central Army Group (HQ CENTAG) NATO, and subsequently received a Juris Doctor degree from the University of Nebraska College of Law where he served as Assistant Editor of the law school magazine, THE NEBRASKA TRANSCRIPT, authoring articles for the publication. A thirty-year career practicing law in Colorado followed graduation, involving multiple and diverse areas of practice including litigation, transactional work, appellate court appearances, and service on legislative committees.

Travel to far flung destinations such as Fiji, Hawaii, Alaska, Belize, Mexico, France, Belgium, Germany, Ireland, Russia, Czech Republic, Italy, Spain, Greece, Turkey and Hungary, fostered an understanding and appreciation of our uniquely-American freedom, opportunity, and prosperity. In particular, a visit to the Berlin Wall and a foray into the underbelly of Russia well off the beaten path underscored the oppression and hopelessness that people suffer under Communist regimes. A recent trip to Israel, Jordan and Egypt reinforced the reality that we should never take for granted the freedoms we enjoy every day which were paid for with the lives and blood of the many veterans who have gone before us.

Before writing BROTHERS IN ARMS, and after a twenty-year period of studying comparative religion, James published his first book, THE EVOLUTION OF JIHAD, under the pen name of H. Davidson, which explores how the search for the one true God of Abraham long ago evolved into the terrorism we face today. His second book, WHY? tackles the question of why the world is so full of suffering if there is a God who loves us. DYING TO LIVE explores what happens to us after our last breath on earth. CROSS ROADS takes a hard look at America's departure from its founding principles that has left us divided after almost three centuries of cohesion and success. All of his books are available at Amazon.

In addition to travel, the author enjoys motorcycling and scuba diving with his wife.

www.ingramcontent.com/pod-product-compliance
Lightning Source LLC
Chambersburg PA
CBHW072148070526
44585CB00015B/1038